The Spanish Caribbean:
FROM COLUMBUS TO CASTRO

The Spanish Caribbean:
FROM COLUMBUS TO CASTRO

Louise L. Cripps

G. K. Hall & Co., Boston, Massachusetts
Schenkman Publishing Co., Cambridge, Massachusetts

Copyright © 1979 by Schenkman Publishing Co., Inc.
Library of Congress Cataloging in Publication Data

Cripps, Louise L
   The Spanish Caribbean, from Columbus to Castro.
   Bibliography: p.
   Includes index.
   1. Cuba—History.   2. Dominican Republic—History.
3. Puerto Rico—History.   I. Title.
F1741.C73   972.9   78-27145
ISBN 0-8161-9003-8

This publication is printed on permanent/durable acid-free paper
MANUFACTURED IN THE UNITED STATES OF AMERICA

"When you deal with the past, you're dealing with history, you're dealing actually with the origin of the thing. When you know the origin, you know the cause. If you don't know the cause, it is impossible for you and me to have a balanced mind in this society without going into the past."

—Malcolm X

"If you don't know your past, you don't have much future."

—Sir Philip Sherlock,
Secretary General,
Association of Caribbean
Universities.

Table of Contents

Introduction	1
Chapter 1, Pre-Columbian History	7
Chapter 2, How the Tainos Lived	21
Chapter 3, The Spanish Conquest	33
Chapter 4, The Settlements	49
Chapter 5, The Indians	63
Chapter 6, Entry of the Foreign Powers	79
Chapter 7, The Revolutionary Era	91
Chapter 8, The Age of Independence, Part One	105
Chapter 9, The Age of Independence, Part Two	119
Chapter 10, U.S. Entry and the Spanish-American War	135
Chapter 11, American Domination	147
Chapter 12, Cuba's Challenge	167
Chapter 13, The Social and Economic Situation	185
Chapter 14, The Political Situation	201
Chapter 15, Future Possibilities	215
Bibliography	229
Appendices	241
Notes	245

Introduction

It is interesting to compare the three Spanish Islands in the Caribbean—Cuba, the Dominican Republic (at one time called Hispaniola), and Puerto Rico. All are neighbors. All have many geographical similarities: backbones of mountains, coastal plains, shorelines of lovely beaches and good harbors; similarities of climate and vegetation; temperatures between 75 and 85 degrees throughout the year; sugar, coffee, cotton and tropical fruits, tropical forests, and palm trees ringing the sandy coves beside deep blue waters. All have the same historic roots. In Pre-Spanish-Conquest days, they were inhabited by Tainos of the Arawak tribes, while most of the rest of the islands were inhabited by Caribs. All have had long ties with Spain, and through language and culture, with Latin America. All have had over the years, since their first discovery by Christopher Columbus and their colonization by the Conquistadores, many similarities of development. All their people are similar ethnically: a melding of Indian, Spanish and Negro.

With the withdrawal of Spain at the end of the last century, all have been dominated both politically and economically by the United States. Yet all have taken, especially in this later period, divergent paths. Today, Cuba is independent and socialist. The Dominican Republic is in name an independent capitalist country, but is governed by a dictatorship supported by the United States. Puerto Rico is a colony, in the form of a "Commonwealth," designated as an "associated free state," but could possibly within the next decade become a State of the Union, or become independent.

So it is fascinating and valuable to trace back the histories of these three islands to their common sources, and then to follow their separate routes and points of departure over the past five centuries: and to wonder if their future paths might lead them back to form a federation with each other; and perhaps, too, with Latin America (as was envisaged by Simón Bolívar) and with the other islands of the Caribbean.

If with the latter, they would form a most important block since their areas and populations are far greater than those of all the rest of the islands put together. Cuba, the very largest island in the region, is 44,218 square miles and has a population of nine million. The Dominican Republic has an area of about 20,000 square miles and a population of about four million (the western side of the island, Haiti, half the size, is 10,000 square miles, but has roughly the same number of inhabitants.) Puerto Rico, the smallest of the three, is only 3,443 square miles and has a population on the island of around three million, though counting those Puerto Ricans who have had to emigrate to the States to try to find employment, the total is four and one-half million.

Outside of the Spanish Antilles, in the Caribbean, only Jamaica is bigger than Puerto Rico, by about 1,000 square miles, but with a smaller population. Trinidad and Tobago together, the next largest of the islands, are fifth in size, roughly half the size of Puerto Rico and also with a smaller population. All the rest of the islands in the Caribbean are relatively tiny. Yet most of them in recent years have attained independence. Among the erstwhile British Islands, Jamaica, Trinidad, Barbados, etc. are all independent. The French Islands are considered part of the prefectures of France. The Dutch still hold sovereignty over their few small islands, though they are to receive independence in six year's time. Amongst the Spanish Islands, however, only Puerto Rico is not independent; and it is the only one of the great possessions once held by Spain in the Western Hemisphere that has never been self-governing.

If Puerto Rico became liberated, a possible federation in the future of the Spanish Islands would form a very viable unit of about seventeen million people, speaking the same language, with a common culture and background, and having ties and great potentialities within the much larger context of a federation with Mexico and the Central and South American countries, as well as with all the Caribbean area.

This could be a far larger Common Market than the European one, and culturally far more homogeneous. This, however, is only a possibility, but a possibility of grand design that is in the minds of some Latin American idealists—one that could be of great significance to the whole area in the future, if it could ever be established.

The concern of this book is more with the past and the present: recounting both the main events that have contributed to the divergences in the three Spanish islands, and also portraying common factors which they have shared in their histories.

Hispaniola was the first island of the three discovered by Christopher Columbus and was the most important in the early years. For Hispaniola, the most crucial happening in its history, following the Spanish Conquest, was the partitioning of the island into French and Spanish sectors in 1697. The second event of major significance was the revolution in 1789 of the negroes in the French part, and its strong repercussions in the Spanish sector. The third highest point was its break with Spain in 1848. And lastly, there has been its latter day history of right-wing dictatorships supported by the United States.

For Cuba, there was the momentous year in 1762-1763 when the British held the island and when immeasurably more slaves were introduced than ever before, which was not in any way ever equalled in the case of its neighbors. Its next most formative step was the long struggle against Spain, in the Ten Year War between 1868-1878, and the revolutionary attempt led by the poet Martí in 1895. Thirdly, was the greatly significant moment in its history, when the United States intervened, on the pretext of the blowing up of the battleship Maine, in 1898, and the then ensuing infringement of Cuba's sovereignty through the Platt Amendment, which gave the U.S. a right to interfere in Cuba's internal affairs, a right it used at various periods to send in its Marines and to occupy the island. Finally, of course, there has been the last momentous occurrence of Fidel Castro's successful revolution.

For Puerto Rico, its main role for four hundred years was as a Spanish stronghold with many fortifications. As its neighbors, with the decimation of the native Tainos, black slaves were brought in early after the Spanish Conquest. Contrary to the later actions of its neighbors, except for an Indian revolt in 1511, there was only one other significant revolt against Spain during the many centuries under her domain. This was the Grito de Lares in 1868. Though there were some movements for independence since 1820, Puerto Rican leaders tended instead to go to Madrid, hat in hand, to seek political crumbs of favor. The island had a continuing influx of Spaniards throughout its history. Later, there was also an influx of Spanish-speaking refugees, usually of the Right, such as those from South

America who remained loyal to Spain at the time of their countries' independence, and recently, of Cuban refugees fleeing Castro's regime. Really, for Puerto Rico, after the Spanish Conquest, the next significant event did not occur until the U.S. Conquest in 1898. With the continuing political and economic domination ever since, it has meant that it passed directly from being the colony of one imperial power into the hands of another, with no break in its servitude.

Thus, there have been over the centuries many different factors and events producing changes in the paths and in the histories of each of the three islands. On the other hand, there have been many similar patterns of development. In the beginning was the almost complete genocide of the Arawaks in all the islands; the quickly dissipated small amounts of gold found; the early introduction of slaves from Africa to fill the laboring role of the original "Indians"; the slave trade; the introduction of intensive cultivation of sugar, the "white gold," into all the islands; the pirates and brigands and the high seas dramas around them, and the galleons, filled with gold and silver and other immeasurable treasures, passing under their guardianship; the Spanish language, the Spanish style in architecture, art, buildings; the plazas and lay-out of towns; the Catholic religion and the Inquisition in early days; the Catholic churches and Catholic teachings by Dominican and Jesuit priests; the dancing, the songs, the music; the mores and manners, the same fashions, the same foods, the same ways of life; and the blending of the three races that made up the islands' peoples over five centuries. These many factors have all been part of a shared inheritance which has mostly differentiated the Spanish Antilles from the British and French West Indies and the Netherlands Antilles, although most of them, too, were unhappy recipients and actors in some of the same events—the iniquity of the slave trade, the monoculture of sugar and the absentee white ownership of their lands.

In the beginning, Spain claimed all the islands of the Caribbean by right of discovery, but after a hundred years, the other European powers began moving into the area, and one by one wrested the smaller islands from her grasp. But once her adventurers had journeyed further greedily to reap the wondrous riches of Mexico and South America, the islands of the Lesser Antilles were not of too much importance to Spain. The large islands of the northern area had, however, of necessity to be retained for their strategic value in the passage of her wealth-laden ships from the Western territories to the homeland. So Cuba, the Dominican Republic and Puerto Rico were fiercely fought for and held. For four hundred years, Spain influenced the life and development of the peoples of these three islands. The peoples were all her subjects and their culture largely showed her viewpoint until at the end of the last century, the Goliath of North America moved in supplanting Spain. In various degrees, the three countries had then to adapt themselves to the new order, the new culture that the hegemony of the United States imposed. Economically, culturally and politically, the islands of the Spanish Antilles were redirected. Not since the original inhabitants, the Tainos, met the Conquistadores in 1492 had the islands faced a situation similar to that faced by Puerto Rico and Cuba in 1898, and the Dominican Republic later; nor had there been, except briefly, foreign troops on their soils during the previous four hundred years.

During the last seventy-five years, however, American armed forces, in particular American Marines, have occupied all three islands in the interest of American business, on a temporary or permanent basis. There are still military bases both in Cuba and Puerto Rico. The U.S. hegemony has evoked far-reaching changes in all the lives of the seventeen million Spanish-speaking people, in what had been called and is still often referred to as the Spanish Antilles. How each of the islands reacted in different ways to the new Anglo-Saxon power is part of present-day history.

This book covers the development of the three Spanish Islands from the Pre-Columbian era to the present epoch and at the end suggests several variants for their possible future paths.

1 -:- Pre-Columbian History

The most recent and generally accepted theory today, according to Professor Jacob Bronowski, about the first inhabitants of the Western Hemisphere, is that people migrated over the Bering Straits, (then an ice-land mass) and filtered down through the upper part of the continent to Florida, into Mexico and Central America, and on down to South America. These first people settled throughout the hemisphere. Much later, it is thought there was a a second migration over the same route, though this second group, for a reason yet unknown to anthropologists, settled only in the northern half of the continent. The two-migration theory explains the existence of a mixture of two blood types in natives of the north, but only one in natives of the south.

Dr. Shirley Gorestein points out that "since aside from man, the New World contains no living or fossil primates more highly developed than the monkey, there is no reason to think that man evolved independently here."

Later tribes from South and Central America ranged over into the islands of the Caribbean. The natives whom Christopher Columbus discovered in islands of Greater Antilles (Hispaniola, Cuba and Puerto Rico) were Tainos from the Arawak-speaking tribes of South America, who had in the previous century displaced a more primitive tribe, the Siboneys. The Arawak tribes were different in many ways from the Caribs, who inhabited most of the other islands, the Tainos being a peaceful, agricultural people, while the Caribs were fierce and marauding, and said to be cannibalistic.

However, all the island tribes must have sprung originally from that same stock that came in the first migration. It is supposed that the migration probably started in Asia, possibly in China. Betty J.

Metgars, of the Smithsonian Institute, writing in 1975 in the *American Anthropologist*, postulates the theory of one civilization coming from China which was carried by the first migration to Mexico, Central and South America. Her thesis is based on similarities between the cultures of Shang China and the culture of the Olmecs, "the mother culture" in South America.

Dr. Leopoldo Castedo too supports this view when he writes: "A parallelism . . . underlies the no less surprising similarity between the broad trends of the pre-Columbian art and the outstanding examples of Orient art," and "Pre-Columbian art (is) in some ways very close to the Oriental, Olmec Masks show the narrow upward tilting eyes of the Chinese." Interestingly too, Christopher Columbus when describing his first sight of natives of Hispaniola, mentions their "narrow upward tilting eyes."

However, it has been suggested that as well as the first migrations, there may have been contact with Asians, Chinese and Japanese at much later times. "There is the question of transoceanic contacts whereby cultural features may have been introduced into the Americas—mainly from Asia by seaborne travellers, well after both continents had been settled," writes scientist and explorer Von Humboldt. Alexander Von Humboldt, who followed Columbus' route from Spain in 1799, wrote that he firmly believed the currents "were capable of spreading the races of mankind across the ocean. . . . I regard the existence of a former intercourse between the people of western America and those of Eastern Asia as more than probable." It should also be realized that "by 400 AD ships sailing from Java and northern China were evidently larger than those used by Columbus."

Von Humboldt, studying the origins of the Incas and Aztecs and the origins of all the American Indians, believed they came from Asia, for another reason. He found "certain analogies between the Chinese-Tibetan concept of the Zodiac and religious symbols of its American counterpart." He found animal signs similar, and also great similarity in certain myths and legends—the myth of the four disasters of the world and the dispersal of mankind by a deluge.

It is probable, according to most authorities, that South America was inhabited by at least 15,000 B.C. and possibly 40,000 years ago. The first established era is the so-called Paleo-Indian period: a flint-age; a hunting stage. Hunters and root gatherers were already living in the Bogatá highlands by the year 10,000 B.C. and had probably developed some form of primitive agriculture, though established communities did not exist till the second period, called Meso-Indian, about 5000 B.C. The oldest date established by carbon-14 of some deposits in Pueblo Mexico, is roughly of this era. Anthropologists José M. Cruxent and Irving Rouse believe that by 5000 B.C. there were communities not only in South America but also in the Caribbean. This would mean the islands were settled at least some 7,000 years ago. In the Meso-Indian period there was fishing and some cultivation of fruits and root vegetables, as well as the gathering of wild varieties.

The making of bread from cassava and the making of vinegar from its juices came from South America. The fact that cassava and not maize was the principal food of the aboriginal population of Santo Domingo is significant of the antiquity of South American cultural influences on the islands, according to anthropologists. Others write: "It is in agriculture that the essential South America culture elements reappear throughout the native provinces of Haiti (Hispaniola)"[1] The succeeding cultures learnt to cultivate more extensively, and the greatest contribution of the Meso-Indian culture was the development of maize or corn. An agricultural society with the cultivation of corn was well established by 2250 B.C. in Huaca, Peru. But Cruxent and Rouse find reasons to believe similar fully established cultivation of manioc and corn existed in the Caribbean by 2000 B.C., at least in Puerto Rico and Hispaniola, and undoubtedly Cuba "and the basis of all civilization is agriculture."

When the Spaniards reached the islands, they found the Greater Antilles inhabited (as already mentioned) by Taino Indians, who spoke Arawakan, and the Lesser Antilles inhabited by Caribs, who spoke Cariban, "both languages that are wide-spoken in eastern South America." The inhabitants' material culture belonged to the final pre-Columbian Age, known as Neo-Indian. They made pottery, knew the art of farming, and were excellent fishermen and skilled mariners.

Authorities tend to agree that these Neo-Indians migrated first to the islands about the time of Christ. But artifacts found in 1933 in the southwestern end of Hispaniola, and a little later in the northeastern end of Haiti, show evidence of the two cultures preceding the Neo-Indians.

An Indian ceremonial plaza in Puerto Rico at Coama dates back to about 600 A.D., according to archeological findings made by Juan José Ortiz Aguila of the University of Pennsylvania. The Coama plaza was built by Ostiones Indians, predecessors of the Tainos, while predecessing the Ostiones were the Igneri Indians, whose presence is dated about 100 A.D.

Ortiz Aquila says, "It has not been fully appreciated how advanced the Ostiones' culture was—and how early—They moved from 15 to 20 metric tons of earth to build their plaza: a mammoth undertaking by any standard." He suggests that these tribes, who preceded the Tainos, were involved in the making of ceramics, in agriculture and inter-island trading. But he believes the Ostiones inhabited only Puerto Rico and what is now the Dominican Republic. His findings bolster the contention of other anthropologists and archeologists as to the well-developed, far from primitive, society that existed in the Greater Antilles before Columbus arrived. He places the basis of society in the islands at more than 4,000 years ago.

In Santo Domingo, researchers have found signs of earlier Pre-Columbian tribes, living in caves along the shore, and eating mainly conches, mussels and other seafood and using shells for utensils and ornaments. Fernandez de Oviedo, who published *La Historia Natural de las Indies* in 1526, mentions a cave population in Western Hispaniola which was not subdued until 1504. So some of the more primitive natives were still living in isolated pockets of the islands at the time of the Discovery. It is thought too that the immigrants moving southward in the Western Hemisphere were from the beginning surprisingly developed.

The civilizations that arose later in the countries settled by the tribes of the first migration were all said to have derived from the "mother culture" of the Olmecs, according to Alfonso Caso, the Mexican archeologist. The Olmec culture, existing at least as early as 1300 B.C. was filled with "dazzling works of art", and "it is in its art that Latin America's essense is to be found," suggests Dr. Leopoldo Castedo. The cradle of Olmec culture is said to have been in Vera Cruz, that is within the Caribbean circle to which the islands belonged.

Thus, Pre-Columbian history and art are as pertinent to the Caribbean and Latin America, as the ancient Greek, Egyptian and Roman civilizations are to Europe. Pre-Columbian civilization goes back to at least as early a period as do the civilizations which arose in the Mediterranean. The oldest date established by Carbon-14 of some deposits in Pueblo, Mexico, is roughly 5000 B.C. First signs of corn were found at that date, and an agricultural society had already been well established by 2550 in Huaca, Peru. The first Egyptian dynasty began in 3258 B.C. Aegean civilization was founded in Crete in 2000 B.C. Rome was founded about 800 B.C. The age of Pericles in Athens was 400 B.C. and Aristotle lived around 200 B.C.

It is believed that the Incas' fantastic architectural skills were derived from an even earlier undiscovered civilization of the Nollo people. The history of the Maya "goes back to at least the middle of the first millennium B.C. but it was not until the Early Classic period (A.D. 300-600) that the record of their remarkable achievements, literally began to be hewn in stone."[2]

Teotihuacau, the first major state-city in America, though founded about 300 B.C. "reached its highest point of development between A.D. 250 and 600",[3] with a probable population of 100,000.

The influence of the early Olmecs was felt in succeeding cultures of the Maya, the Teotihuacans, the Toltecs and the Aztecs. Each succeeding culture, rather than destroying its predecessor, assimilated parts of the previous culture, so that there is a strong thread of continuity through the rise and eclipse of the various civilizations. Since tribes spread from Central and South America to fill the Caribbean Islands, it must reasonably be supposed that a derivative of the Olmec culture, the "mother culture," travelled to the islands too. However, being distant from the centre of that culture, and succeeding cultures, the cultures in the islands would naturally be weaker and more primitive reflections of the originals.

The Conquistadores destroyed so much so ruthlessly. Yet with the discoveries that have been made, especially those in recent years, archeologists today cannot find enough superlatives for the art and culture of those early civilizations. They vie with each other in praise of those past glories.

Two thousand years of rich achievement were almost wiped out by the Spaniards. An idea of the extent of the loss is realized in what has been rediscovered. Beautiful figurines such as the Venus of Tlalico (dedicated to the Morning Star) display workmanship finer than any found in ancient Greece. Pyramids of the Mayan cities are more impressive than those in Egypt. In Tikal, in Guatemala, the highest of the six pyramids rose to 230 feet, each of them an architectural marvel. "But the pyramids were not a uniquely Mayan invention. They were common to all great Mexican civilizations." Dr. Castedo is also impressed by the wonderful friezes on the pyramids.

"Work in stone combined aesthetic achievement with masterful feats of engineering."

"No North American has equalled Inca architecture," according to Edward Dahlberg. The stone sculpture of the Mayan is said by Henry Moore to have been amongst the finest by any group of people. Their wooden sculpture was also superb.

The resplendent Aztec capital Tenochtilan was, at the time of the Conquest, five times larger than Madrid.

"The cities of Spain were small and unimpressive compared with the majesty of the Mexican capital [while] in many respects the city of Curzo surpassed the medieval cities of Europe—the palaces and temples built from enormous blocks of dark stone had at their feet terraces covered with gardens . . . the garden of gold [showed] corn patches, the most characteristic Andean flowers, the flocks of llamas and vicunas. Through the medium of gold, sky, earth, water, plant life, animals and men were all depicted with fantastic craftsmanship."[4]

In Curzo, there were many districts inhabited only by artists brought from distant parts of the Empire. The university was a shrine of knowledge and gathering place for outstanding men who taught and studied the sciences. Architecture and city planning joined together to suit the prevailing social structure. There was a sense of unity and integration of the cities.

"The custom of painting history on the walls of public buildings, manifest both in Teotihuacan and Bonampak, dates back centuries before the arrival of the Spaniards, and mural art is still the medium for revealing to the Mexican people their civil and military history, myths and traditions."[5] Diego Rivera has re-created murals similar to those in Bonampak, whose painted wall treasures were only discovered in 1947. "Bonampak's splendor has rightly been acclaimed one of the classic treasures of universal mural art."[6]

"The Aztecs placed a high value on craft skills, and this is true of all Pre-Hispanic people" says Dr. Leopoldo Castedo. "The Maya developed techniques for making objects of jade, ceramics and terra cotta, and for stone and wood sculpture. The Mixtec's skill in carving hard stone was extraordinary. Rock crystal, jadeite, amethyst, opal, obsidian, jet and agate were fashioned into people with elaborate attire, animals in various attitudes, stylized men. . . . The delicacy, refinement and exquisiteness of Mixtec's applied art are notable. Besides architecture and sculpture, one can trace the evolution of the whole of civilization of excellent craftsmen in bone and wood carvings, the feather mosaics, the metalwork, stone as finely chased as if in soft gold, and especially, the ideographic painting in codices, ceramics, and frescoes."[7]

Sabloff and Rattye say, "[Maya] workmanship of jade is to be marvelled at." The Mexican and Inca were remarkable lapidaries and goldsmiths.

German Arciniegas is enraptured with Peruvian textiles, which, he writes, "compare favorably with the most nearly perfect ever produced. . . . The spinners drew their threads to extreme fineness; the weavers wove a very close web in their primitive loom and they used colored threads to work out designs of birds, llama, fish and stylized jaguars."

"In the course of its 2,000 years of existence, the Huatic culture has probably displayed more continuity and uniformity than any other in Mesoamerica. . . .

"It was probably from the Olmecs, that Tlatico ceramists learned how to fashion hollow pottery and they clearly borrowed stylistic traits from the Olmecs. Today, in Tauhuitz, potters still turn out creamy earthenware decorated in black, as did their ancestors centuries ago."[8]

In addition to ceramics, the ancient Huastics were skilled weavers and worked shell inventively. The Huastics were one of the Mexican Gulf cultures and so because of their nearness are likely to have provided one of the influences on the northern islands. Therefore it is not surprising to find evidence of very fine cream pottery being made at an early time in the era before Christ in the Greater Antilles, along with later evidence of much other ceramic work. The natives of the islands also made shell ornaments and bone carvings and feathered decorations.

"Cotton is found in abundance," writes Peter Martyr D'Anghera, and he testifies that the natives knew how to use it to spin and to weave. The art of dyeing, well-known in Mexico and Peru, was also known in the islands. The use of coloring material certainly long preceded the manufacture of textiles and their application to cloth was a natural extension of an age-old practice of painting. The islanders used vegetable dyes to color the cloth.

This was all part of the Pre-Columbian culture of Latin America. As well as the culture of their own islands, the people of the Spanish Antilles can claim a heritage in those splendid civilizations. It is in

Latin America that the people of the Spanish Antilles have their roots; it was from tribes there that they came to the islands, and so before leaving must have participated in the "mother culture" of the Olmecs. From Latin America have come influences both before the Conquest and up to the present day. Reflections of those impressive cultures, as already noted, can be found in the Pre-Columbian history of the three islands. There was communication between the civilizations co-existing in Latin America and there is evidence that the Tainos were also in communication with the mainland.

Dr. Castedo writes that "long before the advent of Europeans, there was unquestionably communication between the cultures of the north and south—Peruvian goldwork reached Guatemala and perhaps even Mexico; the artistry of Columbian goldsmiths was admired in Yucatan. The Maya imported ceramics from the regions that are today Nicaragua and Honduras, and the ancestors of the present day Panamanians carried on active commercial relations with the tribes of Ecuador, who in turn traded with the Peruvians." He repeats, "For untold centuries before the Spanish Conquest, trade routes from north and south crisscrossed the territories of the present Central American Republics."

This appears to be contradicted by Professor German Arciniegas, who says: "Parallel civilizations emerged in Mexico and Peru, although there was no communication between North and South." Yet most researchers tend to corroborate Dr. Castedo's theories. For example, Dr. Peter Weaver, writing about Columbia, says:

"Of mainland South America's mysterious archeological remains, none are so intriguing as the large stone figures that lie scattered by the hundreds among overgrown mounds at some of 30 major sites, outside the modern city of San Augustine . . . the ancients settled in this hidden valley . . . situated on the Magdalena River about 1,000 miles by river from the Caribbean coast. In other words, hidden in the Andean cove, the 'hidden valley' was situated at the crossroads of major migration and trade routes . . . the nation functioned as a bridge between the two great civilisations that existed before the arrival of Columbus—to the north, the Aztecs, and to the south the Incas."

To arrive in South America, the earliest migrants must have passed from Mexico through Panama to Venezuela and Colombia. These would have been the first logical South American territories they occupied on their long march south. This was of major importance to the Caribbean. During the first millenium B.C. or probably earlier, as mentioned, permanent settlements were established in the Orinoco and Magdalena Valley. Reptiles and fish, combined with root croppings, provided the first food resources. Then maize became a staple food. This, in turn, meant new implements had to be fashioned: grinding stones, pestles and new pottery shapes. Large vessels were used for storing liquids. In the last century B.C., villages were built on stone foundations and from them ran a network of roads. These were the trade roads that the Conquistadores were later to use as their routes.

Taking as "unquestionably" true then that communications and trading existed between the countries of the northern and southern areas of what is now Latin America, one can see that these would surely also have extended in some measure to the islands of the Caribbean. A number of known facts point strongly to this assumption.

It is from Latin America that the first migrations to the Caribbean took place. A tribe of peaceful Arawaks were the first settlers of what is now Curacao, the first of the string of islands off the coast of South America. They were seafarers who conducted a lively traffic in their slim log canoes with Indians of what is now Venezuela. From the first island it would be easy to move to the next.

Most importantly, "The trade winds blow northeast, making voyages in a westerly direction easy in both the Greater Antilles and the South Caribbean chain. The current thus favors movement from South America to the large islands of the north. The effect of the currents is reinforced by the flow of the major rivers of northern South America, the Orinoco and the Magdalena. Both discharge into the sea with such force that debris is carried off-shore for miles, and carried some distance into the Lesser Antilles."

Rafts or boats could easily also have been carried from the Magdalena and Orinoco rivers of South America "to the islands of the north", that is Puerto Rico, Hispaniola and Cuba. Almost certainly groups of men travelled this way from period to period using the force of these great rivers.

There are also early parallels between the culture of the Orinoco River basin and the Greater Antilles. During the first millenium B.C., pottery in Puerto Rico, for instance, was similar to that of the Orinoco: graceful, smooth, finely made, usually with a red or white or black and white design, *showing a long tradition behind it*. It is conjectured that fine pottery declined on the islands in subsequent eras because, unlike South Americans, the men were not hunters. There were no large wild animals on the islands, and the men switched to fishing and farming, though they carried on the stone carving. The women, who were probably the makers of pottery, now also had to help in the fields, and so had less leisure time. The pottery they made then was more roughly hewn and made primarily for household use. The women, however, would have continued to work creatively with shells and gold for ornaments.

The natives of the Greater Antilles like the tribesmen in Colombia "were skilled agriculturists." Von Humboldt writes that "It is in agriculture that the essential South American culture elements reappear throughout the native provinces of Haiti (Hispaniola)." On meeting Caribs still living in the Orinoco Valley in 1800, he wrote that "They were of athletic build, with smooth thick, dark hair cut short across the forehead." His description tallies with that of the Tainos and Caribs Columbus encountered in the islands of the Caribbean.

Their language was that of the Arawakan family, widespread through Colombia, Amazonia and Central America. The Spaniards recounted that the natives spoke with great distinctness and clarity. Many of the words that were first heard on he islands—*canao* (canoe), *hamoaca* (hammock), *hohio* (house), *huracan* (hurricane)—were encountered later on the mainland, proving a similarity of language and means of communication, and so again producing evidence of contact with the Arawaks of South America.

Columbus was able to use the same men as interpreters as he went among the islands of Hispaniola, Cuba and Puerto Rico, and the Conquistadores were also to use them both as interpreters and navigators when they made their first excursions of conquest into the mainland. Columbus noted that the Arawak speech and the Carib speech were understood from Panama to Cuba through the string of islands and down to Venezuela. Columbus also discovered that the natives on the Venezuelan coast knew of the existence of the island of Haiti and of Haitian and Puerto Rican gold. They knew also of the Mona Passage between Santo Domingo and Puerto Rico, which was in daily use by the natives of both islands.

"The Carib language," Von Humboldt wrote, "combines richness with grace, power and tenderness. It knows how to convey abstract ideas like eternity, future and existence. . . ." Their language, he felt, sufficed "to give evidence of a higher civilisation before the Spanish

Conquest." Von Humboldt was convinced of the great antiquity of Indian traditions, far more ancient than historical records. Present-day research has confirmed his estimation. He pointed out these people were not "mere savages," but inherently gifted and spiritually endowed, and with ancient and impressive traditions.

It is not difficult to conjecture how the various tribes reached the islands using the currents and winds and proceeding from one island to another. The islands form a closely linked arc from Venezuela to Trinidad, through the necklace of small islands of the Lesser Antilles to the Virgin Islands, which again almost touches Puerto Rico, the first of the islands of the Greater Antilles, and so on to nearby Hispaniola and then to Cuba. From Cuba and the Bahamas, the arc curves westward towards the mainland in a somewhat longer jump towards either Florida or Yucatan. "It seems entirely possible to us," say Rouse and Cruxent, "that various Paleo-Indians were using rafts for new crossings and coastwise travel in very early times. . . ." But it was not only from the great Magdellena river, that over the centuries the Arawaks arrived in the northern islands, though this is where the first migrations must have begun and where the Arawak culture and language were developed. There are signs of Mayan influences and probably later migrations from Yucatan.

The Mayans invented hieroglyphic writing, invented the calendar, had a metric numbering system, an advanced knowledge of astronomy, and naturally a knowledge of the constellations. "The Maya were able to grope with mathematical accuracy through unlimited millions of years of which Christian Europe had no contemporary comprehension."[9] Much of this knowledge came through the perfecting of the discoveries of the Olmecs, the widespread 'mother' culture. The island Arawaks navigated their boats through their knowledge of the stars. According to Columbus, the Taino Arawaks travelled "all the seas around them." They travelled the ocean in large sturdy canoes handled by seventy or eighty men. Ponce de Leon attests to their being excellent navigators. Both Columbus and Ponce de Leon used the natives for pilots in the area. On his first voyage, Christopher Columbus, first landing in San Salvador in the Bahamas (named Holy Savior because it was the mariner's first sight of land), questioned the inhabitants by sign language about gold. Understanding what he sought, they directed him eastwards. He took six on board to act as pilots and under their guidance he proceeded to Cuba and Hispaniola.

This was only the first of the many occasions he used them as navigators. On his return to Spain on his second voyage, Columbus was driven by bad weather into a Portuguese port. He was captured and taken to the King, who believed the Admiral had trespassed on territory claimed by the Portuguese in the New World. Only by an accurate drawing of the area of his exploration by one of the native navigators whom Columbus had on board, was he able to clear himself and be allowed to proceed on his way.

Some years later Ponce de Leon, sailing from Puerto Rico to discover "The Fountain of Youth," came to Florida. There he found a native of Cuba, who, in the few years of the Conquistadors' takeover of his island, had managed to learn Spanish. He was able to act both as interpreter and pilot for Ponce de Leon on the return journey to Cuba.

"The Indian was quick to learn languages," says Edward Dahlberg. This ability in languages confirms Columbus' view that the natives were men of intelligence. And that a Cuban was found in Florida attests to their not being isolated in their own islands. But most important in the testimony that they knew all the seas around them is the fact that they were fully aware of the phenomena of the currents of the Gulf Stream. They passed on this knowledge to the Spaniards.

"The Gulf Stream flows around Puerto Rico, the Bahama Islands, Florida and Yucatán. . . . According to the navigation logs, the Indians taught the Spaniards how to take advantage of the currents among the islands and in the open seas. It is believed that the Indians used the stars as reference points, because their calendars showed a vast knowledge of astronomy. This knowledge of navigation caused surprise and admiration among the Spaniards who took these excellent Indian pilots on their journeys."[10]

From San Juan in 1513, the Taino navigators guided Ponce de Leon's ship from Puerto Rico through the Antilles current in a straight route to Florida. In 1516, Ponce de Leon again was guided by Indian pilots who knew the current, along the coasts of Central America and from Yucatán to Florida. These trips resulted in the discovery of Yucatan on June 26, 1513, and the discovery of Mexico on June 24, 1516." by the Spaniards.

The first probing Spanish voyages to the mainland were from Cuba to Yucatán. Explorers from Cuba encountered Mayans on Yucatán in 1517. At the time of the Discovery, a sea-going group of Mayans from the Gulf Coast were busily trading around the whole coast of Mexico down to the Gulf of Honduras. These seafarers, named Putans, established for their commerce an "entrepot," or half way storage station on the island of Cozumel. Columbus encountered some of these Putans during his third voyage. From Cuba to Cozumel is only two hundred miles. This is not much more than the distance to Florida, where the Tainos from Cuba, Hispaniola and Puerto Rico are known to have visited, and some possibly immigrated. It is then well within the bounds of probability that they had commerce with this central trading place, an island off the northeastern coast of Yucatán, close to Cuba's western shores.

And this is likely to have been but one other point of contact within the Caribbean circle. The flow of currents in the Straits of Yucatán and Florida swing back northeast to unite in the Gulf Stream. The distances from Cuba to both places is short: 90 miles to Florida and 120 miles to Yucatán. This probably accounted for further, probably later, migrations to the islands. This is one of the reasons Puerto Rican anthropologist Ricardo Algeria also postulates the arrival of some tribes from Florida on the islands of the Greater Antilles. "From one stage of development to the next, from one period to the other, there always existed contacts with the wider scene, by war or migration, trade or marriage, or simply by the spread of ideas." Later successive migrations and contacts added new elements. "Many trends were travelling northwards as fresh influences were still permeating southward," Gerardo Reichel Dolmatole contends. And so in many ways Hispaniola, Cuba and Puerto Rico were influenced, even if faintly, by these civilizations and their cultures, since there would have been migrations from various points within the Caribbean circle from South America, Central America, Mexico and Florida to the Caribbean Islands.

Thus it is supposed that tribes came from different directions at different times to the islands. Their culture derived from these areas. Their skills, then, in many fields—navigation, fishing, stonework, basket work, shell and gold decoration—dated back in long centuries before Columbus "discovered" them.

Indeed, it was not so much a "discovery," as the first time two areas of the world separated by two great oceans first learned of the existence of each other.

2 -:- How The Tainos Lived

The boats of both Arawaks and Caribs were made out of one piece of lumber, a single log. The Caribs of the Lesser Antilles were in the habit of sailing to Puerto Rico to obtain boat-building material, as the trees growing in the Lesser Antilles were not suitable for making large dugouts.

The canoes were squared at the ends and the sides of the boats were heightened with canes and sticks covered with bitumen.

"Use of sails and awnings, decorative designs in paint and carvings—all were traits making the West Indian canoe a highly developed invention." They carried about ninety men, and long paddles were generally used. "Long voyages were not infrequent."[1]

Columbus himself stated that native barter occurred throughout the islands, and included platters, stools, pottery, gold and golden objects. There were many aspects of the islanders' living as they came to be revealed to the Conquistadores that confirm trading, contact, and cultural influences with Colombia, Venezuela, Yucatán, Mexico, Florida and other places within the Caribbean circle. The trading from one point might through that point lead to channels that formed a whole network of contacts.

The wood carvings and sculptures of the Maya have already been mentioned. The Conquerors described the wood carvings as works in which the island natives displayed great art. Peter Martyr D'Anghera, royal counsellor to the Court of Spain, who was a friend of Columbus, and who talked with and was in correspondence with the first discoverers, wrote an account of the "New World" (De Orbe Novo) based on this knowledge.

He writes of "seats, platters, cauldrons, and plates made of black wood, brilliantly polished . . . decorated with representations of phantoms . . . and serpents and men and everything they see about them." He mentions, too, that this black wood, which he identified as ebony, "does not grow in Hispaniola." But they did find ebony in the next island, which the natives called Cuba.

The first chief whom Columbus met in Hispaniola had a head-dress of the plumes of the quetzal bird and was otherwise adorned with them. The quetzal bird and its plumes were used in the Teotihuacán culture. In most architecture and art of Mexico, "the quetzal bird dominates all." A fuller description of the chief cacique says he also was "bedecked with gold jewelry."

On all three islands of the Spanish Antilles, the chief caciques were resplendent in plumes and gold jewelry. The men and women of the tribes also had gold articles, particularly body ornaments such as nose-rings and earrings: "earrings, charmingly shaped such as in the form of golden leaves or similar pleasing designs."[2]

The goldsmiths' art admired in Yucatán included such gold earrings and nose rings, and Peruvian goldwork "probably reached Mexico." A cacique gave Christopher Columbus an ornamental belt with a large buckle on one occasion in Hispaniola. On another occasion in Cuba, a cacique presented Columbus with two golden statuettes. On another of Columbus' early landings, a friendly "King" came to greet the Admiral "wearing a coronet made of discs of gold and copper alloy set with polished stones."[3] The only possibilities to be inferred from the above are: that these decorative pieces were made by local artists on the islands (since small amounts of gold were found there); that they were obtained from the mainland through trading or that they were copied from articles obtained from the mainland. Most probably all three possibilities existed together. But influences from Mexico and Central and South America seem certain. Some pieces could have been brought by the original tribes; others could be the result of later visits.

In the Gulf cultures, existing before 1000 B.C. and up to the time of the Conquest, wide ornamental belts were used by players in ritual games in their ball parks. The gift to Columbus was presumably such a belt. Today an excavated ball park where ceremonial games were played can be seen in Puerto Rico; such ball parks were part of the Mayan culture which though starting in Mexico about 1200 B.C. extended throughout all the territory of what is now Central America. They continued in use until the arrival of the Spaniards. The Puerto Rican ball park dates back to 1200 A.D., three hundred years before

Columbus landed on its shores. There are some fourteen structures consisting of paved walks, plazas and long parallel lines of standing stones of varying heights and colors. Many of these monoliths are carved in low relief into figures of gods. It is believed the Tainos, under the great chief Guaronex, used to gather here for ball games and important ceremonies.

Smaller plazas too may have been put to similar use as ball parks. Perfectly polished rounded stone balls have been found as well as large oval stone collars which are assumed to have been used in the games. "The name of the ball, *vike,* means fruit, and the fruit of the rubber tree." The ball embodies all the fruits which are brought to the festival. The ball is also referred to "as a child of Father Moma, and it is also said that his soul dwells in it."[4] Sniffing tubes of wood which were probably used by their priests for narcotics and tobacco have also been discovered. Many stools were made of carved wood or embellished stone with four short legs and an animal head in front. Some were inlaid with gold or shells. Less elaborate stools were used as grinding mortars.

A beautiful stool inlaid with gold and with a frog's head from Hispaniola is to be seen in the British Museum. All types of frogs abound in all the islands. Indians in southwestern North America made images of frogs as household charms to bring good luck. The Hispaniolan stool was probably meant to bring blessings to an ancient island home. The Indians also made very low stone chairs with high reclined backs and decorated them with carvings.

There was a fairly dense population in the islands of the Greater Antilles. Estimates vary from sixty to six hundred thousand in Puerto Rico alone. The 600,000 figure is given by Fray Bartolomé de las Casas, but historians think he may have been mistaken in the extra zero.

Some Indians built their villages near the ocean or the rivers. Most Spanish towns were built on the old Indian sites, and the Indian squares, the old meeting places, "bateyes" became the Spanish plazas. There were public buildings, as well as houses. There had been a movement from the coastal areas into the interior. There were political and religious hierarchies and the islands were divided into provinces of which the leaders were known as "caciques." The Arawak villages were usually formed of groups of the extensive kinship of one family. (This close sense of kinmanship exists even today. A Puerto Rican will acknowledge two hundred cousins.)

The Greater Antilles were, at the time of Columbus, at the same general level as the "Intermediate" area of Central America, "differing from it only in details. The Indians of the Intermediate area are notable mainly in their skill in working precious metals, in which they surpassed the Meso-Americans, and for their art, expressed in the forms of grave objects and religious figures."[5]

Hispaniola was in a pivotal position which made it "preeminent in West Indian cultural development during the Neo-Indian age."[6] Here the cult of the first *zemies*, household gods, is thought to have arisen and spread to both neighbors on either side. Taino religion centered on the cult of the images and sacred objects as the *zemies*. These included stone and wood idols. Certain *zemies* belonging to the chief were worshipped by the whole tribe; but every man had at least one personal *zemi* of his own. These beautifully carved small household gods in the shape of men or animals, were made of stone, wood, bone or shell; large stone man figure, an "idolo," more than three feet tall and weighing more than two hundred pounds, was recently found in Hispaniola. Recognized as belonging to Taino-Arawakan culture, its date is put anywhere from about 1000 A.D. to 1400 A.D., that is, between 500 and 900 years ago.

Fray Roman Pané, who was with Columbus on his second voyage, writes that the natives of Haiti carved images on their *zemies*, on rocks and in caves. Their houses and the pictographs and petroglyphs they made resemble those of northern South America, while their weaving of cloth and their artistry in ornaments show the influence of Central American culture.

In pre-Columbian times, reflections of the mainland civilizations, however pale, did exist in Cuba, Hispaniola (Haiti in Indian times) and Puerto Rico (Borinquen). There were not just a few thousand savages, as one uninformed North American resident in Puerto Rico recently stated in a widely resented speech. As Montague Ashley says, modern man believes himself so superior to the primitive without realizing "that even pre-historic man of fifteen thousand years ago was in some aspects of life capable of achievements which have scarcely been surpassed by men since."

In South America, far from the big splendid cities, there was wilderness. "A gap of centuries yawned between the hunter of those regions and the courtier in Montezuma's court. The hunter was forced to sustain himself on roots, small wild fruit and raw meat, at a time when the Aztec already had his bread and his cookery."[7]

Indeed, he had much more than his bread and his cookery. In Tenochtitlán, there were canals, bridges, zoological gardens, markets. "Its nobles were so extraordinarily refined that when forced to come near the Spaniards, they screened their nasal passages with branches of fragrant flowers."[8] The native of the Greater Antilles, while far from the development of the Aztec courtier, was also far from being a primitive hunter. He had his cookery, his skills and his crafts, his tribal form of government, his religion and his gods. A corn culture existed on all three islands. Stone tools to grind corn were found both in the islands and throughout South America. The natives grew corn (maize) as did the Mexican and North American Indians. They made bread "with a kind of millet"[9] of maize or yucca or cassava. They cultivated their roots: yams and the manioc plant and others. They cultivated their fruit trees in orchards. They made mats and baskets and sleeping hammocks. They made a variety of tools from stone. They fashioned both large and small canoes.

The men fished as well as farmed. In Cuba, the Spaniards found "fishermen sent to fish by their cacique, who were preparing a festival for the reception of another chief. . . . There were wooden spits arranged about the fire, on which hung fish, altogether about a hundred pounds' weight and alongside lay two serpents (actually iguanas) eight feet long."[10]

The method of fishing was to use a sucker fish (a sea-lamprey or remora) trained for the purpose. It was let down in the sea by a leash cord when turtles or large fish were seen. The sucker fish would attach itself to its prey and then both would be drawn up. A delightful touch was that a piece of fish or turtle was given as a reward to the pirate fish.

The natives also hunted and caught birds and rabbits, wild geese, turtle doves, ducks, but also only to the extent they needed them for food. The huge sea "manatee," they caught and used as their "beef."

During the Gulf culture from 700 A.D. to 1000 A.D., the Huastecs "in addition to ceramics, were skilled weavers and worked shells inventively."[11] Archeologists in the islands have found many remains of early ceramics and pottery. Though no claim is made for such high artistry as in the Mayan and other cultures at the time of the Discovery, a similar, decorative skill is certain. The art had reached greater perfection earlier and then been lost.

"Mexican girls busied themselves spinning and weaving."[12] So did the island girls. The art of dying cloth in different colors was known to the islanders too. The men wore loin cloths of different colors. Cotton grew plentifully on the islands. The women dressed, if at all apart from their jewelry, only in a short width of cloth, over one hip. Columbus says that, as well as being good navigators, fishermen, hunters and skilled in various crafts, Arawaks were good at mechanical arts.

Their houses, which resembled those of the more developed tribes of South America, were sufficiently well-built to be commented on.

At one end of Borinquen (Puerto Rico) some Spanish sailors "found there a handsome house built in the fashion of the country and surrounded by a dozen or more ordinary structures."[13] This was evidently a chief's house. In Hispaniola, there was a chief's dwelling which "upon measuring the large house of spherical form... was found to have a diameter of thirty-five long paces; surrounding it were thirty other ordinary houses. The ceilings were decked with branches of various colors most artfully plaited together."[14] The houses were well-constructed of tall trees for the outside wooden posts, supported by smaller beams on the inside to form a tent-shaped roof. The "King of the mountain country" lived in a "Golden House"—a house in which gold was used for decoration. Many of the native houses "ingeniously built" had wooden statues placed outside, not for religious significance, but purely for ornament. In the houses "were found pots of all kinds, jars and large earthen vessels, boxes and tools resembling ours [the Spaniards]. Birds were boiling in pots."[15] They were a friendly, hospitable people, enjoying entertaining and being entertained.

The mural treasures of Bonampak were only discovered as recently as 1947. In one of the old murals, musicians play a variety of instruments, and actors and dancers disport themselves. Columbus chronicles a playhouse in Hispaniola, where he was entertained by dancing and dramatic acting; other incidents are recounted. One 'queen' in the islands, said to be very cultivated, was held in esteem for the poetry and songs she composed, the 'arreytos', the ballads by which news was passed on and tales of old retold.

The natives, then of the greater Antilles, were said at first by the Spaniards to be intelligent, industrious and relatively cultured people, "the most cultured traits found in the women."[16]

They called themselves "Tainos," meaning gentle. This was in contrast to the Caribs of the neighboring islands to the south, who were warlike. The Caribs existed in St. Thomas, forty miles to the east of Puerto Rico. Professor Samuel Eliot Morison suggests that Caribs had possession of the eastern end of Puerto Rico at the time of the Discovery, and that the Tainos called on the Spaniards for protection against them. Darwin D. Creque writes that some Arawaks from Puerto Rico in turn settled in the Virgin Islands, and that they also had contact with the peaceful Tainos of Hispaniola, "who at times broke tradition by naming the fairer sex chiefs of the tribes."

But even the "less civilized" Caribs knew how to polish stone, make pottery, and drill holes in shells and rocks and softer material, and were considered to have been expert at carving ornaments of bone and coral. They also made baskets and mats and spun a crude cloth, probably of cotton.

The Caribs from the Lesser Antilles met the Spaniards from the first with hostility, with poisoned arrows shot from bows. So naturally it was the gentle Tainos whom the Discoverers first encountered and, again naturally, among whom they first settled. The Taino-Arawaks were described as handsome men and women by Columbus with as already noted, narrow, slightly slanting eyes, suggesting Asiatic forbears. They had straight black hair, were of average height, and were small boned "with long, delicate hands and feet." The men all had lean, muscular bodies. The more mature women wore a type of sarong. Bartholomew Columbus, Christopher's brother, describing a magnificent banquet given by an Arawak chief in Hispaniola to the Spaniards, writes, "as for the young girls, they covered no part of their bodies, but wore their hair upon their shoulders and a narrow ribbon tied around the forehead . . . . They were of a somewhat brunette tint. All were beautiful, so that one might think he beheld those splendid naiads or nymphs of the fountains, so much celebrated by the ancients. Holding branches of palms in their hands, they danced to an accompaniment of songs, and bending the knee they offered them to the Adelante."[17]

These scenes, charmingly described in the early chronicles, give a picture of the lives of the natives. Both men and women were physically strong, both being able to swim out three miles and back to the Spanish ships lying out of their harbors. The manner in which these natives conducted themselves is also well attested to by early reports, as well as the admirability of their character.

The first chief that Columbus met in Hispaniola was welcomed aboard, and during dinner along with the Admiral he behaved with royal poise.

When one of Columbus' ships was wrecked one night because of negligent mooring due to overindulgence at one of the native feasts for the Spaniards, everything the next day that could be salvaged had to be taken off the battered boat. The Arawaks worked hard in helping saving as much as possible, and Columbus records that such were their ethical standards that they did not steal a single lacepoint.

He waxed lyrical about them, of the "guilelessness and generosity of these children of nature. They invite you to share anything they possess and show as much love as if their hearts went into it," and "they are artless and so free of all they possess that no one would believe it without having seen it. Of anything they have, if you ask them for it, they never say 'no'. While they are content with whatever little thing of whatever kind may be given them," even though they were "things so worthless as pieces of broken crockery and broken glass."[18]

The Inca civilization in Peru existing at the time of the Conquest was "communist in general lines."[19] So too were the systems on the islands, though there was a hierarchy of sorts in their government since some chiefs were higher than others. In fact, in Borinquen (Puerto Rico), there was said to be a single king on the island, who was reverently obeyed.

Yet, "It is proven that amongst them the land belongs to everybody, just as does the sun or the water. They know no difference between meum and tuum, that source of all evils. It requires so little to satisfy them, that in that vast region (Cuba), there is always more land to cultivate than is needed. It is indeed a golden age, neither ditches, nor hedges, nor walls to enclose their domains; they live in gardens open to all, without laws and without judges; their conduct is naturally equitable and whoever injures his neighbor is considered a criminal and an outlaw." So wrote Peter Martyr. And he continues: "They seem to live in that golden world of which old writers speak so much, wherein man lived simply and innocently without enforcement of laws, without quarreling, judges and Bibles, content only to satisfy Nature."

Columbus was taken with the islands themselves. In Cuba, "at sunrise [the beauty of the island] was so striking that the Admiral ran out of adjectives describing it in his Journal." Columbus too writes of the excellent harbor he found in Cuba. "He had never seen so beautiful a harbor—trees all fair and green and different from ours, some with bright flowers and some heavy with fruit and the air full of bird song." And there was so "much verdure in so great development as in the month of May in Andalusia, and all the trees were different from ours as night from day. And so the fruits, the herbage, the rocks and all things." About Hispaniola, he was ecstatic, too, writing of "the sweet smell of flowers or trees from the land—the sweetest in the world." Professor Samuel Eliot Morison calls it a good example of his rapturous description of the scenery, the flora, and the natives.

Columbus spoke of Paradise in relation to the Caribbean islands to which he had arrived. He carried Marco Polo's book on the wonders of the Orient with him, "covering its margins with notes" and was convinced he had discovered some outposts of Japan or China. "The inhabitants of Zipango (Japan)," said Marco Polo, "have gold in the greatest abundance, its sources being inexhaustible." Columbus was determined to find that gold.

Being a religious man, Columbus also read his Bible constantly, and on the basis of the Book of Genesis, he thought that he had found the Garden of Eden.

The natives lived in harmony with Nature, of which they considered themselves a part. They were at peace in their fields, their mountains, their forests.

Loren Eiseley says: "If I remember the sunflower forest, it is because from its hidden reaches man arose. The green world is his sacred center. In moments of sanity, he must seek refuge there."

"According to a myth extensively disseminated among Caribs, Arawaks, and other South American tribes, in the beginning of things, sky and earth were as one and man abode within the earth as in a joyous realm."[20]

The natives of the islands adored "the heavens and the stars." They worshiped the gods of the rain, the sun and the wind. Dr. Castedo suggests beliefs were similar in all the southern parts of the hemisphere. "The iconography thus far analyzed indicates that throughout this entire territory the same religion was practiced." This must include the islands. Their gods were the gods of the universe. "Out of the earth rises life, to it it returns. She it is who guards all germs, nourishes all beings. The Aztecs painted her as a woman with countless breasts; the Peruvians called her Mama Allpa, mother earth; the Caribs addressed her as Mama Nono, the good mother from whom all things come."

Huracán was god of the wind in Yucatán corresponding to Quetzecoatal in other parts of Mexico. Huracán was the word used in the Greater Antilles for the fierce wind and the god who caused it. The fierce god Huracán was supposed to reside in the mountain of El Yunque in Puerto Rico. The Tainos believed in what the men in their whole region believed.

In Latin America, the Indians used the term "to grow old or to die," as to "become earthen" or "to change to earth." It is interesting that with almost the same imagery, the Greeks in their national legend said, "The Earth ate up the children of the ancestors."

According to a myth extensively disseminated among Caribs, Arawaks, Wamous, Carayas and other South American tribes, "in the beginning of things, sky and earth were one, and man abode within the earth in a joyous realm, where death and disease were unknown, and even the trees never rotted but lived forever."[21]

The tribes believed in one god, a Supreme Being, though with lesser gods beneath him. They believed in a heaven and a hell. They believed that god modeled the first man and woman in wood. They had annual ceremonies to ask blessing for the seeds they had planted.

The priest would chant: "Mother of Nono, show favour to us. Let us suffer no famine; we call on you each year with our prayers. We have not forgotten you." There were also special dances to induce the spirit to grant them a plentiful crop.

Priests also acted as doctors and knew the local herbs and plants for healing.

The belief of Columbus that he had found the Garden of Eden was perhaps a reflection of the islands' tribes own inner values and serene acceptance of the goodness of the earth by which they lived and from which they believed they originally were derived.

Aztec society astonished the Spaniards by its refinement, community sense and high morality. Columbus was similarly astonished in the islands. During Columbus' second voyage, when the islanders began to perceive what manner of men the intruders were, an old man made the following speech to him. "It is reported to us that you have visited all these countries, which were formerly unknown to you, and have inspired the inhabitants with great fear. Now I tell you and warn you, since you should know this, that the soul, when it quits the body, follows one of two courses; the first is dark and dreadful and is reserved for the enemies and the tyrants of the human race; joyous and delectable is the second, which is reserved for those who during their lives have promoted peace and tranquility of others. If, therefore, you are a mortal, and believe each one will meet the fate he deserves, you will harm no one."[22]

Columbus is said to have been amazed that a man who went naked could know about the mysteries of the soul and he assured him that he would only punish those natives "guilty of crimes" and protect and honor the innocent for their virtues. Here, then were originally people of the same tribe inhabiting all three islands, later to be called the Spanish Antilles, who had the same culture derived from an ancient civilisation; who lived close to Nature as in a Golden Age, on islands so beautiful they were called Eden or Paradise by their discoverers; who had a form of government, a hierarchy within the tribe and among the tribes; who practiced a primitive, or what might be called a "pure" communism; who lived peacefully and with a sense of artistry; whose leaders were men of wisdom; who were physically a fine race of handsome men and beautiful women; who had a standard of ethics and morality higher than the Christians who were to conquer them (in fact, it has been said that it was the Spanish and not the "Indians" who were the "barbarians"); and who were to be wiped out, almost completely decimated, by the greed and treachery and superior fire power of men who had only one motivation—lust for gold. "The hunger and thirst for gold are reflected in Columbus' journal and letters better than in any other contemporay document. Finding it became an obsession with him."[23]

Henry VIII, who was on the throne of England at this time, asked Katherine Howard, the clever, educated woman to become his fifth wife, if she believed in the stories of "The Blessed Islands," and if she would go with him there so that he could forget the worries of Kingdom. The "Blessed Islands" were the Spanish Antilles about which Christopher Columbus had brought tales that spread through Europe of having discovered the Garden of Eden and people of the Golden Age. Katherine Howard said later in regard to a cousin she loved, "When I am Queen I will have the King set him in command of ships to sail westward over the seas. He shall leave the seeking for the Hesperides—where the Golden Age remains to be a model and sample for us all." For such were the first descriptions of the natives of Hispaniola, Cuba and Puerto Rico that they were a people of prime innocence and virtue. It was only later history that depicted them as savages, in the same way as those who later plundered Africa and brought men from there as slaves had to salve their own consciences by depicting them as savages, saved from their barbarism by "civilized" nations.

"Madam Howard" Throckmorton (a courtier) had grinned at the Queen-to-be "If men of our day do come upon any city where yet remaineth the Golden Age, very soon shall be shown the miracle of the corruptibility of Gold. The rod of our corruption, no Golden State shall defy."[24]

And so it truly was as the English courtier foretold. The men of Europe in their lust for gold destroyed the peace and culture and way of life of the Spanish Antilles and later of all the newly-to-be-found countries of the Americas.

3 -:- The Spanish Conquest

In his amusing satire, *The Mouse That Roared*, Leonard Wibberley writes: "By remarkable good fortune Sir Roger had chosen to establish his duchy in a spot which lay on no great sand dunes, possessed no mines or precious metals or metals of any kind, no harbors or great waterways and indeed nothing to recommend it to a conqueror."

The Caribbean islands that Columbus found had the opposite problem. They had good harbors, good beaches; they had much cotton, good hardwoods, and, of greatest importance, they had some gold. If Columbus had not found the gold he was seeking on the islands, there would not have been much likelihood of his raising money for a second expedition. He had had difficulty enough getting his first voyage financed, having unsuccessfully pleaded his cause to most of the courts of Europe. The whole history of the islands and Latin America would have been different if the natives had not been seen wearing gold ornaments, and if "nuggets of gold" had not been found in the rivers of Hispaniola.

With some 100 men and three ships, Christopher Columbus had sailed from Spain, on August 3rd, 1492, and travelling westward, had covered over 3,000 miles of ocean before sighting land. The Spanish were in competition with the Portuguese, who were the famous sailors of their day. They were already engaged in profitable trade with the West Coast of Africa, and had already rounded the Cape looking for a route to the Orient. Columbus himself, who had sailed in the Mediterranean from boyhood, having been born in Genoa, was said to have taken part in at least one of these Portuguese voyages. Columbus believed that by sailing westward, he could find a faster route to the Indies—the Indies then meaning Japan, China, Indonesia, and India—where, as the stories of the great traveller Marco Polo told, there was much gold and precious stones and spices. It was this incentive that caused the Spanish monarchs to underwrite Columbus' first expedition.

There are theories that the Vikings had much earlier reached the northern parts of America; also that some Spanish sailors, going out of Cadiz, had, inadvertently blown by high winds, reached the western continent. There are theories also that the Phoenicians had very early been in South America and Africans had arrived in Mexico. But Columbus set sail with a firm conviction of where he was going, and a certainty that he would arrive in the fabulous Indies.

When his fleet had not come in sight of land after a month, and provisions and water were getting low, his crew were becoming mutinous and desired to turn back. But Columbus had too much at stake, as well as so strong a belief in his own prognosis, that he managed to encourage the crew to continue. They landed in the Bahamas three days later. He named the first island San Salvador, meaning Holy Saviour, for thanks to God for their safe arrival. Indicating his desire for gold, the natives led him, by "their direct canoe" route to Cuba (its native name). On this first voyage, he discovered six islands, but only two of them were large. In fact, he found Cuba so large he thought it might be a continent. After landing twice on different parts of its coast, he decided to leave it for further exploration in a new voyage, and turned back for a stay on the neighboring island of Haiti, which he had named Hispaniola or La Española.

It is easy to imagine Columbus' gratification and sense of achievement when he landed on these islands. He believed then, and until the end of his life, that he had found the Orient. This is why, from that time onwards, the islands became known as the West Indies. He had found new lands. He had found gold, and though the amount he took back to Spain from this first voyage was to be relatively small, he had established its existence at least in Hispaniola.

Upon the second voyage, too, when natives of one of the islands "urged by curiosity, flocked about the ships in their barques, most of them wore about their necks and arms, collars and bracelets of gold and ornaments of Indian pearls, which seemed as common amongst them as glass jewelry amongst our women."[1]

After his initial meeting with the natives of Hispaniola and Cuba, Columbus was full of praise for the guilelessness and generosity of these children of nature.

Originally he had expected to set up a new profitable trading area. However, he now quickly realized that this was unnecessary since he could, with the superiority of Spanish arms, take full possession of the islands and whatever wealth they offered. So that even while he was extolling the natives for their unbelievable amiability and generosity, he was thinking of how well he could take advantage of their virtues. The thought passed through Columbus' mind even as he was entertaining the first cacique, that these people were "ripe for exploitation." And again, "very cowardly and fit to be ordered about and made to work, to serve and do ought else that may be needed."[2]

While he was delighting in the Indians' innocence and friendship and freely offered gifts, he was making plans for their subjection. Even when a chief cacique in Hispaniola gave a great feast for him on his departure at the end of the first voyage, Columbus was treacherously thinking of his return and how he would colonize the island.

Having stayed only a few months in Hispaniola until the approach of Spring, Columbus decided to return to Spain with the news of his discovery of these distant lands. He decided also to leave behind him thirty-six men, who were to use the time until his return in finding out more of the whereabouts of the gold deposits, and to build a first outpost. On the return journey to Spain, he took with him ten islanders, but seven of them either died on the journey or succumbed to the differences in climate, food, and strangeness of the far-off land. Only three survived, and these were presented as gifts to the king and queen. To save their souls, they were immediately baptized.

With the news that Columbus had been right, that there were lands to the west over the ocean, where gold and other riches might be found, the second expedition was quickly organized. This time it was a large fleet of seventeen ships. Included in the crew were twelve hundred foot soldiers, among whom were some who had other skills—artisans who would be able to build a new colony. Such tools as would be needed too, were taken. Included also were horses, cows, sheep, and the seeds of various vegetables and grain, all of which could be developed and reproduced in the fertile earth of the islands. Their imaginations fired by the glowing accounts of Columbus, a few nobles also decided to take part in the adventure. Six priests were included "to save the souls" of the natives. And, of course, there were guns, cannons, and arquebuses, providing proof of the less than peaceful intentions of the voyagers. For immediately on his return, Columbus had presented to Isabella and Ferdinand his plan to colonize the islands, not just to trade with them.

"No Jews or infidels, foreigners or heretics"[3] were allowed, though there were many Moors among Columbus' troops. Every Spaniard who went on the second voyage seems to have concluded from the tales of the mariners who returned from the first venture, that no white men need do a hand's turn of work in the New World: God had provided docile laborers to labor for the "lords of creation."

Yet Professor Morison wrote smugly, with a sort of lock-mostly rough men. Even on the second and later voyages—he made four in all—there were only a handful of nobles and some priests. Some artisans also were taken on these later voyages, men with some skills in carpentry and use of tools, and others who had some knowledge of farming methods. But the majority were tough, illiterate men. Few even knew how to "mark their names with a cross."[4]

On the third voyage, criminals were given pardon from prison to take part in the voyage, and to help in the final conquest and colonization of the Antilles. On this voyage, too, there were thirty women taken, who since they were given no pay, but had to work on the ships, were presumably also either freed from jail or prostitutes.

For his discovery, Christopher Columbus was made Admiral, received a coat-of-arms, and was also made Viceroy of the islands. His financial reward was to be 10 percent of all of the wealth found. Each of the members of the crew was to be allowed to obtain gold from the natives, but with a 20 percent tax going to the King and Queen, the Admiral getting his share, and "something" being given to the Church.

With the announcement of the Discovery in 1493, Pope Alexander VI, a Spanish Pope, issued a Papal Bull that fixed the Line of Demarcation for Spanish and Portuguese possessions: lands one hundred leagues west of the Azores were to be claimed by Spain, and all lands discovered east of this mark were to belong to the Portuguese.

The second voyage started from Cadiz on September 23, 1493, with the three natives of Hispaniola returning home with the Spaniards to act as interpreters. Winds favoring them, it took only twenty-two days for the caravelles to reach the islands, but they came to points south of their original landings. These were the islands of the Lesser Antilles: Dominica, Guadeloupe, Martinique, Montserrat, and the Virgin Islands. Having already been warned that these were inhabited by the fierce man-eating Caribs, Columbus and his men did not tarry to do much exploring. However, when they chanced upon them, they burnt the natives' boats. From some of the islands, instead of the gift-bearing welcome of the Tainos of Hispaniola and Cuba, the Spaniards were greeted with a barrage of poisoned arrows.

In Guadeloupe, "two boys and twelve very beautiful plump girls from fifteen to sixteen years old" were picked up by the Spaniards. Professor Samuel Eliot Morison said the girls had been captured by Caribs in a raid on Hispaniola. He writes the girls "were useful as interpreters; with twelve hundred men on board who had been at sea for several weeks, without any women, it is horrifying to think what happened to the girls.

Yet Profesor Morison wrote smugly, with a sort of lockerroom dig-in-the-ribs, of the uses to which these young girls were put. These were only native girls, who, Professor Morison says, would have been used to produce babies as "hors d'oeuvres" for the man-eating Caribs. Was their fate at the hands of the Spaniards then, one of salvation?

Almost immediately after this incident, Columbus, who was "devoted to the Virgin Mary," began naming successive small islands after one or another of her shrines. (All the islands were claimed for Spain by right of discovery.) Outside Santa Cruz (now St. Croix), Columbus laid anchor for two days, so that he might replenish his supply of water. Thirty Spaniards were placed in an ambush, while this mission was being accomplished.

"From the place where they were watching, they saw a canoe in the distance coming towards them, in which were eight men and as many women. At a given signal, they fell upon the canoe; as they approached, the men and women let fly a volley of arrows with great rapidity and accuracy." One of the Spaniards was killed by a woman and another seriously injured. When the natives' boat was overturned, they swam to a rock and "they still fought with great bravery, though they were finally captured."

A boyhood friend of Columbus named Cuneo conceived "a desire to take pleasure" from one of the captured women. The girl fought and scratched him fiercely with her nails and only after he had severely beaten her, when she raised "unheard-of screams,"[15] was he able to overcome her. The native girls did not submit willingly to their conquerors.

This skirmish, amongst others, gave Columbus a healthy respect for the Caribs and, except with armed parties, he made no attempts to land on their islands. Only later, after the veritable genocide of the gentle Tainos had been effected, was an order given by Charles V of Spain, who succeeded Isabella and Ferdinand, to wipe out all the Caribs.

The next island, called Borinquen by the natives, was named San Juan by Columbus. Here again were friendly Tainos. One of the captains on this second voyage, Ponce de Leon, decided this was the island he would choose for himself. Some years later, in 1506, he became its very harsh first governor; it is difficult to understand why in Puerto Rico today, he is held in reverence.

Fray Bartolomé de Casas writes of him, "He grew rich on the labor, blood and suffering of his subjects."

The next island brought the ships back to Hispaniola. But the outpost left behind had been burnt to the ground in Columbus' absence and all of his thirty-six men had either died of disease or been killed. These Spaniards had formed a gang and roamed the island demanding more gold and more women than the caciques were able or willing to supply. Finally, the Spaniards' conduct passed beyond all bounds of tolerance. The gentle Tainos, who had been so generous and friendly, felt they had to rid their island of the outrageous disturbance of these strangers.

Thus ended the original peaceful relationship between the two peoples.

In any case, Columbus had had in mind to conquer Hispaniola and take its gold by force. He needed no further pretext than the news that greeted him. He ordered cannons fixed and set out himself on a march of vengeance. He despatched a further force of four hundred armed men under one of his lieutenants, Ojedo. "The first thing Ojedo did was to cut off the ears of a native who stole some old clothes." His armed men roamed the island, "extorting gold from the natives, exhausting their food supplies, and carrying off young boys as slaves and young girls as concubines."[6] In fact, he and his men behaved in exactly the same manner as the first Spanish colonists, whom the islanders had decided must be killed. Only now there were not just a few dozen men to be eliminated—there were twelve hundred well-armed soldiers to be fought. Columbus attacked the natives with crossbowmen and armored knights on horseback, and he set savage dogs to hunt them down. "A dog," he said, "is worth ten men against Indians."[7]

He proceeded to round up fifteen hundred of these people who had treated him so well and kindly, and sent five hundred of them back to Spain in one of the boats. Half of them died on the voyage back and the others were put up for sale as slaves, "but they were not profitable since they almost all died . . . the country did not agree with them." One of the tribal leaders then united the natives. "Several caciques sent from different parts to urge Canniaboa (the chief of the mountains and the coveted gold region) not to allow the Christians to settle in the island, unless he wished to exchange independence for slavery; for if the Christians were not expelled to the last man from the islands, all the natives would sooner or later become their slaves."[8]

These were prophetic words, and showed that the Indians had by this time a full understanding of the real nature of the invaders, and of their own mortal peril. The Tainos fought bravely for their lives, and the liberty to continue their lives in peace. But with their primitive weapons they were no match against the Spaniards, armed with muskets, arquebuses, armor and savage dogs. Eduardo Galeano says the Indians "were defeated by terror, by the cannon, which spit balls of fire, by the superiority of arms, by men protected by armor riding in on horseback, pitted against naked men armed only with rocks and bows and arrows." He was writing of Latin America, but this was true also from the first encounters in the Spanish Antilles. In some instances, the Spaniards approached the native villages while the people were asleep and captured the caciques, and put to death those they considered ringleaders. Others they enticed to meet them and caught them by trickery. One of the most important chiefs was put in chains and shipped to Spain, but he died of grief on the way there. The Indians were forced to pay tribute in gold to the Spaniards. Where gold was not to be found, then the levy was made in other produce.

One chief reasonably demanded: "How can you ask tribute from me, since none of the numerous provinces under my authority produce gold?" Bartholomew Columbus, who was conducting the interview, replied, "We know that this country produces an abundance of cotton, hemp and similar things, and we ask you to pay tribute of those products."[9]

The village, in these instances, was forced to produce cotton and hemp in great quantities. In other villages, the Spaniards demanded tribute in bread and other provisions. They had "magnificent trees of great value" cut down for the building of new ships and the construction of houses for the outposts and cities they were building. The natives cultivated the earth, worked in the mines, built the towns, while the colonists with "their inveterate idleness, their tyranny . . . alienated the good will of the natives."[10]

After a revolt was crushed, the natives were warned that "in future, [they were] neither to think nor to plan any hostilities against the Christians, but rather be obedient, humble, and serviceable to them, unless they wished worse things to overtake them."[11] One chief was told by Bartholomew Columbus that his whole country would be devastated by fire and sword if he did not surrender another chief, who had sought refuge with him. But the chief answered proudly: "Everybody knows that Guaronex [the other cacique] is a hero, adorned with all the virtues, and therefore I have esteemed it right to assist and protect him. As for you, you are violent and perfidious men, and seek to shed the blood of innocent people: I will neither enter into relations with you, nor form any alliance with so false a people."[13]

The whole village was burnt, the people put to the sword, and both chiefs finally captured and killed. Similarly, other whole villages were burnt so that the Indians would surrender their leaders.

One queen, who was said to be "gracious, clever and prudent" after the death of her husband and the slaughter of so many of her countrymen, persuaded others "to submit to the Christians, to soothe and to please them" by offering great quantities of tribute. But the Spaniards were insatiable in their demands. It was impossible "to soothe them and to please them." This wise and clever queen, who sought to appease the colonists, was herself later put to a "dreadful" death. The Indians were massacred when they met the Spaniards in open fight. The first pitched battle between Europeans and Indians took place the end of March 1495, and the natives were defeated. Columbus then marched across the whole of Hispaniola conquering it. By 1496, it was "so thoroughly subdued that a Spaniard could safely go wherever he pleased and help himself to Indian food, women, and gold."

This was not totally true. The Indians continued to resist and fight sporadically, so that according to Jesus de Galindez in *Ibero-America*, it was not until as late as 1533, that the last rebellion occurred in Hispaniola. The natives who could, fled to the highest mountains and conducted guerrilla battles from there, while in the plains, in their desperation, the people fought back with a "scorched earth" policy. "When they saw the Spanish wished to settle in their island, they thought they might expel them by creating a scarcity of food. They, therefore, decided not only to plant no more crops, but also to destroy and tear up all the various kinds of cereal used for bread which had already been sown."[13]

They starved themselves hoping in this way to starve also the invaders. But Christopher Columbus' second brother had now joined him, having come from Spain with further supplies. By the end of 1494 too, another four ships with provisions had arrived. So that though the Indians were starving, the Spaniards did not lack food. The scorched earth policy had not succeeded. Indians, who were made captive, were given to the colonists to do what they would with them. Even Cuneo, the rapist, records with some shame how these wretched captives, if released, fled as far as they could from the Spaniards. Women even abandoned infants in their fear and desperation to escape further cruelty. In many cases, there were mass suicides both by the men and their wives and all their children rather than to continue to suffer such oppression.

The colonists "not to lose practice in the shedding of blood and to exercise the strength of their arms, invented a game in which they drew their swords, and amused themselves in cutting off the heads of innocent victims with one blow. Whoever succeeded in more quickly landing the head of an unfortunate islander on the ground with one stroke, was proclaimed the bravest."[14]

A law was passed in Spain, first called "*repartimiento*" and then "*encomienda*." Indians were given with land as rewards. They were distributed as cattle might be distributed. They were worked, too, as animals might be worked, though ironically their masters were supposed to "save their souls" by teaching them the Christian religion of the Catholic Church. They could be punished, tortured; any crime committed against them and their families as their owners wished. They were made into slaves. Each Indian family owed its personal services and economic tribute to a particular Spaniard. Cortez received as many as twenty-three thousand vassals as a reward from the Crown. At first servitude was made for a span of two lifetimes, then to three lifetimes, later to four.

Having made successful war against the natives, Columbus went ahead with his plan to set up a colony even though it was apparent, of course, he and his people were no longer welcome. They set about building a town which they called Santo Domingo on the model of Cadiz, with a plaza, a church, the governor's palace and the town hall on the plaza. "Columbus," to quote Dr. Morison, "impatient to get things done drafted some of the gentleman volunteers for hard labor, which caused great indignation; they had come out to fight or gather gold, not to do menial work." However, "many were appeased by an early opportunity to gather gold. The Spaniards penetrated the interior of Hispaniola and there they found the gold they were seeking." They made merry when they returned to the settlement, "for this blessed gold."

From the general plunder in Hispaniola, Columbus was able to send home twelve ships "with a cargo of sandalwood, pepper, slaves, and gold worth 30,000 ducats."

His second voyage had two objectives: one to colonize Hispaniola and the second to explore Cuba further. He therefore left his brother in charge of Hispaniola and proceeded on to Cuba.

Again in Cuba, the natives were at first friendly. But what happened in Hispaniola was soon repeated in Cuba. The natives were cruelly treated, forced to pay tribute, their women raped, all turned into slaves. They, too, rebelled. They, too, were conquered in the unequal contest. So Cuba was the next island to be colonized. Las Casas, who had joined the second voyage, was made into an *"encomandero,"* that is, he, like others, was given land and Indians as slaves. But in the year 1514, convinced of the cruel injustice of the system, "he decided to sell all his properties in the New World and return to Spain and undertake the defense of the Indians before the Court and its experts."[15] However, when he denounced the cruelty of his compatriots, he was told that these men, who previously had been called beings of the Golden Age, were "too low in the scale of human life to be worth defending." He changed his status as a soldier to become a priest and work among the Indians in the Antilles.

In Puerto Rico, which had originally been named San Juan, the Indians, after their first welcome, offering gifts generously, even of their women, turned against the invaders. Ponce de Leon, who had helped in the brutal suppression of the natives of Hispaniola, was sent as the governor of Puerto Rico. He landed at Anasco Bay in 1506, and had within a year subjugated the natives. He established the first settlement at San German, but later moved to Caparra, and then to the northeastern harbor, which took over the old name of the island itself and became known as San Juan. For five years, he managed brutally to keep relative peace on the island. But in 1511, rebellions and general uprisings of the Tainos took place. These rebellions were quenched only after a great deal of brave fighting by the islanders. They were not quenched easily. Again dogs played their part, as well as armored men, in the campaigns to subdue the natives. Ponce de Leon sailed back to Spain and presented the King with 5,000 gold pesos he had extracted from Puerto Rico. He then was replaced as governor by Diego Columbus, Columbus' son. However, he was given the grant to discover new lands, where there might be greater wealth for him to claim. The small deposits of silver and gold in Puerto Rico had been quickly exhausted.

Ponce de Leon therefore set out for a new land where he was told there was a Fountain of Youth, though he himself was only about thirty-six at the time. The Fountain of Youth is supposed to be at Bimini, an island north of Cuba, "where there is a spring of running water of such marvelous virtue that the waters there being drunk, perhaps with some diet makes old men young again."[17] Ponce de Leon having heard of this land decided he would go there. He called the place he actually landed Florida because it was Eastertime and the land was so full of blossoms and flowers. Las Casas considers Ponce to be one of the most ruthless conquistadores to rule the natives. He never managed to conciliate any native inhabitants of Florida. He landed at various points but everywhere he was met by hostility.

There was another battle and, in it, Ponce de Leon received an arrow wound that festered and his men took him back to the nearest port in Cuba. He died there in July 1521, at the age of forty-seven. Later his remains were transferred to the Dominican church in San Juan, but they were moved to the Cathedral of San Juan in 1908. It was the latter day Puerto Ricans who brought Ponce's bones to San Juan, presumably because he had been the first governor. That they were later put in the cathedral was probably due to their historic significance, rather than any fondness Puerto Ricans might have had for him. Though, as mentioned before, it seems that Puerto Ricans in their history books do offer him veneration. Las Casas says he was one of the cruelest and most despotic of the conquistadores.

It is hard to understand how the image of the conquistadores has been built up as knights in shining armor, as men of valor and refinement, of sensibility and sensitivity. No such image can be made to match with any of the early accounts of the men who conquered the Caribbean and Latin America.

Las Casas wrote that "the Archangel Gabriel himself would have been hard put to govern people as greedy, selfish and egotistical as the early settlers of Hispaniola." Columbus, later defending himself against charges brought against him by some leaders rebellious of his authority, uses the following description:

> They were debauchees, profligates, thieves, seducers, ravishers, vagabonds. They respected nothing and were perjurers and liars, already condemned by tribunals, . . . owing their numerous crimes

... they were given over to violence and rapine; lazy, gluttonous, caring only to sleep and carouse. They were brought to the island of Hispaniola originally to do the work of miners or of camp servants. They now never moved a step from their houses on foot, but insisted on being carried about the island upon the shoulders of the unfortunate natives, as though they were dignitaries of state! They were accused of torturing, strangling, decapitating, and in divers other ways, killing people on the most trifling pretext. [The natives] avoided them as they would fly from wild beasts.[18]

After all the treasure above ground had been taken, the Spaniards began to look for the gold and silver and precious metals under ground, and the Indians in all three islands were put to work as slaves in the mines. It is estimated that they lived no longer than four years, such was the hardship that they endured in this new labor. In the mines, they had the deadly task of sifting auriferous sands with their bodies half submerged in water, or in breaking up ground beyond the point of exhaustion. They had to run to and from the mines and work long hours in a half-starved condition, for they had no time any longer for hunting and fishing and producing their own food. Yet these were the men whose strength and handsomeness Columbus himself had extolled. He had remarked when he had first seen them, that they were "a fine, healthy, upstanding people."

Some hundred years later, in 1601, Charles I of Spain, pretending horror at the decimation of the Indians in Latin America, issued a public decree ordering that there should be no more slavery in the mines in the Spanish possessions. But at the same time as he made the public proclamation, he sent secret instructions to say that the system was to be continued if lack of slavery in any way interfered with the production of gold or silver.

The Spanish, too, brought diseases that had not been previously known in the islands, such as smallpox, venereal diseases, and leprosy. Working in the mines, of course, brought on lung and intestinal diseases. Since the Indians did not have enough to eat, as they had had in the days before the conquerors arrived, their teeth also rotted.

Eduardo Galeano writes: "The Europeans brought with them Biblical plagues like smallpox and tetanus and various lung and venereal diseases, leprosy, yellow fever, and the Indians died like flies because their organisms had no defense against the new diseases."

Arciniegas says: "The imported diseases refused to respond to traditional herb medicines... In some regions more Indians died of measles than of wars." And he adds, "They were defenseless against syphilis, the French disease."

There is some argument on the part of authorities in regard to syphilis. Arciniegas mentions this doubt. But Professor Samuel Eliot Morison firmly puts it to the native's account. He believes the natives Columbus took home with him (of whom only three survived) infected Spanish women. They in turn infected volunteers in the French Army who were on their way to war in Italy. The first outbreak of epidemic proportions was in Naples in 1494. In September of 1493, Columbus had returned to the Caribbean taking the natives back with him as interpreters, leaving the year before the outbreak. It seems incredible that, within a few months, three Indians attached to the royal household in Spain had infected Spanish women of the town, who then infected passing soldiers and caused an epidemic in Italy much later and far away. Morison says the women of the town must have "joyfully received the Indians." But it seems more likely that they would regard them as curiosities and not likely they would be mixing freely with them. Again, if the natives were responsible for the syphilis, did Columbus then unknowingly send five hundred more Arawaks to Spain the next year as slaves further to infect the populace? Professor Morison makes a point that all the crew of the returning ships to Spain were in fine health. "The crew for the return voyage cannot have contracted syphilis for all were healthy and able to work the ship up to the moment of landing." He says on that rough voyage, men with syphilis would have been very sick indeed. But as has been thoroughly indicated, the Spaniards had been continuously raping the native women. How then had they not become infected? It seems more plausible that this was one of the many diseases that the Spaniards brought into the "Garden of Eden."

Though the Spanish conquerors later discovered other sources of wealth, they soon found that there was little gold and silver to be mined in the Caribbean Islands and many moved on to the mainland. In 1519 Cortez had sailed from Cuba to Mexico and discovered there the fabulous treasures of Montezuma. Roomsful of gold and silver were sent back to Spain. Eduardo Galeano in his book *Open Veins of Latin America: Five Centuries of the Pillage of a Continent,* says that the very riches of Latin America have been the cause of its poverty, because it has been plundered from the time the Spanish arrived to the nineteenth century when the countries became independent. Ever since then, it has been plundered by the British in Argentina and in the rest of the continent by the United States. He recalls how Pizarro, whom he calls an illiterate pig feeder, completely destroyed the fabulous Inca Empire in 1533. He quotes an old Indian text, "Firing harquebuses, hacking with their swords, and leaving pestilence behind them, the little band of implacable conquistadores advanced into America." The cruelty and avarice shown in the islands was to be repeated on a much larger scale in Latin America. "After their Tclacluca massacre, Montezuma sent envoys to Cortez who was advancing on the valley of Mexico. He brought gifts of golden collars and quetzel bird feather banners. The Spaniards were "in seventh heaven" says the Nahuatl text preserved in the Florentine Codex: "They lifted up the gold as if they were monkeys with expressions of joy, as if it put new life into them and let up their hearts, as if they were seeing something for which they yearned with a great thirst. Their bodies fastened on it and they hungered violently for it. They crave gold like hungry swine."

Later, when Cortez reached Tenochititlán, the resplendent Aztec capital with three hundred thousand inhabitants, the Spaniards entered the treasure house, "And then they made a great wall of the gold and set a fire, putting to flame all that remained, no matter how valuable, so that everything was burned. As for the gold, the Spaniards reduced it and made fires."[19]

Edward Dahlberg writes: "Pedro de Alvarado a lieutenant of Cortez, annihilated from four to five million natives in the peninsula of Guatemala and Yucatán within a few years. He also had a king and three caciques burnt alive because they were unable to supply him with as much gold as he coveted."

Cortez started his campaign of conquest from Cuba in 1519, from the Antilles when Fall began. Columbus' main purpose—his diaries leave no doubt of it—had been to find gold. "The hunger and thirst for gold [of the Conquistadores] is reflected in Columbus' journal better than in any other contemporary document."[20]

The purpose of all who followed him was the same. Bernal Diaz del Castillo, taking part in the later conquest of Mexico said, "We came here to serve God and get rich." In less than ninety years, the Spaniards had conquered the Caribbean islands, Mexico, Yucatán, good parts of Central America, Chile and Peru and other areas in South America.

In little more than twenty-five years, the native island populations of Hispaniola, Cuba and Puerto Rico "finally stopped paying tribute because they had disappeared."[21] Within a few decades, these friendly people who had done no harm to the Spaniards had either died of disease that the Conquistadores brought, died in the mines from the hard work, or died from the wars that the Spaniards waged against them.

In Hispaniola, from a population of 250,000 in 1492, not more than 3,500 remained alive in 1538. In Puerto Rico the population had been reduced within twenty-five years from 50,000 to 70,000 people at the time of the Discovery in 1493 to about 2,000. In Cuba, the figures were similar.

"The massacre of Indians that began with Columbus never stopped. Las Casas indignantly stated that forty million Indians [were] exterpated by the Spaniards," though Edward Dahlberg suggests this "is doubtless hyperbole."

The American settlers in North America, arriving a hundred years later, came to break their bonds with Britain. They themselves worked hard to establish a new life on a new continent, and they brought their own families with them.

In contrast, the original group of Spaniards (single adventurers) arriving in the Antilles were there for only one object—wealth. They were interested only in plunder, in the treasure they could send back to their Sovereigns, and accrue for themselves before returning home.

They had no desire to do any work themselves so that when they had decimated the Indians, they looked for a new source of labor.

Fray Bartolomé de Las Casas, horrified by all he had witnessed of the treatment of the Indians and now a priest, constantly pleading on their behalf, could yet suggest the substitution of other human beings—Negroes be brought as slaves from Portuguese West Africa.

The slave trade began as early as 1515, even before the final conquest by the Spaniards of the native inhabitants of the Spanish Antilles.

4 -:- The Settlements

The first cities were set up very early in the Spanish islands. In Hispaniola after the failure of the encampment from the first voyage, Columbus chose a new site on a hill near a harbor which he called Isabella. This was started in 1493 and, as well as a few houses, included the construction of a church, which was finished, so that on "the feast of the Three Kings the Holy Sacrifice was celebrated."[1]

He also built a string of small citadels, many of which such as Santo Domingo and Santiago, were later to be developed into towns. The towns were built of limestone from quarries dug in the mountainside, and trenches were dug around the citadels to guard against attacks by the Indians.

Santo Domingo, to become the capitol, was founded in 1496 by Columbus' brother, Bartholomew. It is the oldest complete European settlement in the Western Hemisphere. Not only many houses, but two churches, a cathedral and a governor's palace were built. The church of San Nicolás was built in 1502, then the San Francisco church in 1504. The magnificent Renaissance cathedral begun in 1514 took twenty-six years to construct. The design is Late Spanish Gothic, with fine arches, flying buttresses, vaulted celings and beautiful filigree work on the façade. "Elsewhere in Latin America, plateresque architecture did not attain the vanity it did in Mexico and Santo Domingo."[2] This type of architecture flowered in Puerto Rico and Cuba too, but was modified later in other edifices from Gothic to Baroque. The churches in the beginning were also built on a fairly large scale so that they might serve as fortress-churches, places where large numbers of people could flee for safety. In the Santo Domingo cathedral, the frescos were painted locally. In the rest of the Antilles and in South America, the majority of paintings, known to date from the sixteenth century, were imported. Also in the Santo Domingo cathedral is the ornate tomb of Christopher Columbus. It is interesting that tombs and statues of the Conquistadores were built throughout the Spanish Islands, but no statues were erected to them in Mexico, where the Inca civilization was completely destroyed. The Santo Domingo cathedral was the first site of European culture and, until the conquest and colonization of Latin America, it was also of first importance in the New World. The Alcazár was erected in 1514 as the residential palace of Diego Columbus, another brother of Columbus, who was made Viceroy for all three islands until his death in 1556. After him there were no more Viceroys in the Antilles. The islands then came under the jurisdiction of the Viceroy of Mexico, where the center of control shifted. The Alcazár and other non-religious buildings were constructed in Moorish style, also then prevalent in Spain, since the Moors had occupied the Iberian peninsula for three hundred years from 700 to 1000 A.D. In fact, they still retained large areas of the country until Ferdinand and Isabel, followed by Charles V, finally drove them out. There were Moors in Columbus' army.

Spanish-Moorish architecture with houses built around courtyards and with tiled roofs are still to be seen today in Spain and the Spanish Antilles. Much of Old San Juan, Puerto Rico, in particular still retains the character of the early colonial period. The Alcazár there is supposed to be a replica of that of Madrid, while Santo Domingo was said to be an effort to erect a second Cadiz in the New World. The great Moorish past in Spain is still exemplified in such famous buildings as the Alhambra of Granada and the Mosque of Cordorba. Under Moorish rule the arts, industries and agriculture reached a level never again attained in Spanish history. This Moorish influence was brought overseas along with the Roman and later Italian influences of the Renaissance. The Moorish character was seen in the houses, the Roman and Italian in the churches. Yet none of this could be transported into so different a climate, nor overlay so different a culture without some modifications. All that was Indian was not totally submerged.

The original Indian name for Hispaniola was Haiti. This is now the western third of the island and returned to its indigenous name when Tousaint L'Overture, the rebel Negro leader, conquered it in 1801. When it had been seceded to the French at the end of the seventeenth century, its name was Saint Dominique. There is a certain confusion of names on the islands.

Columbus landed on this end of the island on December 6th, 1492, and built a fort, La Navidad, which was later to become the capital and the present town of Cap-Haitien. Port-au-Prince replaced Cap-Haitien as the capitol in 1770. The town of Gonaives also erected early was built on the site of an Indian village.

Puerto Rico was settled when Ponce de Leon arrived as governor in 1508. An encampment was begun inland at San Germán, where another of the oldest churches in the Western Hemisphere, Porta Coeli, was built in 1606. Ponce de Leon then moved nearer the north coast to Caparra, but finding this not too satisfactory moved again nearby, where two rocky islets formed an ideal, almost landlocked harbor. Here the city of San Juan was founded in 1521. La Fortaleza, a fortress, now the Governor's palace, was begun in 1523, the Casa Blanca in 1523 and the Cathedral in 15b2. The Dominican friars, the first Order on the island, built the Santo Domingo Convent in 1523 and their chapel, San José, adjoining it. The island was originally called San Juan Bautista and the town Puerto Rico, the rich port, but in time the names were changed, and San Juan became the capitol and Puerto Rico the name of the island. Between the time of discovery and that of Ponce de Leon's arrival in the colonies, some fifteen years, the island had been almost completely neglected by the Spaniards, and the natives had continued to live as they had in the past.

In Cuba, a settlement was first built in Baracoa, then soon after Santiago. One year later, a settlement was started in Havana and finally developed in 1519. However, with Diego de Velázques as governor, it was soon to become an important assembly point for the fleets arriving with treasure from the mainland. The reports of Velázques to the Crown are amongst the important documents that provide much information of this era.

The islands were the first centers of Spanish domination, and it was from them that the conquest of Latin America began. The expeditions of Velázques, Cortéz, Balboa and others all started from Cuba and Puerto Rico. It was a quarter century after the founding of Santo Domingo that the first city in Mexico, Mexico City, was built on the destroyed Azetc city of Tenochtitlán in 1521, with the first erection of the Christian church in 1525 on the site of the main Aztec temple. In South America, Buenos Aires was founded in 1536 but not refounded until 1580, and Caracas was started in 1536, abandoned and not refounded until 1567. So, the longest history of Spanish domination in the Americas has been on th Spanish islands: It started there first and ended there last.

The towns in the New World were built around a square, called a plaza. This was not only a Spanish tradition, but was similar to the squares built by the Indians in their villages and called by them *"bateyes"*. Again as the Indians had done, straight lines were used in forming the towns. Streets were drawn straight and then at right angles, forming greater squares whereas in contrast, streets twisted and turned in Spanish towns. In the plaza, the church was erected on one side and usually the *alcazar* on the opposite side. This middle square became, again as it had for the Indians, the centre for the social life of the people. It was a place to meet friends, to gossip, to market. High and low, white and colored, laborers and people of leisure mingled around it or passed time under the shade of planted trees. It was a place for religious processions and the civil pronouncements of the town crier, informing the people of the news or of the latest royal proclamations. The erection of these imposing and often beautiful edifices in the towns was accomplished in a very few years. The old Indian 'bohios' and villages were succeeded with remarkable rapidity by all aspects of Spanish civilization. Many of the fine buildings erected by the Spaniards in the sixteenth century still remain today.

At the time the cities were being built in America, the Church in Spain, though powerful, was subservient to the Crown. It was a powerful ally but not the supreme authority. Yet their Spanish Majesties were among the strongest defenders of the Catholic faith, then threatened in Europe by arising protestantism under Charles V, who succeeded Ferdinand and Isabella in 1500 and was elected Emperor in 1519, there was a great expansion of empire. His realm finally stretched throughout Spain to the Netherlands, Austria, Italy and across the seas to the Philippines and over almost all of South America. It was the period when Spain was at the peak of its power. Charles drove out all the Jews and finally all the Moors from Spain. He captured the King of France and put the Pope to flight.

In the circumstances the Pope was in a weak position and he allowed the Emperor to make his own choices of bishops. The Emperor was all-powerful. He elected the viceroyalty and the governors and they acted always in the name of the Crown. They had total power in their regions but were accountable to the Spanish rulers. They were their surrogates. The Emperor gave to the conquistadores land and slaves commensurate to the extent of their services to him. There was no self government in the islands and no elections.

Now pronounced savages the Indians and the Negroes had recourse to no justice except through their immediate masters, and they were therefore subject either to the will of a cruel man or some beneficence from a more humane one. However, the Crown had ordered that all Indians and slaves should be "saved" and brought into the Christian church.

The priests, among the earliest settlers, must have made the children, whose parents were of different races, their first converts.

The Indians drew their religious strength from the natural resources around them; the sun, the wind, the rain, the earth, the ocean. The Spaniards' religion was a ritual that had to be practiced not under the open skies, but in the buildings that they fashioned for the glory of their God. Indians were forced into the making of these rising cathedrals, monuments to the God of the Western religion.

The descendants of the conquistadores and the Indians and the Negroes were to continue to worship in the cathedrals conceived by the former and built by the latter for the next 500 years. The Catholic Church still was to have a continuing power and influence during these centuries over the inhabitants of all three islands. In the Dominican Republic, the church was in later years to support the cruel dictatorship of Trujillo through the 1960's. Even in Communist Cuba, the Church was to continue its influence and the Vatican representative became a friend and supporter of Fidel Castro. In Puerto Rico, the Marxist party suggests that their theories can go hand in hand with Christian beliefs.

In the beginning, the church was another weapon used against the native people. As well as by its superiority of arms "Espana conquisto America a Cristazos." (Spain conquered America with blows of the crucifix).

The Indians were forced to accept the new God and the new symbols of worship. They were brought before a public notary and were required to adopt the Catholic faith in a language of course, that they did not understand, except by its obvious threat. They were told the following:

> If you do not [adopt the holy Catholic faith] or if you maliciously delay in doing so, I certify that with God's help I will advance against you and make war on you whenever and wherever I am

able, and will subject you to the yoke and obedience of the Church and of their Majesties, and take your women and children to be slaves, and as such I will sell and dispose of them, as their Majesties may order, and I will take your possessions and do you all the harm that I can.[3]

In Spain, the Inquisition was established in 1478. By Papal Bull, the King of Spain was authorized to control the prosecution, conviction and execution of the heretics. These ceremonies were attended by the King, the count, the clergy and the people. Thus human sacrifice by gladiatorial combat which had been suppressed as a pagan ritual by Christian influence was now restored in its full vigour by the Christian Roman Church. Soon after the settlements in the Spanish Antilles were established, it was asked that the Inquisition be brought the islands.

There were innumerable trials of poor "blasphemous" Negroes. "The most frequent occupants of the Inquisitional jails were the native people."[4] When some Indians were said to have profaned a church, Bartholomew Columbus had them publicly burnt. But it was San Juan, upon the urgent request of its very first bishop, which was the first bishopric in the New World to receive into its hands the authority of the Catholic Inquisition.

Under the circumstances, the Indians, and the Africans after them, accepted the Catholic faith. "Catholic priests, friars and monks . . . abetted the slaughter of the Indians when conversion was the object. But when conversion had been achieved and their rule accepted, they devoted themselves to preserving the people of converted races."[5]

As the churches stood on their old ceremonial grounds; as the crucifixes and the small effigies, the "Santos," replaced their *zemies;* as their old dramas and songs were replaced by Christian pageantry and hymns—a replacement of new forms of old symbols and holy places and actions—the transition might not have been so difficult. The forbidden old religion was artfully intertwined into the commanded new. Old peasants of the islands up in the hills, where the last Indians fled, still fling the last drop of their libations to the ground in long-lost memory of the necessity of tribute to be paid to Mother Earth.

The exhaustion of the gold mines in the islands coincided more or less with the decimation of the natives and with the exploration and discovery of much greater wealth in Mexico and the rest of Latin

America. Since the Spaniards did not intend to work themselves, Negroes were brought in to perform the necessary labor.

The slave trade was authorized by a Papal Bull as early as 1442, that is, before the Discovery. Thus, when a new source of labor was needed, it had already been prescribed by the Church.

The Spaniards then could have "trabájadores más robustos que los Indios"[6]—workers more robust than the Indians. The importation of slaves began as early as 1501 in Hispaniola, 1505 in Cuba, and 1515 in Puerto Rico.

Though the role of the priests who were brought to the islands was primarily to teach the new religion to the people, they had of necessity also to teach them Spanish, to develop a means of communion through a common tongue. The natives of the three islands had come from the Arawak speaking tribes. The Negroes ranged from princes from Dahomey to men from more primitive tribes in the interior of Africa. There was no common tongue among them. Now began the first cementing of people throughout the whole new empire of Spain by means of a common language which has been part of the heritage of all of Latin America for the last four and a half centuries.

In bringing religion—their religion—to the people, the monks also became their educators. The first school was founded by Franciscan monks in Santo Domingo in 1505. Many of the priests in their first attempts to communicate with the Indians used the art of theater, and it was said this helped to bring a great many of the Indians to accept the Christian religion, though in fact, they were given no choice. "The catechism and the abstractions of Christianity succeeded the drama of Indian pagan rites."[7] When the priests used drama to communicate, then, it was more comprehensible to the Indians, for playacting of history had been part of their own tradition. So it was acceptable to them, when some monks "staged mystery plays presenting scenes from sacred history." The priests as well as giving lessons in Latin and Spanish helped "train bricklayers, stone cutters, carpenters, blacksmiths and musicians."[8] Various artisans in different fields had been brought over on the voyages from Spain by then, and the priests' workshops were set up and apprentices taken and taught a trade or skill. As has been recorded, the Indians were quick to pick up languages and were generally intelligent. Along with their own art in carving and making their own homes and household goods, they must have been quick and apt pupils; that is, those that had survived.

With the beginning of schooling and a common language, from which a new hemispheric literature would develop later, and a common religion, the melding of races had also commenced. The hybridization began with the Spaniards mating with Indian women. "The civilizations and races of the Old World and the New World were for the first time brought face to face," and they were "quickly interbreeding with one another."[9] This was followed by the intermarriage of Indian and Negro, and Spaniard and Negro.

The Spanish settlers, unlike those of North America, had no prejudice against intermarriage with the Indians, nor later with mulattoes or Negroes, though white skins were the most socially acceptable. Also, the Spanish had originally brought to the islands few of their own women. They had also had Moors, both dark and light, living amongst them for centuries, so that a colored skin was not strange to them.

In the countryside, many of the people lived Indian-style in small cabins, with hammocks as beds, and living on native fruits and vegetables and planting a few cash crops of coffee, cane and tobacco.

One writer reveals "the rather surprising fact that, in 1765 Census, there still remained 2,000 pure blooded Indians in Puerto Rico."[10] There were degrees then of mixing, percentages varying in the three islands, but in geenral there arose a mestizo population that, according to Professor Darlington, could be considered a separate race in its own right.

The Instituto de Cultura Puertorriqueña has for its emblem the Indian, the Spaniard and the Negro standing side by side, all having made their contribution to the island—all having intermarried over many generations to produce the present day Puerto Rican. The same is true of the making of present day Cubans and Dominicans.

In the art forms that evolved in the Spanish Antilles, the influences of all three races can be distinguished. The Indian heritage persisted. "Even today there are noticeable traces of Antillean Indian blood, although the Indians as a civilization, were wiped out centuries ago by the conquistadores. Enough of them survived, however, in hidden mountain enclaves to intermarry with blacks and whites, leaving a unique—and often strikingly handsome—racial imprint." This is by a modern writer on Puerto Rico. Also, he continues, "even in the eighteenth century Indian music was made by banging hollow tree trunks with sticks, shaking a type of gourd known as a *maraca,* or scratching the notched surface of another type of gourd called, *guiro*."[11] This same type of music, using the same types of gourds, persists in the islands today, only in a more sophisticated form. The tree trunk drum has changed to an African steel drum, and the music given an African rhythm. A Spanish guitar, or its modified version, exemplifies the third influence in Antillean music.

Fray Roman Pané, living in the islands soon after the Discovery, reported that "their laws are set down in ancient songs through which they rule . . . and when they wish to sing their songs, they play a certain instrument that is called Maiohana."

While the towns were built, the mines worked, and the agriculture produced by the labor of Indian and Negro slaves, the crafts and artisan items tended to be in the hands of the mestizos in the early days. The young man with a Spanish father and an Indian mother was likely to be among the first recipients of the monks' schooling. He would also tend to learn the new trades that were needed in the new society: leather-work connected with the horses, grillwork for the houses, the beautification of the churches, and the making of furniture and clay pots like those of his ancestors. Into all of these would go some not-forgotten skills of the past.

"Although it is possible to dispute the extent to which pre-Columbian artistic values survived the Iberian Conquest, there is no doubt an atavistic instinct persisted."[12] Also, considerable adaptations in religious art were necessary because of lack of craftsmen trained in skills and traditions of the Old World. The people, the newly melded people, provided the adaptations and new forms, the popular mergings.

European art of the sixteenth to eighteenth centuries was an aristocratic art created by elegant artists attuned to the temper of wealthy nobles, ecclesiastics of pomp and fortune, and royal courts that monopolized power, riches, and standards of taste. In the Latin American colonies, art became more and more popularly based as the Church succeeded in penetrating into the souls of its parishioners, without distinction of race or social condition. For example, Ricardo E. Alegría, ex-Director of the Instituto de Cultura Puertorriqueño, writes,

> Santos, devotional images of saints and other holy figures, are among the most individual expression of folk art in America. They have been found in the countries of Central and South America, in Mexico, New Mexico, the West Indies—almost every area colonized by Spain in the New World. . . .

All means of intensifying religious zeal were encouraged, and Santeria, the art of making santos, became an important and prolific art form.

Santos were carved for churches and cathedrals, and for domestic altars of both rich and humble families. . . . Due to the difficulty of obtaining religious images from Spain, people began to carve their own from the hardwoods of our [Puerto Rican] forests . . . and thus the *jibaro* was forced to draw upon his own skills, experience and inspiration for the devotional figures.

The Magi or Three Kings have always been Puerto Rican favorites from the earliest days. The Kings always ride horses, and Melchoir, the black King, rides a white horse.

Santos were worshipped to invoke the intercession of the holy figures they represented. The *jibaro* "kept his santo in a special place of honor where it was venerated by all the family and rewarded for its favors with ex votos of silver and other metals."[13]

This account of *santos* is interesting to compare with the Indian religious traditions: "One rather advanced aspect of their culture was the Taino belief in a Supreme Creator. They also worshipped lesser dieties known as *zemies*. Each village and each family had its own *zemi*, and the Tainos made carvings of these in wood, stone, clay or gold."[14]

The shift to the Catholic religion therefore, was made by an adaptation of the Indian forms of worship. The shift from the *zemi* to the *santo* is not too wide a gulf. The Indian was used to making carvings in wood and making carvings of his gods as household objects. It is interesting too that the Magi were so popular. The horse that the Conquistador rode had helped him be "more tall," more powerful, than the Indian. So a black king riding a white horse would have been a symbol of satisfaction to those of Indian descent, and to the Negroes, too.

How some of the Indian ways were passed on is easy to conceive. It is not hard to imagine that an Indian woman, taken against her will, and hating the conquerors who had killed her husband, would take the only measures open to her for retaliation, that is through her children. They would be in her care, and it would be her pride to pass on to them such of the old ways and the old beliefs of her tribe as she could secretly do so.

"The new religion infused the fear of a new god, who, like the old gods, favored the ruling class. It brought the terror of hell, and of the new authority of Spanish justice,"[15] for "the American in the new society had to renounce all his freedoms."

Yet as he carried his cross, the Indian or Negro could hide within it his old fetishes. "The Indians hid fetishes inside crosses so that they might worship their ancient god while they appeared to be adoring Christ."[16]

Within himself, the slave would nourish some traditional faith from which he could draw comfort in his extremity. Like the Indian, the Negro also united with the Catholic religion and its holy figures some of the symbolisms he had brought from Africa, so that there was "voodoo" existing in Haiti, and other forms of "spiritism" in other islands.

Though the building of the cities was progressing swiftly, the countryside had been neglected. The "governing class had little idea of agriculture. They had come for gold and silver and what there was they took. But when this precious stuff was gone, they were somewhat at a loss in their country . . . it was hybridization that saved them."[17]

The Indians had been self-sufficient with crops they grew. They were an agricultural society. In Hispaniola, they had destroyed the crops and done no replanting in an effort to starve out the invaders. In all the islands where the Indians had primarily been forced to work in the mines, they had no time to tend the fields. Thus, the rich, fertile lands were for a long time left uncultivated.

It was the mestizo who began again to farm the land as his Indian forbears had. The age-old roots and crops were again grown.

Actually, in the Western Hemisphere, "maize, beans and squashes all appeared first as wild plants eaten by man in Mexico in the fifth millenium B.C. The squashes included gourds and pumpkins . . . the same is true of the sweet potato from crossing . . . several scattered wild species. The third and second millenia B.C. brought a diversity of crops . . . on which village life and later city life could be based . . . Manioc and sweet potato, as well as tobacco and cocoa (moved) from Puerto Rico to Mexico."

It happened also in all the islands. The natives cultivated all the same produce. Some of the plants that the natives grew were taken to Spain to see if they could be transplanted. Columbus and his men had seen the Indians smoking tobacco. They themselves liked it and this habit spread throughout Europe. Columbus had found that "melons, pumpkins, cucumbers and other similar products were ripe for the picking thirty-six days after they were planted, and nowhere had our people tasted any finer flavor."[18]

This was a time of transportation of plants and crops over the oceans. For, in turn, the conquerors brought their own seeds and plants, especially those from Southern Spain. They tested wheat, beans, flax, alfalfa, and a number of citrus trees—oranges and lemons—as well as a variety of flowers. In Puerto Rico, at King's Garden, a tropical experimental station was begun. Rice, too, came to the tropics by way of India from China, and the mango was brought also originally from India. Bananas came from Guinea, and a certain type of banana is still called a guinea. They were first tried in Hispaniola, but they grew so well, they were soon developed in other islands. And of course, the greatest success came from the planting of the sugar cane. This after awhile was to become the new "White gold" which, with increased Negro slave labor to sow and cut it, was to be the basis of new wealth for the Spaniards in all the islands. Columbus brought the first seeds to Cuba.

The conquerors also brought horses, cattle and chickens, asses, donkeys and oxen. Pizarro, the erstwhile swineherd, was responsible for the introduction of the pig into the New World. The ships arriving at the island harbors were like Noah's Ark with suitable pairs, male and female, of each animal. The Spaniards also brought the plow to the New World and the wagon, and with it, the wheel.

With the growth of the settlements, many of the mestizos had greater social mobility, moving up into the wealthier classes, and adopting their mannerisms and their style of living. From native communism, there was now a stratified society of rich, middleman and poor—owner, freeman and slave—with those at the bottom always the vast majority. They built the cities, worked in the mines and cultivated the fields. It was from their labor that the wealth of the islands was produced, and from the gold of the islands, that the money for the beautiful cathedrals, the palaces and the fortresses was raised. With the growth of the settlements, there arose a new attitude in the ruling class. The sons of the old conquerors began to settle down in the new countries. They were not so anxious to return home to Spain since there was no gold to take with them. Many did go on to the new areas of America where treasure was now found in abundance, but a royal edict soon forbade further immigration, fearing that the islands would become depopulated. The second generation then found the life on the plantations, riding around on horseback master of all they surveyed, not an unpleasing life. They had houses built for themselves in the cities that were developing as well as their haciendas in the country. They lived a life of wining and dining well, of fiestas and dancing. Card playing particularly was a favorite past time. With plenty of slaves in the houses as well as in the fields, there was nothing the masters and mistresses needed to do.

Within a half century, there was a complete transformation in life in the islands, both for the original inhabitants and the invaders.

Latin America had been colonized in this short time. So now, where previously the long native canoes had gone out on fishing trips from the shores, galleons laden with gold and silver stopped over in the fine harbors. Columbus had recognized how well suited the local hard woods would be for shipping, and shipbuilding was started in Cuba. The great forests of the islands were cut down for their lumber for ships, houses and furniture.

The islands became the crossroads between Spain and the western mainlands: the stop-over points for the treasure galleons. There were all the activities of busy ports in all the larger harbors.

The lure of the treasure ships brought pirates, and soon all the capital cities of the Antilles were raided by them. With pirates on the high seas the Crown realized that the strategic position of the islands must be protected.

The gold found in the Caribbean was soon exhausted, but islands became important gateways to the larger continent where the incredible treasure was found.

For the defense of her empire, Spain had to start building fortresses in the coastal regions of her new possessions and especially in the northern islands in the Caribbean. An El Morro Castle was built both in Cuba and Puerto Rico. With the continuing dangers to her treasure ships as time went by, these fortifications were multiplied. This was particularly the case in Puerto Rico where, as well as El Morro, six other large fortresses and several small ones, with gun emplacements, powder magazines, portcullises, and walled enclosures were built over the years. "Add to all this about two miles of subterranean passages, barracks, penal quarters, living quarters—and multiply this up and down the Atlantic Coast—the total is staggering."[19] Mostly Italian engineers were used to design and supervise the construction. The building went on year after year for more than two centuries.

These castles and forts were built by slaves, as the cities themselves had been. So within a half century, there was a complete change in the islands—the building up of the cities, of fine churches, cathedrals, houses; and the intermingling in two or three generations of peoples, so there were no longer just the Spaniards and the blacks and a few Indians, but mixed groups of the children, the grandchildren, and the great-grandchildren who had come of three races in the islands. The Catholic religion dominated the whole area. The single language was used in both the Antilles and Latin America. The generations of local arts and the beginnings of literature appeared in the islands.

Quickly then, the culture and way of life of the original inhabitants had been overthrown. Quickly, a new civilization and a new culture had arisen in its place. Except for the greater importance of the first found colony of Hispaniola, in all cases, those ways of life, the old and the new, were the same for all three islands. Changed by the Conquest, the people of all three islands had the same stratifications, the same mixings. It was not until the next century, the seventeenth, that differences in each of the islands were to occur. These were to come mainly from challenges from Europe and from the rapid rise in the slave trade.

5 -:- The Indians

"Of the formations that history gave to the Caribbean life, two may be considered of extreme importance . . . The first is the colonial experience . . . The second important historical inheritance in the Caribbean, intimately related to the first, has been slavery."[1]

The Indian experience was in many ways repeated in the Negro experience. A modern black writer suggests that it would be wise to see America through the eyes of an Indian. "Indians had a commodity—their land. Blacks were required for the use of their commodity—labor."[2] Though he is writing of North America, this view is equally pertinent to the Spanish Antilles. There, the Indians not only had their land, but at first, gold.

"Whereas the native Arawak Indians perished so fast that one hundred thousand of them in Haiti were reduced to a very few thousand after only twenty years of Spanish occupation, Negro slaves died at only about three fourths of this rate."[3] The Indians were irreplaceable; there was an inexhaustible supply of Africans.

Within less than twenty-five years after the Discovery, the first slave ships started coming from the west coast of Africa to the Caribbean, bringing their human cargo. The first slave ships arrived in Hispaniola in 1515 with a cargo of fifteen thousand blacks. The demand from Puerto Rico for Negro slaves, started earlier, was soon increased after an Indian uprising in 1511. Very soon, too, slaves were brought to Cuba. At first, the Negroes were brought in to fill the place of Indian labor. Oddly, it was Friar Bartolomas de las Casas, soldier turned priest, who, in pity for the cruelly treated Indians, petitioned the Emperor to allow the importation of Negro slaves.

"Thus, through the intercession of God's holy minister, the

African slave trade to the New World was begun."[4] The fifteen thousand slaves brought into Hispaniola in 1515 were the beginning of this slave trade. It ended in millions and millions of Africans being brought, over a period of three and one half centuries, to the Caribbean and America as slaves. The Negroes were first shipped from the west coastal areas of Africa in the hands of the Portuguese. Later the banditry extended into areas in the interior to bring out captives. Later, too, African chiefs themselves, both through coercion and bribery, made raids in the interior of their own country to capture people from other tribes. Black was set against black, tribe against tribe.

Before the slave trade, a traveller could cross the whole of Africa unmolested. After it, there were dangers, wars, general dislocation, hatreds bred and fostered, and the breakdown of old ways and cultures. In the ensuing long periods Africa was to remain "undeveloped," not only because it was later to be colonized and its wealth of copper, cobalt, manganese, tin, uranium, gold, platinum and chromium stolen, but because it had lost millions of its ablest sons and its own civilization had been destroyed from the sixteenth century.

In his book, *The Black Jacobins*, C.L.R. James quotes the works of Prof. Emil Dorday, an African scholar, who said that "in the sixteenth century Central Africa was a territory of peace and happy civilisation. The tribal wars from which the European pirates claimed to deliver the people were mere sham fights. It was a great battle when half a dozen men were killed. It was on a peasantry, in many respects superior to the serfs in large areas of Europe, that the slave trade fell. Tribal life was broken up, and millions of detribalized Africans were let loose upon each other. . . . products of an intolerable pressure on the African peoples, which became fiercer through the centuries as the demands of the industry increased and the methods of coercion were perfected."

The great continent, which may prove to be the cradle of humanity from which man evolved, was fractured and ruined by the capture and sale of its people. What would have happened to their civilization and cultures without the abomination of the slave trade one can only guess. But the trade in slaves that continued for three and a half centuries and involved the tearing of millions of people from their families, their tribes, their gods, their land, had its terrible destructive effect in Africa. Though a mild feudal form of slavery had existed in some parts before the Portuguese settled in the west coast and started the slave trade to the Spanish Antilles, with the enormous proportions that trade developed, the tribes were forced to prey on each other. As the civilizations in Latin America had been destroyed by the Spanish Conquistadores so those in Africa had been destroyed by the Portuguese and those that followed them. "Much of the later despotism [within African tribes] arose out of anarchy brought by the slave trade and the advent of firearms."[5]

Before the slave trade, "Advanced cultures had rapidly developed in West Africa—the Nok culture is thought to have begun well before 2000 B.C." There were Bantu areas. "The great kingdoms of the interior . . . . The mining civilisation of Katanga, the stone city of Lunbabive in Rhodesia, the lake kingdoms of Uganda, Ruandi, and Urandi were Bantú domains. Their philosophies were in no way primitive."

In the Yoruba tribes, ancestor kings were men of wisdom, devoting their lives to the metaphysical concepts. "Ifa, along with many other divinities of the Yoruba, came to the New World in the fetid holds of slave ships. Although this difficult art of divination tended, for obvious reasons to fall into disuse, it was preserved in Cuba. The metaphysical assumptions out of which Ifa evolved transcendental ethical systems are shared by all traditionally educated Black Africans, whose forefathers perceived themselves to be part of a continuum of forces both seen and unseen."[7] They had their own arts. "The Mangbetta, a tall Negro people [from the north Congo] are noted for their highly developed artistic sense. The murals with which they have decorated their court buildings are particularly impressive." There are the bronzes of the Benin and Shango cultures to consider.

"Africa was not some sort of blank page in the history of humanity." Africa has a "history that contains certain cultural elements of great value . . . . Its values were values that could still make an important contribution to the world."[9] This is at last being recognized. Just as today's archeologists cannot find sufficiently high praise for the culture of Mexico and South America, of which the Spanish Antilles were a small derivative part, so today's artists of magnitude—Picasso, Vlaminck, Braque, and Henry Moore among others—have been greatly influenced by past African culture, though Gauguin claimed his talents were derived from the Incas.

The main cultural contribution of the United States has been the music based on Negro music, and Negro music has been a strong element of the music of the Spanish Antilles.

Africa's social formation, its educational level, its artisan skills, though varied from area to area, were by no means primitive.

"It is a fundamental error to consider other cultures as inferior to our own, simply because they are different," says Professor Otto Klineberg of Columbia University. African society "had evolved from the family through the clan to the tribe. Until the end of the Middle Ages, there were kingdoms like Nelle and Songhai where culture was so rich and vigorous that their schools and universities attracted scholars from Asia and Europe. Among the people of these kingdoms, the weaving of cloth, the working of metal, the making of pottery and the turning of wood had long been common skills. Indeed, they had clanked into the iron age before Europe climbed from the age of stone."

"The general structure of society was socialistic," as it had been with the Indians. "They were communal societies, never societies of the many for the few. . . . They were cooperative societies, fraternal societies."[10]

However, "In some tribes the political system was monarchal, in others, aristocratic. There were courts and kings, chiefs and headmen, and all degrees of lesser folk. Craft guilds and trade guilds prescribed markets, the common ownership of land and a monetary system based on the cowrie shell proved not only that living was complex but that sustaining life meant doing more than stretching open-mouthed under a mango tree." There were considerable differences among these people. "They were, these slaves, people of at least four great races — the Negritiens, the Fallatahs, the Bantus and the Galles — and many tribes whose names make a kind of poetry."

These were the men, then, of great variety and culture, who were thrown like cattle into ships and brought to the Antilles to provide slave labor for the islands. Such were these men, handsome, vigorous, proud, who were wrenched from their homeland, deprived of their manhood and all human qualities, to serve the whims of the indolent and mostly ignorant conquistadores and their successors in the New World. Like the Indian, so too should the African inheritance in the islands be reevaluated.

"They came in chains and they came from everywhere along the west coast of Africa and from a thousand nameless villages inland."[11] The slaves were collected, in the interior, fastened one to another in columns loaded with heavy stones of forty or fifty pounds in weight, and then marched on the long journey to the sea.

The conditions under which they were brought in ships to the New World were indescribable in their horrors. The captains, afraid of revolt of the Africans, kept them in the holds, huddled together in the stench in the burning heat. A great portion of each cargo, this human cargo, died on the voyage. Probably a third of those captured died on the voyage.

In the holds of the ships with a space of only four or five feet in length and two or three feet in height, for each person, so that they could neither lie at full length nor sit upright, they were chained together, right hand to right leg, left hand to left leg, and all attached in rows to long iron bars. Thus, they lived for the long voyage, allowed only to come up once a day for exercise. Negroes escaping from the hatch when food was put down, would run to the side of the boat and throw themselves into the sea, and commit suicide rather than continue living so intolerably. "No place on earth has concentrated so much misery as the hold of a slave ship."[12]

The Negroes died not only from enormous hardships, but also from rage and despair, having been wrenched from their families, their tribes, their traditions, force-marched for hundreds of miles, then herded together in these ghastly ships. They were taken far across the ocean to unknown lands; there, to be put to work as beasts of burden. Arriving at their destination first in the Caribbean and later in America, they were put on display like cattle. At the ports and in the plazas of the Spanish islands, the white purchaser would often treat the individual black man as he might treat an animal: look at his teeth, feel his muscles, even his genitals, to see if he was a good and healthy specimen; estimate how much labor would be obtained from him; and then make his bid in this human market. He usually decided it was better working a man to death in ten years and then buying a new slave, than to think in terms of a slave's life for twenty years.

Naturally, revolts and attempts to escape, both individual and collective, occurred: from the place of origin of capture, at the point of embarkation, aboard ship, at the stop-over points, in the markets and finally on the plantations. There was no opportunity that was not taken to escape, despite immense risks and fearful punishments. In Santo Domingo, all the slaves of the son of Diego Columbus revolted, but all ended on the gallows.

Slaves ran away in the islands to the mountains, as the Indians had done before them. They formed marauding bands who swept down to villages and plantations to obtain food and anything else they could get. Some were called "Maroons," and it was of such fighters that the Black Republic of Haiti was to be born.

"Fear of the slaves was the permanent psychological feature of slave trader and slave owner."[13] All feared the vengeance which might be wrecked on them in a revolt. Because of this fear, the captured people were kept in chains on the long journey from the interior to the coast of Africa and on the ships, even though shut down in the holds. Whips were used freely, too. Fear of that strong black African, who in the Antilles had come to replace the less robust Indian, was ever present. The fear bred cruelty. Force, brutality, sadism were used.

The Spanish were notorious for maiming slaves for small offenses. As the Spaniards had cut off the heads of the Indians for sport, now for the slightest infractions of rules, or just for the whim of it, they mutilated the Negroes.

"Mutilations were common: limbs, ears and sometimes the private parts [were cut] to deprive them of the pleasures which they could indulge in without expense.... Their masters poured burning wax on their arms and hands and shoulders; emptied the boiling cane sugar over their heads, burned them alive; roasted them on slow fires; filled them with gunpowder and blew them up with a match; buried them up to their necks and smeared their heads with sugar that the flies might devour them; fastened them near the nests of ants or wasps; made them eat their own excrement." Many were whipped to death. "The slaves received the whip with more certainty and regularity than they received their food."[15]

Galeano writes bitterly on the subject. "Priests, who received five percent of the sugar production price, gave Christian absolution to overseers who administered punishment like Jesus Christ castigated sinners." The slave owners, to justify to themselves their own inhumane behaviour, said the slaves were thieves and drunkards, treacherous and lazy. But a Swiss writer, describing his travels in the Caribbean wrote after seeing slaves at work: "There were about one hundred men and women of different ages all occupied in digging ditches in a canefield. The majority of them naked or covered with rags. The sun shone down with full force on their head. Sweat rolled from all parts of their bodies, their limbs weighed down by the heat, with the weight of their picks and by the resistance of the clay soil. They tried hard enough to break it with their implements, strained themselves to overcome every obstacle. A mournful silence reigned, exhaustion was stamped on every face, but the hour of rest could not come yet. The pitiless eye of the manager patrolled the gang, and several foremen armed with long whips moved periodically between them, giving stinging blow to all those who, worn out by the heat, were compelled to take a rest—man or woman, young or old."[16]

The reason for the ditch digging was that a ditch had to encircle each area that was planted. As the cane grew up, new cane would be planted, so there was constant digging of ditches, as well as the actual labor of the cutting. The slaves worked like animals and were housed like animals. They were fed a starvation diet. "When the herrings were unfit for the whites, they were brought up by the planters for the slaves." These fish, together with a few handfuls of corn, were the standard slave ration in the Caribbean.

Late in the eighteenth century, sources of starch were brought into the islands, such as the breadfruit tree from Tahiti, and mangoes from Africa, to help feed the slaves.

They were sometimes given small pieces of land, which in their infrequent hours of freedom from their work on the plantation, they could cultivate for themselves. It was only by these means, by the extension of their labor, that they managed to keep themselves alive by raising a few chickens and cultivating a few vegetables. Since men and women both toiled eighteen hours in the field, where then did they find the strength or the time to till and grow for themselves?

"The stranger in Santo Domingo was awakened by the cracks of the whips, the stifled cries, and the heavy groan of the Negroes, who saw the sunrise only to curse it, for it signalled their labors and their pains. Their work began at daybreak. At eight, they stopped for a short breakfast and worked again till midday. They began again until evening, sometimes until ten or eleven.

"Day after searing day, week after week, year after tortured year, the slaves toiled and died." And ever more and more were brought in. "Natural increase played almost no part in supplying the Antilles and Latin America with slaves."

To some extent, this was due to the sterility caused by hardships the Negro women endured: but part of it was a measure of revolt. The Negroes could refuse this: to produce children to be born in slavery. This was not total, of course, but once abolition occurred, it is interesting to note that a natural increase in Negro families occurred.

The owners took some care of pregnant women. In Cuba, "Overseers applied their thongs of hemp to the backs of pregnant female blacks, who had erred, but not before stretching them out with their bellies over a hole to avoid damaging the expected little creature. They still wanted to keep the progeny for future use."[17] And here is a description of the slave's condition a century before emancipation in Puerto Rico. "The coarse cloth which covers part of his bare body neither defends him from the heat of day nor the harmful night dew: the food that is given him — cassava, sweet potatoes, bananas and such things — scarcely suffices to sustain his wretched existence; deprived of everything he is condemned to continuous labor, always subject to experiencing the cruelty of his greedy and fierce master. A white insults any of them with impunity and in the most contemptible terms; some masters treat them with despicable harshness; getting pleasure out of keeping the tyrant's rod always raised and thereby causing disloyalty, desertion and suicide.[18]

"Colonization," says Aimé Cesaire, "dehumanizes even the most civilized men—the colonizer in order to ease his conscience gets into the habit of seeing the other man as an *animal*, accustoms himself to treating him like an animal and tends objectively to transform *himself* into an animal."

As the Indians, in the Spaniards' expressed views, had changed from loveable, gentle people into savages whose souls needed saving, and whose wickedness made them unfit for anything but work in the mines, now the same calumniations were extended to the Negroes. Though they worked hard from morning till night under broiling sun, they were essentially "lazy." Though it was their labor in every field that created wealth, they were incompetent—and ignorant. Further, it was necessary that the existence of their own culture and civilization be blotted out and denied, as that of the Indians had been. It led to the justification by the white man—first by the Spaniard, then by other Europeans, then by North Americans—of his inhumanity. It led one Frenchman to write: "It must not be forgotten that [slavery] is no more abnormal than the domestication of the horse or the ox." And another wrote: "The regeneration of the inferior or degenerate races by the superior races is part of the providential order of things for humanity." This quotation is from Renan, the Western humanist, the "idealist" philosopher. A clergyman wrote, "Humanity must not, cannot allow the incompetence, negligence, and laziness of the uncivilized people's to leave idle indefinitely, the wealth which God confided to them, charging them to make it serve the good of all."

Louis Philippe, later to become King of France, in exile after his father was guillotined by the French Revolution, was appalled by George Washington's shabby treatment of his three hundred slaves. A surprising indictment from the man whose mother had said of the poor who had no bread, "Let them eat cake."

Thomas Jefferson believed in the institution of slavery and was himself a slave owner. In 1858, Lincoln said in a speech in Charleston: "There is a physical difference between the white and black races which I believe will forever forbid the two races living together on terms of social and political equality."

"No one colonizes innocently," says Aimé Cesaire. This was true of the Spaniard in relation to the Indian. It was true of the Spaniards and later of the other Europeans and Americans in relation to the Negroes. Every possible means had to be used to prove that the Negro, like the Indian before him, was an inferior human being. In religion, he was a pagan, outside the white pale. However, the religion of colonizers had little to do with the teaching of Christ, who was himself a revolutionary and crucified as such. "Religion provided the dishonest equations. Christianity = civilization: paganism = savagery." Yet, Frobenius wrote: "Civilized to the marrow of their bones, the idea of a barbaric Negro is a European invention."

The slave trade resulted in tremendous wealth for the Spaniards; tremendous fortunes were made in this inhumane trade of man. And the labor of the slaves also created great wealth in the sugar plantations that were developed in all the islands. So, while the islands did not any longer have gold resources, these two trades of black men and sugar produced great wealth. Tribute had to be sent back to the Spanish crown, but the traders and the plantation owners in the colonies became rich.

The plants of the sugar cane were brought to Cuba by Christopher Columbus on his second voyage. From that time, even to the present day of Fidel Castro's regime, sugar has been the predominant crop. From Cuba, sugar growing spread to the other Spanish islands and throughout the Caribbean. Cultivation in Puerto Rico started in 1514, and by 1850 was to be worth four billion pesos.

In the early 1700s, a Frenchman introduced coffee seeds into Puerto Rico. Coffee, too, was then grown on the islands and needed slave labor; cotton, too; and tobacco, which the Indians had cultivated. All became profitable exports to Europe, though Spain allowed her colonies to trade only with the homeland.

As sugar, called "white gold" as today's oil is called "black gold," was producing such fabulous wealth for the islands, so more and more of the land was planted with sugar and more and more slaves were brought into the islands to work in the sugar plantations. "The slaves were the most necessary, most valuable and most mobile part of the planter's capital."[19]

Though sugar gave immediate riches to the few, the general growth of the islands was retarded by this monoculture. With the growth of the settlements, there was also a need for house servants which the Negroes filled. Some social distinctions appeared amongst the slaves on the haciendas. These social distinctions related to the role of the slaves in the social and economic organization of the plantation. There was a distinction between those who served as house slaves, and those who toiled in the fields. House slaves had a certain superiority, and dressed in the hand-me-downs of their masters and mistresses. If they displayed individual talent and skill as artisans, these were sometimes recognized by their masters, which gave them a superior status among their fellow bondsmen. Also, the house slaves often acquired some elements of education from their masters' homes.

Although they were often treated better than the field hands, they still lived under miserable, degrading conditions. One elderly woman in Puerto Rico, in an interview in a newspaper in 1975, to illustrate the liberalism in her father's household when she was a child, related how Negroes in her home did not have to kneel, as they did elsewhere, when they wished to talk to their masters. But some of the slaves absorbed a little education.

The early monks had set out to educate the Indians. With the Negro slaves, there was neither time nor desire to educate them. In general, it was felt that education would be dangrous and it was better to keep them ignorant.

A few Jews on the islands, some of whom had come from Spain (having been driven out by Charles V), and Jews from Holland seeking refuge in the New World, gave their slaves instruction in their religion and thus offered a little education. Bernard Shaw once wrote, "Ancient Hebrew history and literature, half fabulous as it is, is better than no history and no literature."

In St. Croix, the island next to Puerto Rico, it was suggested that the benign influence of the doctrine of the United Bretheren would be a fine sedative for the fractious Negroes "who do not fully seem to appreciate what a good thing was being done for them."[20]

Once the European powers were taking part in the trade, it was said that amongst them in the Caribbean, the Spanish treated the slaves best. The Spanish had a policy that a "slave had a right to his freedom, as soon as he could repay to his master the sum he had cost."

"In order to allow the slave to do this, he was not only allowed the undisturbed enjoyment of the Sabbath, but he was allowed also one day in the week for the cultivation of his provision-grounds, his master being entitled to the labor of the other five. As soon, however, as the slave, by his industry and frugality, had accumulated the fifth part of his value, it was usual for the master, on being paid the amount, to relinquish to the slave another day of the week, and so on until he had repaid the whole of his original cost, and thus become altogether free.... In consequence of this admirable system, the whole Negro population of the Spanish possessions were so rapidly approximating to emancipation that about the year 1790, the number of free blacks and people of color somewhat exceeded in all of them, the number of slaves."

This was written by an English abolitionist, Tachery Maucauley, in 1823, thirty years later—a time when talk of both abolition and revolution was in the air, and when Spain's power was in sharp decline.

The almost inhuman labor needed to achieve the price of freedom is hard to imagine. It also shows how dearly, and with what patience, the Negroes sought that freedom. Even so, it meant that 275 years after the first import, half the populations in the Spanish Antilles were still slaves. The mestizos were often free men from the beginning. Only the percentages varied from island to island due to varied circumstances in their histories. Differences in the populations in the Spanish Antilles were formed to the degree to which they imported slaves and themselves engaged in the slave trade.

In Hispaniola, the first Negro slaves arrived in the western ports, which continued to be the main arrival centre, and that side of the island became predominantly black. In western Hispaniola and in the area of the town of Santo Domingo, in the ensuing years Negroes far outnumbered mestizos and whites. Thus, Toussaint L'Ouverture, who was to create a Black Republic in that part of the island (and give back its old Indian name of Haiti), when asked by a timid follower how the slaves could be successful in their revolt, answered by showing a flask full of beans. There were both white beans and black beans in it, but when it was vigorously shaken up, the white beans scarcely showed.

In the eastern side of the island, later to become the Dominican

Republic, the Negroes were not so prolific. After the black revolution, the Spaniards there were joined by many fleeing Frenchmen. Later too, because of the pressure of overpopulation of the blacks in Haiti, the Dominicans invited European refugees to emigrate to their territory.

Cuba imported large numbers of Negro slaves because of the size of the island and because of the extent of the sugar plantations. "In twenty-one years, 320,000 slaves were taken to Cuba alone."[21] Also, during one year of British rule in Cuba, when the British had become the chief slave traders, the number of Negroes imported was ten times that of any similar period.

In 1975, Castro was to tell his countrymen that they were not just Latin Americans, but Latin Africans. Thus some distinctions arose in the islands with the introduction of slavery and according to the number of slaves imported. Puerto Rico, the smallest of the islands and therefore the most easily held, emerged as one of the most formidable Spanish strongholds in the New World. Spanish and mestizos were used as soldiers for guarding the fortresses in San Juan. It was not a slave trading center and the area for plantations of sugar, coffee and tobacco was smaller, so fewer slaves were needed. There were more immigrations of Spaniards to fill military and administrative positions over the centuries. In the period of the Latin American revolutions, Spanish loyalists were to flee to Puerto Rico for safety, and most of a garrison of Portuguese were to remain.

By 1550, it is estimated there were fifteen hundred Negroes on the island. From 1664, when there was competition from other European powers in the area, the Spanish governors instituted a policy of giving refuge to run-away slaves from neighboring islands. These Negroes were given their freedom on the condition that they embraced the Catholic Church and swore allegiance to Spain. Of forty-five thousand Blacks, only about five thousand were slaves at this time. Most Negroes then in Puerto Rico had a long heritage as freemen. There has been an enclave of Blacks, in Loiza Aldea, just east of San Juan, for the past four hundred years, providing the largest concentration of Negro population in the island. Here they live today as they have for generations with their home-made huts amongst palm trees on the shore, using the coconut palms and fibres for thatching; fishing; keeping a few goats and chickens; living a settled rural life within a few minutes' ride of the present metropolis.

But in the beginning, as in the other two islands, all Blacks were slaves and worked first in the mines, then in the fields in unrewarded labor under the constant lash of the whip. At first Portugal had supplied Spain with slaves, but Spain had then rapidly entered into the slave trade herself. The Spanish Antilles were to become a stop-over for slaves from Africa, as they were for gold and silver from South America, Havana being a great gathering place for the Spanish treasure fleet. The Negroes were so sick on the voyage that those who survived needed their health restored or they would be valueless to buyers. They were rested and fed, so that they would be in better shape when presented in the human market elsewhere.

When the three islands had absorbed all the Negroes they could use for themselves, they sold those they had made "tractable" by the whip and various means of torture to the southern states in America. There a great new need of labor had arisen, and it was on the labor of the Negroes, first in the south and then in the north, (in addition to European immigrant labor) that the wealth and power of North America was to be constructed.

From the first fifteen thousand slaves imported into Hispaniola in 1515. "Within a century slaving had grown into a commercial enterprise of such proportions that no civilized nation could ignore it as a lucrative source of trade. . . . In the twenty years from 1571 to 1591, Brazil imported fifty-two thousand slaves. More than three hundred ships out of Liverpool, England, were engaged in the trade by 1744; by which time, too, the British West Indies alone had imported two million black slaves."[22] In the American colonies, by 1776, there were over a million. In 1664, a private company given the monopoly of trade to Santo Domingo supplied two thousand Negroes each year. By 1720, the colonists of the island needed eight thousand per year. Estimates vary, but in all from fifteen to fifty million Africans were enslaved overseas.

The Spaniards only led the way that was to be followed by other Europeans—English, French, Dutch, Danish—and then by North Americans. Yet the Spanish colonies always had fewer Negro slaves than the British and French colonies. There were also at various periods new influxes of Spaniards into the island, and there were marriages between whites, mestizos, and blacks. The social stratification was always more fluid in the Spanish Antilles than in the rest of the islands of the Caribbean.

The Spanish, surprisingly, until the nineteenth Century—the century in which slavery was to end—did a relatively small trading on the West African coasts themselves, preferring to buy slaves from the other European powers.

In England, several members of the Royal family were shareholders in the Negro-buying enterprise. The price in Africa for a slave was three pounds. His selling price in the West Indies was seventeen pounds. This was the price of one ton of sugar. How many tons did one Negro produce in his lifetime? The French originally received the "Asiento," the monopoly on the Spanish slave trade, but with the treaty after the War of the Spanish Succession, the concession went to the British. One of its interests in that war had been to obtain this valuable trading concession.

The problem of organizing a regular and reliable supply of slaves became a major preoccupation of governments. If supply failed, even for a year or two, sugar production suffered, for slaves in those days were short-lived.

Von Humboldt describes Havana in 1800 as almost the size of New York, with a population of 44,000, of whom half were Negroes and mulattoes. The harbor was "still the most important strategic base of the Spanish colonial navy." He visited for weeks its sugar plantations and factories, and its indigo, tobacco and cotton fields, "where the slaves labored in unspeakable miseries." In 1828 he published his *Political Essay on the Island of Cuba*. In it, he called for the abolition of slavery. He estimated that in the fourteen years between 1811 and 1825, Cuba received some 185,000 Negroes from Africa. He wrote in a letter to his brother, describing a slave market of the nineteenth century, "The slaves exposed for sale were young men from fifteen to twenty years of age. The people who came to purchase examined the teeth of these slaves, to judge their age and health, forcing open their mouths as we do with horses in a market." The slaves were then marked with a hot iron like cattle, so they could be identified in case they ran away.

In Havana, he obtained government statistics for 1786. Into the English islands in the West Indies alone more than two million slaves from Africa had been forcibly introduced in the preceding hundred years. In the year of 1806, the English West Indian slave trade involved some 53,000 Negroes, and in the United States, 15,000 blacks. "It would be easy to prove," he wrote, "that the whole of the West Indies which now comprise scarcely 2,400,000 Negroes and mulattoes (free and slaves) received from 1670 to 1825 nearly 5,000,000 Africans.... These revolting calculations do not include the number of unfortunate slaves who perished on the passage or were thrown into the sea as damaged merchandise." In his book on Cuba, he continued, "If the legislation of the Antilles and the condition of the colored population does not experience some salutary change the political power may well pass into the hands of that class which holds the might of labor, the will to throw off the yoke."

A Black Republic already existed in Haiti. He thought a federation of black states might well arise. He also warned that Cuba's wealth could not be continued without the end of slavery. Interestingly, Lord Palmerston in England in 1851 urged that slavery be abolished in Cuba as this would "create a most powerful element of resistance to any scheme of annexation to the United States."

The first English colony in Africa was financed by a company in 1787 to establish Sierra Leone as a home of freed slaves. At this time in England, there were some 10,000 Negro slaves, the property of West Indians who lived in England.

Wilberforce, aided by Fox and Pitt, won an agreement with the Houses of Parliament that the slave trade should be abolished within four years, by 1792, though in fact abolition did not take place until fifteen years later, in January 1808. The Abolition Act put England out of the slave trade at least legally, while half the slave trade was still in its hands.

The United States government declared the slave trade illegal in 1808, though many Americans managed to evade the law by selling them their ships to Spain. Spain belatedly declared the trade illegal in 1820. In Cuba, the trade even increased after that date and continued until 1865, for the demand for slaves both in Cuba and the United States continued with the expansion of the sugar, cotton and tobacco production.

Louisiana as a sugar state by 1830 was producing half of the sugar needs of the United States, while the American south became the world's greatest supplier of cotton.

The Methodists and Baptists were the first to preach abolition in the colonies, the Quakers the first to denounce it in England. By the mid-nineteenth century, slavery existed only in the Spanish Caribbean islands, Cuba, the Dominican Republic and Puerto Rico. Slave traders of any nationality who imported slaves were allowed to export nine other commodities free of duty.

Eduardo Galeano says that by about the end of the seventeenth century, two hundred years after the Conquest, pillage having taken place continuously since the first invaders, 99 percent of the mineral exports from South America was silver. Latin America still constituted a huge mine.

The plundered gold and silver from the Caribbean and Latin America spread through Europe, and provided the accumulation of capital which made possible its historic advances in world economic evolution. While for North America, "the triangular trade in sugar, rum and slaves is an instance of programmed accumulation of wealth such as the world has never seen."[23] For there was this second source for the accumulation of capital, that came from Africa in the form of the slave trade. The western world's development and North American growth were based on these two sources—pillage and slavery—both of which had their beginnings in the Spanish Antilles.

6 -:- Entry of the Foreign Powers

Spain had conquered the New World in an amazingly short time. Columbus discovered Hispaniola in 1493. Colonization began there in 1501 and swiftly followed in Puerto Rico in 1508 and in Cuba in 1511. Cortéz conquered Mexico in 1519; Central America was claimed in 1523; Peru was conquered by Pizzaro in 1533; Chile came into Spanish hands in 1540; and the silver mines in Bolivia were opened in 1545. The Pope had ruled that the Catholic Kings of Spain could claim all the land her envoys discovered, beyond a tracing he made, which gave Brazil to Portugal. Within fifty years, the vast area of the New World, from Florida through Mexico down through Central and South America and encompassing the whole Caribbean area, was part of the new Spanish Empire.

At first all Europe, amazed by the Discoveries, was content to benefit indirectly from the fabulous fortune Spain was amassing from her new colonies. For the Spanish luxuriated in what was a never ending stream of gold and silver. The Spanish aristocracy devoted itself to extravagance. The upperclass Spanish representing Spain "became a nation of people living on a fixed income, a nation of gentlemen, who lived in parasitic dependence on the gold and silver which came to them from the Indies. They were a people maintained by the shipment of wealth from the colonies to the mother country."[1] The squanderings of the aristocracy condemned Spain to economic impotence.

"The Duke of Medinaceli had seven hundred servants, and the Duke of Osuna to score off the Tsar of Russia, dressed his three hundred in leather cloaks. . . . The laces of Lille and Arras, Dutch fabrics, Brussels tapestries, Florentine brocades, Venetian crystal, Milanese arms, and French wines and cloths, swamped the Spanish market." The silver and gold from the New World went to France, England, Holland.

"Every year from 800 to 1,000 ships unloaded in Spain the products of other countries' industries." Thus, despite the enormous wealth Spain acquired and continued to acquire from its colonies, it remained backward. It developed little industry of its own. Yet as late as the eighteenth century, "the economic surplus drained from Mexico (alone) between 1760 and 1809"—a bare fifty years—"through silver and gold exports has been estimated at some five billion present day dollars."[2] The industrious burghers of other countries reaped the benefits. The resources usurped from Latin America by Spain laid the capital foundation for expansion of industry in England, France and Holland. It is said that without the tremendous gold reserves England had acquired indirectly from Latin America, she would not have later been able to confront and defeat Napoleon.

"Latin American silver and gold," as Engels put it, "penetrated like a corrosive acid through all the pores of Europe's moribund feudal society—for the benefit of nascent mercantilist capitalism."

Spain used her wealth for lavish ostentation. The enormous amounts brought into Spain spread through Europe. It was channelled into other countries. England, France and Holland thriftily used the money to build up the rising bourgeois classes in their countries. The European Industrial Revolution was built on the destruction of a civilization going back three thousand years in America, from the plunder of its resources, and from the inhuman trade of other men—black men from Africa, whose sweat, blood and tears produced that foundation. Industry and capital investment, so lacking in Latin America and the Caribbean and Africa today, were built for the Western Europeans from these countries in the preceeding centuries.

Greed grows upon itself. The profits from trade alone could be expanded. It entered the minds of men in power in other European countries, that as well as these indirect benefits, they might take the wealth from Spain at its source. The small gold mines in Hispaniola alone were said to have yielded twenty-five to thirty million a year. So, "Soon after the Conquest of a great part of the New World, Spain and Portugal had to defend their colonies from North European rivals. This rivalry began with the coming of the corsairs in the sixteenth century and ended in the early nineteenth century with the last of a half-dozen imperial wars and with independence movements these wars helped to generate."³

The Caribbean area was the main centre of rivalry. The settlements and new cities were no more than fifty years in existence when the peace in the area was shattered by the invasion of pirates. No port in the islands or the Spanish mainland was safe from these marauders of the sea. The pirates were of many nationalities and though they acted in the beginning as individuals, they had the unwritten support of their various countries. All the Caribbean islands and countries of South America were threatened. Spain could no longer safely allow single ships to sail with gold and silver from Columbia, Peru and Mexico. For safety, she had to send whole fleets and build assembly stations and have naval ships standing by the harbors for protection against foreign intrusion.

"By 1543, French corsairs in the South Atlantic obliged Spain to adopt the Venetian fleet system, which displaced the sailing of individual ships to America."⁴ The French were the forerunners but the English soon followed.

It was necessary to build a series of fortresses on the islands and on the threatened coastal areas. Antonelli, the first of a number of Italian military engineers that Spain sent out, recommended fortifications in Havana, Cuba, and San Juan, Puerto Rico, since these were the most important ports of call for the arrival of treasure fleets.

Twenty-five years after the first settlement in San Juan, the first fort, La Fortaleza, was built, to be followed six years later in 1539 by the start of El Morro, the huge fortification at the northeast headland. A similar El Morro was built in Havana. These were the initial fortifications. Year by year, they had to be extended as European piracy mushroomed. In Puerto Rico, El Cañuelo, San Cristobal and Fort San Jeronimo were constructed for protection around San Juan. Finally a wall was built all around the town. Most of the inhabitants lived within those walls during the years the island was under attack.

"In 1582, a military garrison was established at El Morro, thus converting Puerto Rico into a military base. This meant that San Juan was from its early days a military society, its tone set by Spanish soldiers."⁵ There was a continuous influx of Spanish personnel for the garrison. Puerto Rico was in essence a military island with San Juan a military town, valued for its strategic position. The governor, a military man, was in complete command, surrounded by other military men. His job was to keep the island safe as a gateway to Spain for the treasure galleons. Puerto Rico was to develop within this authoritarian framework. The island's economy was insufficient to support the military necessities. An annual sum was sent, therefore, from the Viceroy of Mexico, the overseer of all the Spanish islands, to aid in these expenses. This bounty from the Mexican treasury was continued until the independence of Mexico from Spain.

The pirates, with single ships flying the skull and crossbones, were succeeded by buccaneers openly supported by their European powers. They had whole fleets of ships with a hundred soldiers or more aboard and equipped with cannon and other armory. They were commanded by such men as Sir Francis Drake and Henry Morgan, who became famous for their exploits in the Caribbean. Spain's treasure galleons were constantly menaced, not only on the high seas but in her ports. In 1595, for instance, Drake tried to capture a treasure ship in San Juan.

In Puerto Rico in 1595, the famous buccaneer, Hawkins, was killed in one of the many fights in which the island was embroiled. In 1598, the Earl of Cumberland attacked the city of San Juan and held it for three months. He came with a great fleet but his troops were defeated by an epidemic, as well as by the valiant fighting of the defenders.

The attempted capture of the cargo of silver and gold from the Spanish fleet on the high seas led almost naturally to trying to take over Spain's colonies. The occupation of the islands and some of the other territories by North European powers began. In the sixteenth and seventeenth centuries, there were numbers of attempts to wrest the islands of the Greater Antilles from Spain's grasp. Spain could afford to let some of the islands of the Lesser Antilles go, but the three large islands in the north were of major importance and they were fortified and defended. In 1586, Hispaniola, St. Augustine, Florida and Cartagena, Columbia, all towns fortified by the Spanish in the Caribbean, were attacked and sacked. But none were held. The attacks of the buccaneers on Spanish ports in America coincided with the long wars in Europe between Spain and her enemies. Her position as a dominant power was on the wane. Her armies were overextended, her navy costly. The Crown was in financial difficulty.

In 1543, three quarters of all royal revenues were used for the payment of annuities on debts. Isabella and Ferdinand had consolidated sections of Spain by their marriage and had helped finance the exploration of America. Under Charles V, their successor, who was elected emperor, the expansion into other countries made Spain powerful both in the Old and the New Worlds. The Netherlands, Austria, and parts of Italy were all encompassed in the Spanish Empire within a short period, as well as the whole of the Caribbean, Mexico, Central and South America, Florida and other parts of North America.

Charles's son, Philip II, far less able, tried to introduce the Inquisition in the Netherlands. By 1585, he was attempting at the same time, "to save France from heresy, defeat the Dutch rebels and bring England to her knees for daring to support the rebels."[6]

William of Orange expelled the Spanish from the northern area, now Holland, and declared her independence in 1581, though this was not recognized until 1648 after the Thirty Years' War, in which Spain also took part. Southern Netherlands, now Belgium, was reconquered and remained Catholic.

But the most crushing blow was the defeat of the Spanish Armada in 1588 in the English Channel. It was the beginning of the Spanish decline. Philip had launched his armies against heresy but "the war against Protestantism was also the war against ascendant capitalism in Europe."[7] This mainly meant against the Dutch and the English. The wars were fought as much in the Caribbean as they were in Europe. When war broke out again between Holland and Spain in 1625, the Dutch came in the same year to Puerto Rico with a fleet of seventeen ships and a thousand men. They took the city, but not being able to hold it, burnt the town, including La Fortaleza. They were defeated with nearly half their men dead and several of their ships captured. In 1611, the English captured Jamaica, and Henry Morgan, a notorious buccaneer, was to become one of its governors. During these early years of the seventeenth century, the French, English and Dutch began their occupation of the Atlantic coast of North America, the Lesser Antilles and the Bahamas.

The English interest in the New World began with Henry VIII's weary suggestion to his fifth wife, Katherine Howard, that they run off and find a peaceful existence there. His daughter, Elizabeth I, gave her blessings to Sir Francis Drake in his pirating and ventures in the Caribbean. During the Civil War in England, there was some respite from British attacks in the West Indies, but in 1655, under Cromwell, the attacks were renewed. The English successfully took Honduras, but their efforts to take Hispaniola were rebuffed.

On their side, the Spanish, using Havana as a base, made attempts to get Jamaica back, but the British could not be dislodged. Finally, in the two treaties of Madrid of 1667 and 1670, piracy was outlawed, and the King of Great Britain was granted all lands in the West Indies and America that the English then occupied.

Piracy ended, however, only for some fifteen years, and then began once more. Not only were England and Holland involved, but the French and Danes too. There was perpetual petty war in the Caribbean, and there was wondrous booty to be snatched from Spain, too. It is estimated that the loot Morgan and Drake and other Caribbean buccaneers were able to take in the capture of such cities as Puerto Vello and Panama easily equals the booty of contemporary European warfare.

"It was as if the peoples of Europe had come into a splendid legacy. . . . The powers of Europe began a frantic 'claiming' of the new realms.. . . That the Papacy had divided the American continent between Spain and Portugal roused the hostility of the excluded nations. The seamen of England showed no respect for either claim. . . . The Hollanders, as soon as they had shaken off their Spanish masters, also set sail westward to flout the Pope and share in the good things of the New World. His most Catholic Majesty of France hesitated as little as any Protestant. All these powers were busy staking out 'claims' in North America and the West Indies.

"Most of the territorial changes by treaties of peace were at Spanish expense."[8] After the War of the Spanish Succession, Britain received Newfoundland, Nova Scotia, and the Hudson Bay Territory in America from France, and the Rock of Gibralter and the island of Minorca from Spain. Britain was also granted the *Asiento*, a special and highly remunerative contract for British merchants. The *Asiento* permitted merchants to export several thousand slaves a year to Spanish America, giving them a temporary monopoly of the Spanish slave market, a very lucrative concession.

It was during this war that England, Scotland and Wales decided to form a union with one ruler, one parliament and one flag—"The Union Jack." By 1750, the British held the east coast of North America from Savannah to Newfoundland, and included in their shores the Bahamas. Barbados and Trinidad were taken by 1789.

The English settled on the North American continent in Jamestown in 1607, with the Mayflower sailing from Plymouth in 1620. Canada was claimed as "New France" by Jacques Cartier in the second of his voyages of 1541 and 1542. Quebec was founded in 1608 by Samuel De Champlain, but the number of French settlers grew slowly. Even by 1660, there were only twenty-five hundred people in the city. The French held Louisiana and a stretch behind the coastal area of the British up into Canada. In the Caribbean, they had acquired Martinique and Guadaloupe and other islands as their prizes. The Dutch held Nievo Amsterdam until 1674, when the English took it over and renamed it New York. But the Dutch obtained Surinam in exchange and also, in the Caribbean, took over Curacao and Aruba. The Danes amassed some small islands, including St. Croix.

There were innumerable conflicts among all the powers during these two centuries and much changing of allies. The War of the Spanish Succession, when Louis IV placed a Bourbon on the Spanish throne in place of a Hapsburg, changed Europe, and produced the beginnings of the modern states as we know them today. Spain was the greatest loser. But though she lost on the European battlefield, she was able to retain most of her American empire—Florida, Mexico, nearly all of Central America, and South America, except for Brazil. Within a few years of Spain's occupation of Latin America, the Portuguese had settled in and claimed that country. This was in accordance to the treaty in which the Pope had traced the dividing line between the two powers.

Spain had also kept the most important Caribbean islands: Cuba and Puerto Rico and two-thirds of Hispaniola. The French had by this time encroached on the other third.

Smuggling was a way of life in all the islands, as much a way of life as fighting pirates and buccaneers. Smugglers of all European nationalities had their special coves and enclaves throughout the Caribbean. The famous classic *Treasure Island* by Robert Louis Stevenson was based on the smuggling and piracy that pervaded the islands at this period.

Pirates were known to occupy Mona Island—one of the islands off the west coast of Puerto Rico—because it was very lush, growing a great deal of fruit and there were wild boars to be had. The mixing of native women and these adventuring men added new racial elements to succeeding generations. "The great variety of people, customs and traditions has been one that has always provided much of the fascination of the whole Caribbean."[9]

Tortuga, an islet off the northern coast of Hispaniola was a famous lair of the buccaneers. First it was in British hands but a Spanish force attacked and threw them out in 1635. However, the French then moved in and the Spanish were less successful against them. The French not only established this toe-hold, but proceeded to use it as a base for moving into the larger island. They continued to expand their hold until they occupied roughly one third of the country. It was a very prosperous part of the island.

In continued retreat from her former might, Spain had to sign a treaty giving away this territory to her enemy. Under the Treaty of Ryswick in 1697, the western part of Hispaniola became French under the new name of Saint Dominique. This division of the island was to have a profound effect on her future history. Further, a great many more slaves were introduced. In 1786, twenty-seven thousand slaves were brought in; in 1787, forty thousand. Revolution broke out in 1791, and in the one month of September, two hundred sugar plantations went up in flames.

The Haitian Revolution coincided with the French Revolution. The revolution and the destruction of the plantations in Haiti (the Indian name being reused and Saint Dominique dropped) produced, in turn, a sugar boom in Cuba. In eastern Hispaniola now named Santo Domingo, the revolution had greater consequences. From the time of the French take-over and through all the continuing years, there were rivalry and fighting between the two parts of the island. But after the Black Revolution, the Spanish ceded their part to France. Toussaint L'Ouverture, the Black leader, then over ran all of Hispaniola, and the French were forced to withdraw. Spanish rule was not reestablished until 1808.

The presence of Spain's enemies in the area changed in different measure each of the islands of the Antilles. The government of Puerto Rico became military because of the many attacks on her. England was so anxious to obtain the island that she offered Gibraltar, given to her in the Spanish succession wars, as a trade. The Spanish refused and offered instead their dwindled area of Hispaniola, but the British turned this down. When Spain declared war on England again in 1796, Sir Ralph Abercrombie arrived with sixty ships and six hundred cannon in a new attempt to take San Juan, but failed and was forced to withdraw.

From this time, for the next one hundred years until the United States entered with troops in 1898, Puerto Rico lived in peace, with no more attempts by European powers to capture it.

As much of Puerto Rico's budget went into fortifications, so "the complete absorption of Cuba's revenues went into the maintenance of a huge military and naval establishment out of all proportion to the ability of its citizens to sustain."[10] Puerto Rico had been occupied by the British for only three months and this was too short a period to induce much change. But Cuba was captured and held by them for a whole year from 1762 to 1763. This was a significant occupation. England by then was foremost in the slave trade, and she brought nine times the number of slaves into the island than there had been in any previous year. It drastically changed the ratio of blacks and whites. Before abolition, there were nine times the number of slaves in Cuba as there were in Puerto Rico, and though the difference in size of the two islands must be taken into account, the numbers were largely the continuing result of the British seizure. The British also intensified the cultivation of sugar during their occupancy. Previous to this, Cuba's economy, though sugar was grown, included also tobacco plantations and cattle ranches. (There was a similar situation in Puerto Rico, where there was a diversification of crops and cattle raising during the seventeenth and early eighteenth centuries). Havana too, as a military bastion, possessed an important cannon foundry. It was the first harbor in the Caribbean where shipbuilding was begun, and shipbuilding, too, had become important in the island's economy.

Because it was a better investment, bringing greater profits, larger and larger areas were given over to sugar cane. It led to the destruction of much of the magnificent forests of mahogany, cedar and ebony in Cuba. Similarly, Puerto Rico was later to lose many of her coffee plantations, to make way for the more profitable sugar.

"The Cuban upper class on the profits of sugar, were able to go to Europe and bring back dresses from Paris, works of art from other countries, and have their portraits painted by fashionable artists in London."[11] It was the British who had stimulated the great increase in sugar production while they held the island, and this was continued by the Cubans at the end of the eighteenth century. It led the Cuban planters in 1789 to oppose a more humane Slave Code.

Harsh treatment in all the Spanish islands tended to increase in boom sugar years. Repression of Negroes, too, tended to increase as the ratio of slaves to the white population increased. Both these factors were at work in Cuba and in the French portion of Hispaniola. The plantation economy in the Spanish islands was geared mainly to domestic consumption; that in the French and English islands was geared to export. The long years of wealth acquired from the sugar plantations from a wageless labor force were also a source of wealth to the emerging bourgeoisie in Europe.

Intermarriage between Whites and Blacks, Mestizos and Creoles in the Spanish islands influenced society and encouraged the growth of free colored groups. "They gave the name of creole indistinctly to everyone born on the island, no matter what race or mixture he comes from. The Europeans are called Whites, or to use their own expression 'men of the other band'."[12] Society was less rigid and less slave-centred than in the rest of the Caribbean. It was quite different, too, from the English colonies of North America, where the colonial assemblies were dominated by the planter class that regarded slavery as essential to survival. Another difference between the Spanish islands and Latin America, and the islands now occupied by other European nations, was that of language. All the communities spoke Spanish and there was little difference in accent and speech between the rich and poor. In the English and French islands, there was a definite class distinction in speech. Another difference was that in the British colonies, even before the Revolution, there was a measure of self-government. The Spanish colonies had no government of their own. Spain appointed viceroys who represented the King. All officials were selected in Spain and sent out to govern. "The Spaniards came to America in the service of the Crown and the Church."[13] The King ruled the colonies through a special agency, the Council of the Indies.

The American colonies had a large degree of local independence before the Revolution. But the Spanish "colonists had no voice regarding taxation. They had to pay to the Crown poll taxes, customs on imports, and excises on goods exchanged within the colonies. In addition, the king received rich revenues from the sale of monopoly rights to trade in certain natural products and in slaves and was entitled to a fifth of all gold and silver mined."

"The Spanish colonists were not allowed to participate in making their own laws, paying their taxes or choosing their own governmental officials.

"Broadly each of the colonial societies came in time to mirror the personality of its metropolitan model."[14] This was not only because its government, religion (Spain barred all the heretics) speech and traditions came from the overseas center, but because its trade was also rigidly restricted to the mother country. Spain allowed no trading with other countries by the colonies. All shipping back and forth had to be in Spanish vessels. Goods had to be purchased from the home source to help the national economy. The English Navigation Laws equally disallowed colonial trade other than in English colonial ships.

The mother countries sent to the Caribbean islands all the exports they needed in the way of flour, wheat, wines, etc. It was estimated that by the late 1700s, the livelihood of at least three million Frenchmen depended upon what was sent to the colonies. In very much the same way in 1978, the exports from the United States to Puerto Rico represent the livelihood of a quarter million workers in the States. It is the continuation of the policy as it existed with Spain and the earlier European powers.

"The mercantilist policy of the Hapsburgs of Austria and Spain forced isolation on all the islands . . . that led to stagnation of agriculture, and industry, and imposed a monoculture.

"In return for imports from Spain of wines, olives, figs, oil, iron, quicksilver, dry goods, etc., the colonists exported gold and silver, sugar, gongs, cacao, vanilla and other nature products. Trade was strictly limited to Spanish vessels and merchants."[15]

It was because of this restriction that "a long smuggling trade grew up between Spanish colonists and English, French and Dutch traders."[16] This smuggling formed a considerable part in these times of the economies of all three islands of the Spanish Antilles. A particularly heinous part of the illegal operations was a New England triangular trade that involved sending men from Africa to be sold as slaves in the West Indies, then sending contraband molasses from the West Indies to America to be made into rum.

The events then in Spain and Europe, particularly the wars, were to have their effects in the Antilles as the other European countries entered into the Caribbean, fighting in its waters, and as they challenged or captured some of Spain's territories in the New World. But Spain retained its control in Mexico, and in great part in Central and South America.

In the eighteenth century, it was still a vast empire that had to be defended for the treasure that these colonies continued to produce for the mother country. The three islands of the Spanish Antilles were vital in the defense of that wealth. Not until the Wars of Independence in the first quarter of the nineteenth century did Spain finally, after more than three hundred years, at a time just following her own occupation by Napoleon's army, lose her empire in the New World. She was to retain only two of those islands she had first discovered and colonized. In pride then, she clung to them more fiercely than ever.

7 -:- The Revolutionary Era

By the middle of the eighteenth century, the feudal system in Europe was showing cracks in its structure. A bourgeois class was rising and gaining strength. England was experiencing the beginning of her industrial revolution. Agriculture was giving way to industry, with many new inventions helping, especially in the textile industry and in the steel mills—using coal. New ideas were being promulgated for the advancement of the new class, or at least, there were new concepts being put forward that fitted the need of the growing middle class. Factories were being built that led to agricultural workers leaving the farms for the cities. Artisans and craftsmen were thrown out of work. The old mercantile ideas were being challenged. There was a demand for free trade and fewer restrictions in the flow of goods.

New philosophies were being expanded. In England, Locke defended England's revolution when the King had been beheaded, stating that "if any government should fail in preserving men's natural rights or should infringe on those rights, a revolution is justified."

Jeremy Bentham and his followers, the "Utilitarians," called for the greatest good of the greatest number. There were those who asked for a state of perfect freedom to order their actions, and dispose of their persons and possessions as they saw fit.

The divine right of Kings was a concept never again to be tolerated in Britain. In France, similar theories, put forward in this period by many men, led to its being called the Age of Enlightenment. There were whole groups of philosophers—Rousseau, Diderot, Montesquieu, Voltaire—who gave expression to new social theories, which, becoming widespread, led to the questioning of the existing systems.

These ideas were to find expression in the sentiments of a new humanitarianism in the French Revolution: *Liberté, Egalité, Fraternité*. They were to cross the seas. These ideas were to be used as a rationale when the American colonies were to break away from England, and form a new independent country. They were to infiltrate to the slaves in Hispaniola to spark the Black Revolution. They were to inspire Simon Bolívar, who looked not only to the independence of the countries of South America, but of the islands of the Spanish Antilles too.

There was no doubt that the literature of protest was reaching the Americas. Though the majority of the upper society in the Spanish islands was interested only in balls and card games and frivolities, there was then, as always, a minority interested in ideas. The printing presses in Mexico turned out translations of European pamphlets. Though most were forbidden reading by the Catholic Church, they were read, their ideas were discussed, and their influence spread. Bolívar's tutor was greatly influenced by Voltaire and Rousseau, and the revolutionist himself corresponded with them and journeyed to Europe to meet men with similar ideas.

Rousseau objected to methods that turned a child into a repeating robot and felt the object of education should be to help a child to think and judge for himself.

"If nature is to be the tutor's guide, he will give the child as much freedom as safety will allow." He suggests that the child should be encouraged to love nature. "Let us lay down as an incontrovertible rule that first impulses of nature are always right. There is no original sin in the human heart." He dreamed of a perfect state and held up a pattern that "he who desires may behold it."[1] The idea of the noble savage and his lifestyle based on Columbus's early writings of a people living in a Golden Age was re-expounded by Rousseau. The ideal was revived that man must live in harmony with his natural environment as the Arawaks of the Spanish Antilles were said to have done before western civilisation was thrust upon them, an idea being revived again today. Many of Rousseau's ideas on education were borrowed and expanded by Bolívar, in the hope that he could put them into practice in Latin America. Similar ideas have been expressed and put into practice by Fidel Castro in Cuba today.

Yet underlying all the new ideas was the new economic reality. The stage of economic development in any country at any period of history is the infrastructure on which ideas are built. In France, politics and finances were in the hands of the nobles and the King. The French

Revolution "was essentially a struggle between the privileged orders and the middle class for political power."² The bourgeoisie was challenging the feudal system.

Beaumarchais in his opera *Marriage of Figaro* addresses the nobles of Spain (and France) with almost revolutionary scorn: "What have you done for so much good fortune? You gave yourself the trouble to be born, and nothing more; for the rest you are sufficiently ordinary"

In Spain, there were popular feelings of discontent, such as the revolt of the people of Saragossa in 1766, when they sacked and looted the town. Such news, even if belatedly, reached the Spanish colonies and had different effects on different sections of society. These were the preludes to the revolutions. When the French army of Napoleon first entered Spain, it would be welcomed by about half the populace. Only after invaders were occupying the country did the Spaniards move together to resist them. The mercantilist policies of France, England, Spain and other European countries were being challenged as restrictive for economic growth. Adam Smith wrote of the North American situation, "plenty of good land and liberty to manage their own affairs, their own way, seem to be the two great causes of the prosperity of all new colonies." The proposition of "managing their own affairs in their own way" was heard by receptive ears in the Spanish colonies as elsewhere.

"The tradition of resistance to oppression, and the ideals of liberty and equality were to grow everywhere into radical movements at deeper alterations of the social order than the revolutionary movement had achieved," write Professors Gottschack and Lash in describing the effects of the French Revolution. The French Revolution was to affect St. Dominique, and the revolution there in turn was to affect not only the other part of Hispaniola that remained Spanish, but the other Caribbean islands and Latin America too.

Before the Revolution, "part of [French] mercantile prosperity, as in England, came from the capture or purchase of slaves and their sale there for work on the plantations. In 1788, French slave dealers shipped 29,506 Negroes to St. Dominique alone. French investors owned most of the soil and industries there and in Guadaloupe and Martinique. In St. Dominique, thirty thousand whites used four hundred eighty thousand slaves. In France, as in England, with the new humanitarian ideas, there was a call for the abolition of slavery, but it was strongly opposed by traders and planters."³

In 1789, the Chamber of Commerce of Bordeaux declared:

"France needs its colonies for the maintenance of its commerce, and consequently it needs slaves in order to make agriculture pay."[4]

Nevertheless, humanitarian ideas were gaining ground. In England, William Wilberforce formed an anti-slavery league in 1787. But, "it was not our Christian Parliament, however, but the deist Assembly of the French Revolution that first abolished slavery in 1791, thirty-three years before England, and eighty-two years before Spain."[5] And it was Toussaint L'Ouvertures successful revolution that ended slavery in Western Hispaniola, despite Napoleon's efforts later to turn back the clock. The American Revolution also was tied into developments in the Spanish Antilles. The American colonists were not so much concerned with "no taxation without representation." The New Englanders wanted to continue their lucrative trade in rum and slaves without interference. This was directly linked to the West Indies.

"The relationship between West Indies rum and the American Revolution is one often ignored by the history books. It is a complicated tale of smuggling, slave trading and the evasion of the British Acts of Trade—all of which were respectable New England occupations at the time."[6] The Molasses Act in England in 1733 demanded a tax that would lower the profits of New Englanders in their West Indian trade, most of this trade being in the non-British islands. It was a trade in molasses, rum, and slaves that brought in considerable wealth and was continued even though illegal.

John Hancock was one of those mixed up with this contraband trade (and John Adams was his lawyer). If the Revolutionary War had not broken out, he would have been brought to trial. "Trial might have brought half a million dollars penalty if he had been found guilty."[7] Two important figures of the American Revolution then were directly connected with and gained wealth from the slave trade, which was conducted in great measure from Cuba and Hispaniola.

The southern states in their turn wanted to expand westward their economy which was built on slave labor. French traders had spread into the Great Lakes region and there was a struggle between the two nations, France and England, on behalf of their settlers for control of the Ohio Valley. George Washington had been sent by the English governor of Virginia to warn the French to stay out of the region.

During the Seven Years' War from 1756 to 1763, the Anglo-French struggle spilled over once more into the Western Hemisphere. It was during this war that England captured Havana for a year and enormously increased the slave trade. They then fought the French in North America and drove them further westward on the continent. The English, having gained this further territory for the colonists, felt the latter should carry some of the financial responsibility. "But if the colonists were not keen about incurring heavy financial obligations in the prosecution of the war, great numbers of them were all too ready to carry on their lucrative trade with the French West Indies." This included, of course, French Hispaniola and St. Dominique. "Ships from almost every American port were engaged in trafficking with the enemy,"[8] even though the colonists were to gain from the lands won for them by British soldiers. The colonies being prosperous, Britain felt they should help carry the burden which fell otherwise heavily on English taxpayers.

Thomas Paine in his pamphlet *Common Sense* published in January, 1776, sought to prove that any economic prosperity of America was not based on any ties with England, but that America would be better off without the interference of the mother country.

Further, exports from the North American colonies were in competition with those of Britain. North American ships by their smuggling were hurting the revenues of English trading ships. There gradually developed an increasing economic friction between Britain and New England.

A Frenchman as early as 1747 said "She [England] will call upon them to contribute to the burdens they have helped to bring upon her, and they will answer by striking off all dependence."[9] Yet according to John Adams, in the War for Independence, one third of the colony remained loyal to England and one third was "lukewarm." Other estimates claim that as much as four-fifths of the population remained loyal to the Crown. Washington was constantly short of ammunition, food, clothing, and medical supplies. He did not receive the support of the country. He actually had no standing army and was dependant on ill-trained volunteers. There were large numbers of profiteers and speculators who created acute shortages. There was plenty of black marketeering. There was, as Washington bitterly described it, an "abominable lust for gain." In war, as in peace, the shippers of New England continued trade with the enemy.

It is certain that the colonies could not have won their war against England without both the financial and military help of France. There were twenty-eight thousand French soldiers at Yorktown. There were on the American side only eleven thousand, that is only about a quarter of the total force. And of these there were only four thousand regular trained soldiers.

A secret agreement with France made by Benjamin Franklin was that in return for help, France would be given a free hand in the Caribbean. Yet when Napoleon was fighting to put down the revolt of the slaves in St. Dominique, the North Americans would break the promise given twenty-five years earlier and give support to the Black Revolution. The French must have regretted their generosity, for it was a factor in their own worsening financial situation, and gave revolutionary impetus to the aspirations of their own bourgeoisie.

As the English Navigation Laws had been hurting the English colonies, so too were the Spanish ones economically restricting the Spanish colonies.

The pronouncements and the English colonists' revolution were enthusiastically supported in the New World.

The famous lines of the Declaration of Independence signed by John Hancock as President of the Congress on July 4th, 1776 were quoted and endorsed by other revolutionaries. They found these truths similarly "self-evident, that all Men are created equal, that they are endowed by their Creator with certain inalienable Rights, that among these are Life, Liberty and the Pursuit of Happiness— That... whenever any Form of Government becomes destructive of these Ends, it is the Right of the People to alter or abolish it...."

When the Venezuelans declared their Independence and their first republic was born, the creole concept of the new society was revealed in the constitution of December 1811, a constitution strongly influenced by that of the United States. But they, like the North American Union, did not extend their concepts of equality to the slaves. Only Bolívar "the most daring and idealist of the creoles [saw] the need of fusing the creole, pardo (White-Negro parentage) and slave rebellions into one movement."[10]

In the fateful year of 1789, the Spanish government had issued a new slave law, which sought to improve the condition of the slaves and to define the relationship between master and slave. All over the Caribbean and in South America, planters resisted the law and procured its suspension in 1794. But by the next year, Venezuela had to contend with a revolt led by free Negroes and fought by slaves. This was only one of many slave revolts in the New World, engendered by the ringing sounds of those words, Liberty and Equality, fired by the spirit of the French Revolution, and more particularly by the successful black revolution in Hispaniola. Slaves believed those words applied to themselves.

At the time of the French Revolution, both sections of Hispaniola were prosperous. "No colony ever became rich so quickly. Because of this wealth, young French noblemen came out for a life of ease and luxury in this beautiful, fertile land in the tropics. Part of each year, they spent in St. Dominique and the other part in Paris and other capitals of Europe.

"Never before, and perhaps never since has the world seen anything proportionately so dazzling as the last years of pre-revolutionary San Domingo. Between 1783 and 1789 production nearly doubled. Between 1764 and 1771, the average importation of slaves varied between ten and fifteen thousand. In 1786, it was 27,000 and from 1787 onwards the colony was taking more than 40,000 slaves a year.... The enormous increase in slaves was filling the colony with native Africans, more resentful, more intractable, more ready for rebellion than the Creole Negro. Of the half million slaves in the colony in 1789, more than two-thirds had been born in Africa."[11]

The Negroes of Hispaniola were a widely scattered African people. Not of Congo stock alone, but royal Dahomey strain and many tall Zulu warriors. The population of St. Dominique consisted of thirty-two thousand whites, twenty-four thousand freemen mostly mulattoes with mixed background of white-Spanish or French and Negro parents and four hundred eighty thousand slaves.

Toussaint L'Ouverture who became the leader of the slave rebellion was a slave on a plantation of a humane French count, who lived mostly in France. Toussaint's father had received some training from the Jesuits, that is, he had some education, which he passed on to his son. Toussaint's own ability with horses led him to be made coachman for the manager of the estate. He used every free moment to read and write, an almost unheard of accomplishment for a Negro slave.

He showed the influence of Rousseau in declaring. "I was born in slavery but I received from nature the soul of a free man."[13] He read the French philosopher, Abbé Raynal, and was greatly influenced by a passage in the Abbé's writings.

"Nations of Europe, your slaves are not in need of your generosity or your councils in order to break the sacriligious yoke which oppresses them. The Negroes lack but a chief." Toussaint came to believe he was that chief. In the beginning, he did not join the revolt. His master was away and had entrusted his wife to Toussaint's care. Only when he had fulfilled that obligation and seen her safely sent to the Spanish end of the island, and done some self-questioning, did he join his fighting brethren. Because of his superior education and his superior abilities, he soon became a leader. He added L'Ouverture, meaning 'opening' to his Christian name.

"I open the door of liberty to you," he told the slaves.

The first reaction of the colonists to the news of the French Revolution was one of confusion. When the new National Assembly convened in Paris, a delegation from the planters attended. Previously, the Governor General had had absolute authority. Now the planters wanted the right to select their own officials, run their own affairs in St. Dominique, and send their own representatives to the National Assembly. But also the French Revolution led mulattoes to believe they could become free by legislation, and have a chance to gain some political power. They too sent a representative to the National Assembly. A decree in 1791 allowed Assembly for the colony. Men of color born of free parents could be admitted to seats. On the island, this aroused the planters. There was armed conflict between the two groups. The mulatto revolt was suppressed by the governing forces and their leader publicly executed. For a long time, the mulattoes did not see that they had to join forces with the Negroes for any revolution to become successful. For a long period, they preferred to side with the planters when the slaves in turn revolted.

The planters talked freely of the French Revolution while Negro servants waited at table. Through them, the news spread, and on the plantation, African drums sent the message through the entire region. When the colonial planters claimed seats in the National Assembly, Mirabeau had challenged them: "You claim representation proportionate to the number of the inhabitants. The free blacks are proprietors and tax-payers, and yet they have not been allowed to vote. And as for the slaves, either they are men or they are not; if the colonists consider them to be men, let them free them and make them electors and eligible for seats; if the contrary is the case, have we, in apportioning deputies according to the population of France, taken into consideration the number of our horses and mules?"

On August 14, in 1791 the drums carried the message to the slaves to revolt. Eight days later the uprising began. The leaders were three slaves, Jean Francois, Bookman and Bissau. Toussaint was not yet among them. The slaves set houses afire. With flaming torches, they ran out in the fields, where stalks of sugar cane caught fire and carried the blaze forward. The revolt spread with one hundred thousand slaves taking part. The whole northern province was laid waste by fire. The slaves scorched the land. In the towns, too, the slaves rose up and began rioting.

Two years earlier, a mulatto had written to his brother, the mulatto commisioner in Paris. "The Revolution has penetrated here, most of all among the Blacks. To them, the national cockade stands for liberty and equality. They were ready to revolt, but several have been sent to the scaffold and things have quieted down."[13] They had quieted down only temporarily. The slaves continued their preparations for their own *Liberté* and *Egalité*.

At first, the mulattoes sided with the terrified, horrified whites. Then some began to join the negroes.

"In the first two months, 2,000 whites were killed, 180 sugar plantations destroyed, and 10,000 slaves died either by fighting, or by famine, or the executioners hands."[14] The total white population was estimated at 200,000.

The whites appealed to France for an army, but the Jacobins, in power by September 1792, sent a revolutionary army to carry out the rule of "liberty, equality and fraternity" for all. Their leader placed himself on the side of the slaves. A conditional emancipation was called. Whites fled the country, particularly to Puerto Rico, and in Mayaguez on the West Coast still exist descendants of these French.

As the French Revolution itself moved forward, and the masses and their leaders took control, the National Assembly abolished slavery in the colonies and declared all slaves free. The planters and many mulattoes then no longer felt any loyalty to France. They appealed to the British to come in and help "to restore order."

The Spanish from their side of the island began to cross the border into French territory, hoping to take advantage of the situation and restore the whole of Hispaniola once more to Spain. For some seven months, Toussaint accepted an alliance with them. The Spanish governor offered "Liberty, now and forever and the rights of citizenship," as well as offers of land. In accepting, Toussaint was welcomed by Spanish officers and given high rank. When he found that Spain was not granting freedom to all blacks, he broke the alliance. The Spanish campaign collapsed soon after his departure from their ranks.

With the declaration of war by England against France, the British moved their armies into St. Dominique. Toussaint sent a note to the French general, that his forces were prepared to help in pushing out the invaders. They could do nothing but agree, and Toussaint battled against the British until they withdrew. By his military victories, he became commander-in-chief of the French troops. In 1800, the Spanish governor handed over the colony to Toussaint, and by 1801, he was supreme commander of the whole island.

The whole of Hispaniola was once again joined and was independent again, as in 1493, when Columbus had discovered it. Now it was inhabited by a different people, yet with some slight traces of the original natives.

Toussaint set about the rebuilding of the colony. He safeguarded the whites. He gave San Domingo a constitution. The Church was subordinate to the State. He sent a group of mulattoes and Negro children to France to be educated, so that they could return and help in the education and government of the country. But he kept the ties to France. San Domingo would have local government under his rule. It would, however, be a totally changed country, a totally changed situation. For "Black men who had been slaves now negotiated with the French and foreign governments. Black men, who had been slaves, filled the highest positions in the colony. Toussaint, the former slave, incredibly grand and powerful was incomparably the greatest man in the colony. They had no need to be ashamed of being black. The revolution had produced the possibility of further achievement, of confidence, of pride... That psychological weakness, that feeling of inferiority with which the imperialists plague the colonial people everywhere, was gone.... The Frenchmen, who still lived in Santo Domingo and knew the people created by the revolution, never ceased to warn the French government, of the catastrophe that would follow any attempt to restore slavery."

Having defeated the planters, and then the British, Toussaint now had to contend with Napoleon. The French Revolution had abolished slavery, but in the several years since Toussaint had been building his revolution, the peak of the French Revolution was past, and Bonaparte was now in power.

The leaders of the French Revolution had supported the Negro desire for freedom, but Bonaparte did not share this sentiment. Bonaparte arranged for an expedition of twenty thousand of his men to go to St. Dominique and capture Toussaint and restore slavery on the island. He put in charge of the expedition his brother-in-law, LeClerc. Toussaint's reply was, "Our liberty is no longer in her—France's—hands. It is in our own. We will defend it or perish." Dessalines, one of his lieutenants, also made a speech to his army. "If France wishes to try any nonsense here, everybody must rise together, men and women.'[15]

At the sight of so formidable a French army, the black army and the people took as previously to the hills. But before they left, they burnt Santo Domingo to cinders, so that the French found a ruined town. Yet the French were able to score some victories, mainly because Toussaint himself did not recognize that he had to break his ties with France, and call for independence. His vacillation caused dissension amongst the commanders within his own army. However, as the French put down the insurgent army in one part of the island, it would arise in another. They spent an endless year in trying, by force of arms, to defeat the black revolutionaries. France in the Paris Convention under Napoleon restored slavery in Martinique, but Santo Domingo's name was omitted from this decree, since it was still uncertain who would be the victor in the war. Slavery was also restored in Guadaloupe. By an act of treachery, Toussaint was captured. Despite this, the revolutionary spirit of black slaves remained alive. The generals whom Toussaint had appointed carried on the fight against the French.

In many cases, as the Indians before them had done, they continued to use the scorched earth policy by which, rather than let the French take possession in any place, they set the cities or the plantations on fire. Some blacks and mulattoes went over to the French, and joined LeClerc's army, hoping thereby to consolidate their position with them. But the peoples' instinct was such that they knew that if the French won, then slavery would be their fate once again. LeClerc had to ask for reinforcements. He had few of his original expeditionary force left. The black armies had decimated them. LeClerc himself became ill and finally died. But before he died, he knew Santo Domingo was forever lost to France.

In a letter which he sent back to Napoleon before he died, he wrote: "Unfortunately the condition of the colonies is not known in France. They have a false idea of the Negro ... you have in Europe a false idea of the country in which we fight, and the men whom we fight against."[16] LeClerc had come to understand the revolutionary fervor of the black slaves, and that whatever the seeming victories, in the end he could not overcome these men who refused to go back into slavery—they knew that they were fighting for their lives and their liberties and the liberties of their children.

According to Eduardo Galleno, General LeClerc had written to his brother Napoleon in 1902, soon after taking prisoner the slave Toussaint L'Ouverture: "Here is my opinion about this country. All the blacks in the mountains men and women must be suppressed, keeping only the children under twelve. Half the blacks in the plains must be exterminated and not a single mulatto with epaulets must be left in the colony." The French were unable to enforce this massacre.

After LeClerc's death a new general, Rochambaud, with twenty thousand men was sent to put down the revolution in Santo Domingo. He also brought fifteen hundred dogs with him to hunt down the blacks, as the Spaniards had done in Hispaniola against the Indians. The French cut up Negroes and gave their bodies to the dogs, to encourage in them a desire for Negro blood. They tortured and put to the sword and fire thousands of blacks. They decided that they had to destroy the Negroes or they would lose the colony. Dessalines was now in charge of the army. He had no longer the feeling of allegiance to the French that Toussaint had kept. When the French put to death five hundred blacks he went out and hanged five hundred whites —his was an eye-for-an-eye attitude—the philosophy of Judea. He burned the whole of Santo Domingo rather than give it up.

Napoleon could not win against these determined revolutionaries. Dessalines now took the French tricolor and tore off the white part and instead of the initials RF, meaning Republique Francaise, he inscribed 'Liberty or Death.' Santo Domingo was declaring its independence.

The English and Americans, at that time fighting Bonaparte, supplied the revolutionaries with arms and food. Dessalines, like Toussaint before him, did not wish in any way to become their dependent, and he paid for all the supplies that he received from them.

In the end, Rochambaud decided to retreat, and prepared to retreat to Spanish Santo Domingo. Dessalines warned him that he must evacuate the whole island, while British ships standing off the harbor demanded that the French surrender to them. Of the sixty thousand French troops that had been sent to suppress the revolution few remained. These in the end were to finish their days in English prisons. Meanwhile, Dessalines issued a proclamation of independence.

The new country broke completely with France. By this uncompromising ferocity, Dessalines had won the final victory. He put the remaining whites on the island to death.

The country was in ruins after the war. The French were later to demand indemnity, which was paid; the country was never to rise out of the ruins. But the Negroes had won their freedom and had won it by their courage, almost bare-handed against the plantation owners, the mulattoes, the British, and the Spanish ruling class in Santo Domingo who had helped the expeditionary forces of Napoleon, which were proving unbeatable in Europe.

But Dessalines could not hold all the island and he was forced to retreat and consolidate his power in the old French region, where he proclaimed himself emperor and renamed the country Haiti. This was the old Indian name for the island, meaning 'land of the mountains'. Dessalines thus identified himself with the earlier inhabitants who had fought and died under Western conquerors.

After Dessalines' death, the countryside was divided between the Negro, Jean Christophe, who reconstructed the sugar plantations on his side of the island, and Petión, a mulatto, who decided on diversified crops and small landholders, with coffee the principal crop.

After Dessalines' army had been withdrawn, Spanish rule was again established in the other part of the island. But the effects of the independence proclaimed for Haiti in 1804 by Dessalines naturally had its effect upon the Dominicans.

The reverberations from the French Revolution had originally had faint echoes on the Spanish side. Now the situation was different. Within five years, in 1809, the Dominicans were to set up their first Republic, naming the island Spanish Haiti. It did not last long, but the desire for independence had been ignited. Though Spain was to reclaim the country later, and for a longer period the Haitians were again to take over the whole country, the fire for independence would never be put out.

The Dominican Republic would now also have a largely mulatto population. There had always been a smaller number of blacks in that part of the island, and after the Haitian Revolution, many slaves ran away from their Spanish masters and joined the new free country, further depopulating the Spanish side of Negroes.

There were various effects of the Black Revolution on the other islands of the Spanish Antilles. Many French Royalists and many Spaniards fled from Hispaniola to Puerto Rico. This had the two-fold affect of increasing the ratio of whites and blacks and of increasing the already existing conservatism of the upper classes. In 1765, there were only five thousand slaves in a population of fifty thousand. While the population increased to one hundred fifty thousand by the end of the century, the ratio of slaves remained similarly small.

As part of a contigent of Spanish royalist troops, soldiers from the garrison town of San Juan were used to help in putting down a slave revolt in Venezuela in 1812. This was the time that all of Latin

America was waging wars of independence. But the slaves everywhere were fighting not for some new found patriotism, but for themselves, for their own personal liberty. For this reason when the short-lived revolt, the Grito de Lares, occurred in Puerto Rico in 1868, Negroes took little part in it. The first movements for independence from Spain were begun in the 1820s in Puerto Rico, but abolition of slavery did not occur until 1873.

There was also an economic effect of the revolution on the other islands. With the loss of sugar from Haiti, the price of sugar rose. A great expansion of sugar plantations took place, with forests destroyed and other produce diminished for the sake of the "white gold."

In Cuba, "the expanding sugar economy depended on slave labor, the supply of which in turn depended on the continuation of Spanish rule. The demographic strength of the Negroes, moreover, recalling as it did the black revolution in Haiti, deterred the white aristocracy from promoting change and persuaded them to place their trust in a reformed colonial administration backed by strong military force."

A Spanish decree in 1765 had, moreover, given Cuba a special concession to trade with Spain on the same terms as Spaniards.

There was a diminution of the flow of wealth to Spain. The colonies now appropriated more of their own production, and employed their capital in their own administration, defense and economy. They gave less to Spain. They sold or wanted to sell their products to other colonies and other countries. Smuggling and contraband trade were considerable parts of the islands' revenues.

"When in 1808, Spain collapsed under the onslaught of Napoleon she ruled an empire stretching from California to Cape Horn, from the mouth of the Orinoco to the shores of the Pacific, the site of four vice-royalities, the home of seventeen million people. Fifteen years later, she retained only Cuba and Puerto Rico . . . [they] remained Spanish enclaves in an independent America."[17]

8 ∴ The Age of Independence

PART ONE: THE EARLY NINETEENTH CENTURY

It is interesting to speculate at what point a people develops a national identity. The Tainos, living a settled agricultural life, fighting only against the warlike Caribs to retain possession of their islands, undoubtedly identified themselves with their own territories, and probably had fraternal feelings towards the Arawaks on the neighboring islands. The Spaniards, when they first came, were interested only in plunder. Spain remained their homeland. They did not in the early years identify themselves in any way with the islands. Even though they took Indian women, they had no real links with the land. The Negroes, brought in as slaves, must have looked back with longing to the different regions in Africa from whence they came.

When then were these three different races sufficiently melded to have a sense of nationality? Within the islands, at what point did the people begin to think of themselves as Cubans, Haitians, Dominicans or Puerto Ricans?

The attitude of the child in the first generation must have depended on the attitude of the parents. If the Spanish father accepted the child as his own and planned to take him back to Spain, then the child must surely have tended to identify with his father and with the "motherland." If the native woman was raped, her attitude to the Spaniard would be hostile and this feeling would likely be carried on by the child or children. If the woman willingly accepted the man, then the offspring would naturally have a more harmonious relationship with the parents: they could identify themselves with the island through their mother and still have a feeling for far-off Spain and the land about which their father would tell them.

With the introduction of slaves from Africa within a quarter century, the mixing of the races again took time. It presented no conflicts within the population. It is unlikely then that a feeling of Puertorriqueñismo or Cubanismo or Dominicanismo appeared until the seventeenth century. It is unlikely that the Mestizo in any of the three islands had any feelings of 'patria' until a much later date. It would not be until the third, fourth or fifth generations that the people would stop hearing echoes from Africa or Spain or an earlier heritage. But by 1798, even Toussaint L'Ouverture, the Black slave who led the successful revolt in the western part of Hispaniola against the French colonists, and later against the new upperclass mulattoes —even he was not able to break easily the ties which the island had developed with France.

It took a Negro with less ambivalence to proclaim the republic.

Is this sense of nationality just a question of time? Is it brought about by fighting against invaders, or fighting for freedom? Is it a question of contiguity? Until trade restrictions under George III became too confining, the colonists of North America, three thousand miles from England, thought of themselves as Englishmen and were loyal to the Crown. Yet on the same small island with England itself, the Scots to the North, the Welsh to the west, and the Irish, separated by a narrow channel of ocean, have always thought themselves separate people from the English, even after the unifying influence of more than 300 years under a king or queen.

Common language binds, but begets changes in different areas. The patois spoken in Brittany and the dialect in Cornwall differ from the French and English spoken in metropolitan Paris and London. Yet the Bretons consider themselves Frenchmen and the Cornish, Englishmen. Does the rise of culture—music, poetry, art—springing from the spirit and the lips of local sons and daughters, provide the cement between groups of men and women in different parts of the globe? Certainly Spanish spoken in the three islands provided ties to Spain and Latin America, which were lacking in the rest of the Caribbean, where English, French, Dutch and Danish had taken the place of the language of the original conquerors.

Is nationalism even more basic? Is it the process of identification with a particular aspect of nature—the actual earth, the ground, the seas, the rivers, mountains, ocean—that gives rise to a common feeling? At what point does nationalism arise? The consensus of opinion seems to be that nationalism in Latin America and the Spanish Antilles began in the eighteenth century and was in full flower by the beginning of the nineteenth century. The great liberators called for the support of "La Patria" in overthrowing oppression. Writing in this general era of awakening nationalism, Sir Walter Scott puts the emotionally potent question:

'Breathes there a man with soul so dead,
who never to himself has said;
This is my own, my native land?'

How long does the feeling of belonging to a particular land take to develop? Recent European immigrants to the U.S. still retain ties to their native lands. Second generations often become aggressively 200 percent Americans. However, ties to the land of origin often extend in some closely knit communities even into the second, third, and fourth generation. Puerto Ricans in the states, for instance, a second generation, unlike any other second generation Americans, are usually fiercely nationalistic not to the land in which they have been born, but to the land of their fathers and mothers. One observer writes: "In the States, especially those who have never been in Puerto Rico, would even kill for the freedom of Puerto Rico. Most share hopes to go back."[1] What part do the arts and education play in nationalism and demands for independence? At the end of the eighteenth century and the beginning of the nineteenth, there was an increase in education. Among the younger generation of the well-to-do, many were going to the universities of Europe and being exposed to new ideas of nationalism and of liberal thought.

What part does religion play? The church, stronger in Spain than elsewhere in Europe, was being challenged by Protestantism, and in the northern countries, by the deism of the French philosophers and the doubtings of others. In Spain and her colonies, the alliance of the sword and the cross had been common from the beginning. Religion had been used to prevent the spread of ideas, to suppress rebellious thoughts. Up to that date, "religious practices rivaled the pursuit of bread, and probably exceeded the pursuit of sex, as part of the substance of life. The people, including the prostitutes, crossed themselves a dozen times a day. The worship of the Virgin far surpassed the adoration of Christ; images of her were everywhere. In Spain above all rose the popular demand that her 'immaculate conception'—her freedom from the taint of original sin—be made part of the defined and required faith."

In the Spanish colonies, the Catholic religion was also a unifying factor. The Church was rich, having received its portion from the plunders of the conquistadores onwards. The people were made docile by the priests. The Jesuits dominated education and the Dominicans the Inquisition. The poor were told their poverty was God's will and they gave their centavos towards the beautification of their churches. "The cathedral was their creation and they loved to see it gorgeously adorned."[2]

Now this was changing. In 1817, the first Protestant church was allowed in Puerto Rico. Freemasons' lodges, which played the role of radical political clubs, grew up everywhere during the struggle for independence. Priests were often on the side of the revolutionaries. Hidalgo, a rural priest, rang the church bells of Dolores in Mexico, urging his congregation to fight for freedom. "Will you stir yourselves to the task of recovering from the hated Spaniards, the lands robbed from your ancestors three hundred years ago?" The people then were no longer considering themselves Spaniards.

Books and pamphlets of a political nature were increasingly written and distributed. Poetry of protest against Spanish domination appeared throughout Spain's colonies. These writings were forerunners of Spanish American independence, as the writings of the Encyclopedists had been forerunners of the French Revolution. Antonio Nariño, a wealthy young Creole of Bogotá, translated the French Declaration of the Rights of Man into Spanish in 1793 and printed it on his own press. He was put into prison for this, but on his release, he issued a gazette called *El Bagatele* which in 1811 became the mouthpiece for independence. Francisco de Santa Cruz Espejo, an Indian doctor and lawyer in Quito, in 1795 also published pamphlets on the need for independence. Though he was imprisoned, he too continued his work after his release.

These and similar writings found their way to the islands. By this time, too, the three Spanish islands were producing their own writers. People there were not only reading the material that came out of Europe and Latin America, but building up a group of philosophers, and poets and playwrights who were developing their own distinct artistic forms. Though much of this derived from the Spanish culture and was influenced also by Latin America, it was still individual in that it reflected in each case the conditions and aspirations of the people of the separate islands.

One of the Cuban writers of the time (1803-1839) was José Maria Heredia. He helped to organize a secret society named, 'Suns and Rays of Bolivar' to plan rebellion and union with the famed

Liberator. He was exiled and while away from home in Niagara Falls, wrote a poem by that name "which evokes with nostalgia his greatest love, the land of Cuba."[3]

> But what do my eager eyes seek
> With vain desire? Why can I not see
> All around mine immense cavern
> The Palms, ah! The delightful palms
> That are born and grown in the guile of the sun
> On the plains of my warm country
> And the wave to the breath of the breeze off the sea
> Under a cloudless sky?

The same expression in Spanish of love of country could as easily have come from Puerto Rican or Dominican lips.

Printing presses proliferated throughout the Spanish colonies at this time enabling the spread of ideas of nationalism and independence. "Less than a hundred years after Guttenberg invented his press and fourteen years after Cortez completed the conquest of Mexico, [South] America had a printing shop, opened by Johann Gromberg in Mexico City in 1533."[4] Printing shops were opened in the eighteenth century in Santo Domingo and Havanna; and in San Juan by 1808. The Mexicans gave space in their journals to reviving the memories of Aztec heroes. No colony had as many printing presses as Mexico.

Miguel Hidalgo y Costella published *El Desperador American* (The American Clarion), but the Bogotá *Papel Periodic* (The Daily Paper) was started by a Cuban. Costella also directed the public library. Further, he started discussion societies which were at that time spreading throughout Spain and were to spread through the colonies. Francisco Jose de Caldas edited the *Diario Politico* which gave information of the progress of the revolution all over America, and was eagerly read throughout the Spanish colonies.

Thus it can be said that after a welding process through ten or twelve generations, there was in each country a definite sense of nationality, each peculiarly its own, which in turn gave rise to a desire for independence from Spain.

In regard to Puerto Rico, Professor Maldonado-Denis says: "The nineteenth century marks the decisive period in affirmation as a people, a nationality. Literature, music, painting—in short, all the cultural expressions—offer evidence that in this century a culture we can call Puerto Rican came together." He quotes a fellow Puerto Rican writer, Pedriera, as believing that this nineteenth century was one of "an awakening and a beginning. In the first moment, we were nothing but a faithful extension of Hispanic culture. In the second, we began to reveal an independent manner within that culture." Maldonado-Denis says there was an increasing division between the Spaniards and the native born Creoles, between the well-to-do Spaniards and the Puerto Ricans, and this took the form of social strata translated into political terms. Those in control of the island were still Spaniards. The mass of the people below now thought of themselves as Puerto Ricans.

A Spanish minority ruled the island. It was so in the other islands too and in all the colonies of Spain in the New World. Cruz Monclova in his *Historiá de Puerto Rico* writes:

> In the heart of the conservative sector were the civil and military leaders of the colony; the great merchants, generally speaking Spanish, who had control over the relations with peninsular Spain's exporters and the means to finance and to buy the island's products; their agents and associates; and some landlords and professionals who, in conjunction with the supporters of merchants formed the demographic element of greatest economic importance in the colony. In the liberal reforming sector were grouped the majority of the professionals, small farmers, cattle men, native industrialists, and merchants . . . and the great mass of the middle and lower class, all of whom as a unit constituted the demographic element of greatest social importance in the island.

The same groupings appeared in all three islands.

Professor Maldonado-Denis analyzes the colonial policy of Spain with respect to Cuba, Puerto Rico, and Hispaniola: "First, extermination of the indigenous race. Then, enslavement of the black race. Finally, oppression of the Creole, or with his consent use of the Creole in the governing process—as long as he served the interests of the colonial power faithfully."

Now there was change in the air. The Spanish colonies were awakening to a consciousness of themselves as a people. They also turned back to discover themselves. "In South America, the process of introspection went back at least to 1780, the year of the Indian rebellions and the scientific missions because of the rediscovery of their history."[5]

In the Spanish Antilles too, the revolutionaries identified themselves with their first roots. With independence, Saint Dominque became Haiti. Spanish Hispaniola became the Republic of Spanish

Haiti. The Puerto Ricans often referred to their island by its Indian name, and their patriotic song was *La Borinqueña*.

The purpose of a colony is to obliterate the identity of the subjugated peoples, to make them believe they are nothing without the oppressors. Despite such efforts, nationalism arises and the deep sense of a people's own roots produces its own culture, distinct from that of the colonizer, though naturally incorporating traits from it. With this sense of nationalism, there arose too the desire for separatism from Spain and from Spain's overlords on the islands. As Hispaniola was the first country of the New World to be discovered and, after valiant fighting by the natives, conquered by Spain, so was it the first to gain its independence.

In Santo Domingo, after Dessaline's Black army had withdrawn, Spanish rule was again established in 1808. But the independence proclaimed in 1804 by Dessalines for Haiti naturally had its effect upon the Dominicans. With the help of the British, who had also helped the Black revolutionaries, the Dominicans set up their first Republic in 1809. It was short-lived but it was followed by all Latin American countries breaking away from the motherland between 1810 and 1825.

Events in Europe had their contributing effects. In the Peninsular War of 1803 to 1814, Napoleon's armies occupied Spain, and deposed Ferdinand VII, thus disrupting Spanish rule both at home and in the colonies. The discontented new classes that were rising in Latin America seized this opportunity to declare independence. One after another, new Republics were proclaimed. "The independence of the Spanish colonies in America did not begin with an overt military uprising—the process went much deeper and went far back—and it still goes on. The freedom cry, uttered in 1810, when the main city councils in Spanish America issued a formal declaration of separation from Spain, came after forty years of popular protest, always echoed by new federations in the universities and their teachers. The actual fighting lasted some fifteen years, an episode of physical violence essential for driving the representatives of the Spanish government from American soil."[6]

During the whole era of independence there was an intertwining of events and sentiments throughout the Spanish colonies and the Spanish Antilles. The revolutionaries in one island were to find sympathizers and supporters in the others. For instance, Eugenio de Hostos, Puerto Rican patriot, was also a prominent figure in Cuba. When in exile in New York, he joined the Cuban Junta Revolutionarios. He also taught for many years in the Dominican Republic. He was highly regarded as a poet, essayist, writer and teacher in all three countries.

Simon Bolívar intended that the Spanish Antilles should be included in his design for a confederation of states of all Latin America. Betances, another Puerto Rican patriot, went into exile to the Dominican Republic and here formulated his plans, and attempted to take an armed force from there. When José Martí organized a new revolt in Cuba in 1895 from New York, Puerto Ricans there formed a chapter of the Cuban Revolutionary Party. And the Puerto Rican poetess and patriot, Lola Rodriguez de Tio was to write:

"Cuba and Puerto Rico are one bird with two wings,
They receive bullets and flowers through the same heart."

Earlier in 1823, Puerto Rico and Cuba had joined together to ask for more autonomy from Spain. And in 1862, Puerto Rico's separatists were encouraged once more by a rebellion in the Dominican Republic. Though there was an essential nationalism in each of the islands, a common tongue and common roots made for a generally warm rapport between them all, and the camaraderie between the revolutionaries of the three islands was even greater.

So too in Latin America. "The fight was for a common cause carried on in common by the people of all countries. San Martín took his Argentine troops to battlefields in Chile and pacified Peru with them. Bolívar united Venezuelans, Colombians and Ecuadorians in his march to Peru and Upper Peru. When Mexico's independence was in danger, Santander, Bolívar's companion in the Colombian campaign, offered his sword to the Mexican Republics. This spirit lasted as late as the Cuban War of Independence (1895-98) almost a hundred years later, when [Latin] Americans from the entire Caribbean zone appeared on the island battlefields."[7] These were not battles for conquest, but for ideals and for unity of all the colonized peoples. The leaders had no desire to change frontiers or to be crowned emperors, but to serve as liberators. This phase of political culture, original in South America, has never been sufficiently stressed.

The word 'liberty' rang with magic in South America. No hymn to any republic is without its salute to liberty. Liberty meant independence of the country from the shackles of all forms of exploitation. Liberty meant the opposite of slavery; liberty meant a national extension of man; liberty meant the road to democratic justice. Liberty meant the recognition of the dignity of all men.

'Dignidad' has always been of great importance to Latin Americans. It is a special word in the language with a far deeper connotatation than its English equivalent. So the cry for liberty too had a different significance—a profound cry evoking a profound response from people who had been under a conqueror's heel for centuries. It was not the imitative cry that oppressors themselves used in shallow patiotism to disguise their intentions of plunder. The cry of liberty became a call for the liberation and independence of all the Spanish colonies: the southern continent and the Caribbean islands.

Following the lead of Haiti and then the Dominican Republic, Central America took up the call to revolution. "The Spanish-American Revolution exploded in 1810, after forty years of preparation, as the freedom cry rang and was echoed from bell tower to bell tower, in all town halls, from the village of Dolores in Mexico to Buenos Aires, the capital of the viceroy on the Rio de la Plata."[8] Central America's goal in the revolution was not only to separate itself from Spain but to create, like its northern neighbor, a great federation of all the Spanish colonies including the Spanish Antilles.

The Latin American armies that came into being during the War of Independence against Spanish rule from 1810 to 1826 were *patriotic* armies, inspired by the ideas of independence, freedom and continental solidarity. They were not professional soldiers. "The officers were talented peoples, leaders and patriots, some representatives of the urban population, and rich Creole families influenced by the Enlightenment of the eighteenth century and [by] the French Revolution of 1789."[9]

General San Martín was almost the only Liberator who had previous military education. "The 'generals' of the War of Independence often were students, farmers, even village priests, who stepped forward to lead the rebellious masses of Creoles, Indians and Negroes. They received their rank by popular acclaim and started campaigning without weapons or uniforms. All they had in the beginning were sticks, stones and lances made in the village smithy."[10]

Rebel forces in the new Republic of Spanish Haiti were reminiscent of the inadequate armies of the Indian inhabitants of Hispaniola in their first fight against the Conquistadores. In Mexico, the first generals were the two rebel priests Miguel Hidalgo y Costilla (1783-1811) and José Mará Morelis y Pavon (1765-1815). Many battles were fought by troops in rags. They were of the same class with the poorest of the poor, the ragged men, the sans-culottes (those without trousers), who had fought to bring about the French Revolution.

Peru, almost last to fall to the revolutionaries, became independent in 1812. Armies brought from Argentina led by San Martín, and the troops from Venezuela led by Bolívar, converged on Lima for the final effort to achieve complete liberty for South America. Neither of the Liberators entered Lima with the intention of seizing the vacated viceroy's palace; instead they visited the university. San Marco is the only university in America whose classrooms were honored by the two men. Both went there to affirm the authentic ideal of the revolution. San Martín founded the national library and the Patriotic Society of Lima. At the ceremonies inaugurating the library he said: "As the Spanish Government is convinced that ignorance is despotism's doughtiest column, it has placed the strongest fetters on [Latin] American enlightenment and kept thought in chains to prevent [Latin Americans] from becoming aware of their dignity."[11] Bolívar declared: "An ignorant people is the blind instrument of its own destruction." A hundred years later, Fidel Castro in freeing Cuba would similarly put the greatest emphasis on education. The universities, founded more than a hundred years before the oldest in the English colonies, were the breeding ground, and still are, for the fight for liberty and independence. "Bolívar founded the University of Trujillo after he had gained control of all Peru. He decided that every province should have its normal school, and he established a college for the study of jurisprudence, philosophy and mathematics in Icá, and one for science in Cuzo, where he also founded the first women's college in Peru."

When the short-lived republic was established later in Spain, it was enthusiastically supported in Cuba. A decision was made to found a chair at the University of Havana of constitutional law. Father Balear, taking over the chair, called it, "A Chair of Liberty and the Rights of Man."

When at the beginning of the century Napoleon deposed Ferdinand VII, a group of Spaniards formed the Cortes (parliament) and asked the colonies to send deputies. A new, liberal Spanish Constitution was adopted in 1812 with deputies from Puerto Rico and Cuba taking part. Both islands made demands on the Cortes, some of which were granted. Tariff-free goods were allowed into the islands. All Cubans and Puerto Ricans were made full citizens of Spain. Seeds and agricultural tools were sent to Puerto Rico, and the island began to flourish in a way it had not done previously, when it had been isolated as a garrison citadel.

When the British defeated Napoleon in 1814, the crown was restored in Spain. Ferdinand VII, having learned nothing from the fate of his fellow Bourbon, Louis XIV—who had had his head chopped off in the French Revolution—was determined to rule once more in the old despotic terms. All printing presses were shut down. The king revoked the constitution. It was a year of executions and wholesale repressions.

Spain took possession of Santo Domingo in 1815, and a Spaniard was again made governor of the island. But the attempt by the Spanish monarchy to turn back the clock of history failed.

In his book *Faces of Nationalism*, Boyd C. Schafer writes: "In 1815 the guiding principles of high statesmanship were restoration and legitimacy—return to the dynastic religious and class arrangements and to the territorial division of the old regime. For 33 years, Metternich [connived] from the old seat of empire in Vienna— [with] the Bourbons and their followers in France, the Romanoffs, their officials and their churchmen from Russia, and to a lesser extent the Tory landlords and their allies in Britain—to preserve the world as it had been. In the short run, they had successes. In the long run of course they failed. They failed because an industrial, urban world was taking the place of the rural, agrarian one that had produced them. Because new elites, living under new conditions and an increasing number of people, demanded different political, economic, social arrangements, and because the old doctrines and practices no longer suited their desires or fulfilled people's needs. The new and then revolutionary doctrines, were liberalism, and nationalism. Of these two, nationalism proved the stronger, the more universal, and the more dominant." Spain could hold only her colonies of Cuba and Puerto Rico, which because they were all that were left to her, she ruled now with greater repression.

In Santo Domingo, though the Spanish Crown took over the colony again in 1814, the mood for independence was strong, and Spain was forced again to yield. This time independence lasted only from 1821 until 1822, but during this period the Dominican Republic proclaimed iself part of Bolívar's Federation of Colombia. The White Spanish aristocracy fled in the next years to Puerto Rico and Cuba, and the island became dominated largely by mulattoes.

Spain was unsuccessful in getting back her Latin American colonies. Independence had been achieved. Nationalism had won. The ideals of Federation were also known for a while. José Antigos, who fought for the agrarian reforms so vitally necessary, held all the territory of Uruguay and some of the Argentine provinces from 1811 to

1820. Guatemala included all of Central America for a short time from 1821 to 1823, and was called the United Provinces of Central America.

"San Martín planned a state that would comprise all lands south of Panama. Iturbide established a short-lived empire that embraced all the Spanish lands north of Panama; Bolivar managed temporarily to unite most of the territories that had made up the viceroyalties of Peru and Colombia, Venezuela and Ecuador. The goal of an abortive Pan-American Congress in Panama in 1826 was to form a federation that would compromise the entire old Spanish Empire in America."

But a series of betrayals followed independence. Latin America was split apart by new frontiers and was doomed as before to monoculture and dependence. This time dependence was on a new imperial power. For each group of Creoles preferred a state, an army, and a flag of its own. The Creoles still thought like colonials. Behind the scenes, the U.S. used its influence to foster this mentality.

It was dispossessed of Latin America who, with spears and machetes, really fought against Spanish power at the dawn of the nineteenth century. Independence did not reward them; it destroyed the hopes of those who had shed their blood. Peace came, and with it a new era of daily misery. Landowners and businessmen increased their fortunes while poverty grew among the classes. The intrigues of Latin America's new master grew, and the four viceroyalties of the Spanish Empire blew up and gave birth to various new nations, splinters of what might have been national unity.

The revolutions so bravely fought for independence against Spain had after a while to be turned against local conservatives and the local reactionaries. The "ragged ones" who had fought for the revolutions were not to gain by them. The spoils of victory went to their own upper classes, and then to the United States allied with the reactionaries in each country. "After the officers who had taken part in the War for Independence had died, the only desires of the second generation of militants were for power and booty. Naturally, they let themselves be led by whomever could fulfill their wishes, and that meant the Creole oligarchs. Consequently, the common people remained disenfranchised, and the oligarchs acquired a supplementary police force to protect their social system."[13]

Meanwhile in Hispaniola after a fresh invasion in 1822, Jean Pierre Boyer, President of Haiti, ruled the whole island until 1844. Although his rule was a cruel one, he freed the slaves, severed ties with Rome, forced out the traditional ruling class and tried to weed out Hispanic traditions. On the east side of the island, however, Juan Pablo Duarte, known as the father of the Dominican Republic, began in 1830 to organize secret societies to fight the Haitians and free his country of all outside rule. After a long struggle helped by an outbreak of a civil war in Haiti, independence was restored. The Dominicans had had a stormy history for nearly fifty years.

In 1844, the Dominicans marched against the Haitians and pushed them back to the old boundaries. At the same time they declared themselves a republic and seceded from Spanish rule for the third time. Some 20 years later in the 1860s, Spain regained the island for a short period, but the Dominican Republic had really been firmly established since 1844.

But as in Latin America, so it was in the Dominican Republic: those who had fought for the revolution were not the gainers. Duarte and other idealists were soon exiled. From 1844 to 1899, there was a series of dictators, Pedro Santana and Buenaventura Báez among the two most prominent, who ruled for many years. They amassed their own fortunes and sold out the interest of their country to foreign and domestic entrepreneurs. They brought the republic almost to ruins. There were several new skirmishes with Haiti, and to avoid futher assaults, Santana returned the island to Spain. In a weakened condition itself, Spain withdrew its troops after a short while. The occupation having been highly unpopular, Báez, then in power, asked the U.S. for protection. President Grant favored taking over the island, but because the questionable activities of a U.S. land speculator outraged the public, the U.S. failed to ratify the treaty. Báez resumed the presidency and then was succeeded by President Herveark, another 'strong man', from 1882 until 1898, the time of the Spanish-American War. He was to be in the continuing line of dictators, enforcing order and suppressing revolts with a spy system and a private army, and with the island coming more and more under American control, both financial and military.

In Latin America, after the achievement of independence and the futile attempts to establish larger confederations on the basis of the liberated colonies, the armies fell apart. New national armed forces arose, which were the only organized national force, and so the cult of the army arose in almost all the liberated countries. The military took an active part in political life, usually upholding reactionary dictatorship in the ensuing class struggles.

The Federalists in the Spanish colonies had envisaged the Hispanic continent as a whole, including the Spanish-speaking islands: a unit that would be equal in power to North America and Europe. The United States, fearing that Spain would still try to regain her lost colonies, hoped to keep other powers out of the area, and found it in her interest to keep South America 'balkanized'. She therefore proclaimed the Monroe Doctrine in 1823, and later the idea of her "manifest destiny."

The new bourgeoisie of Latin American countries soon were to become mere surrogates of international imperialism. Only Cuba and Puerto Rico remained now to attempt to obtain their independence from Spain, and later in the century they too would be engulfed in the United States' growing sphere of influence in the Caribbean.

9 -:- The Age of Independence

PART TWO: THE LATE 19th CENTURY

"The new independent republics [of Latin America] served only to tighten more than ever the Spanish grip on the remaining Caribbean colonies and to inhibit any reform movement."[1] Nevertheless, with the end of Spanish rule in Latin America, "the despotic rule of Spanish viceroys, who during their tenure of office thought only of enriching themselves,"[2] was over. With the independence of Mexico in 1820, after ten years of bitter fighting, the viceroyalty there, which had been in charge of the Spanish Antilles, was abolished. Puerto Rico had received a military grant from Mexico for nearly three hundred years. This now stopped and Puerto Rico was the poorer financially.

As elsewhere in the colonies, the poets, painters and writers of Puerto Rico helped to develop the island's own culture during the final hundred years of Spanish domination. The last effort of a foreign power to conquer Puerto Rico was made unsuccessfully by the British in 1796 with 7,000 troops led by General Ralph Abercromby. After that, the island had no further external enemy, and a long period of peace ensued. This was the period, according to Tomas Blanco, when "the foundations of Puerto Rican society were laid down." It was during this period that new classes developed and stratified; when poets and writers and patriots appeared; when there arose the beginnings of Puerto Rico's desire for independence, the assertion of its own nationhood. This period started when the U.S. War of Independence was finishing. During a period of revolutions occurring all around, both Puerto Rico and Cuba were relatively quiet. In fact,

Cuba, "the Pearl of the Antilles" was called "the ever faithful island of Spain."

As a garrison-controlled island, Puerto Rico had had a particularly authoritarian existence. Its own Spanish conservatives had been joined by French royalists fleeing Haiti, by Dominicans in fear of more black invasions, and by Spanish loyalists fleeing the revolutions in Latin America. The influx of conservatives gave a reactionary atmosphere to the island, and with the people more strongly suppressed, the concept arose they were more docile. Yet this was far from the truth. Several small rebellions broke out on the island in the years that followed. The most outstanding fight for independence was the *Grito de Lares* (*grito* meaning "cry," the cry for independence).

The reverberations of the Black Revolution in Haiti were felt in the island, though Puerto Rico's slave population was small in relation to the far greater numbers in Santo Domingo and Cuba. Everywhere the success of the Black Revolution put fear into the hearts of the white governing classes. Everywhere too in the Caribbean, it inspired other slave revolts. Although Blacks did not manage to gain their freedom anywhere else, slavery and the slave trade would be ended in roughly half a century. During the period of the restoration of the Spanish Crown, a period of great repression, there were several slave revolts in various parts of Puerto Rico from 1820 to 1840. But not being united and lacking a leader like Toussaint, the slaves were harshly overcome.

The plight of the 'free' laborer was not much better than that of the slave at this time. The plantations belonged to owners who ruled in a feudal fashion. The field hand, the *campensino*, had either a tiny plot or no land of his own, and was restricted by the patron in all his movements. A *bolito*, a sort of wage and passbook, kept him tied usually to one master. However, the winds of change blew even in Puerto Rico. Changes and advancements were to be made in the nineteenth century. A sense of nationalism was to grow, and the beginnings of a separatist movement to appear.

"The island was ruled like a fortress by a captain-general, who had total control, both military and civil. His power extended into the economy and the judiciary; he was in charge of the royal treasury and its tribunal and was a decisive influence in church affairs."[3] The governors in the islands felt themselves little kings and ruled in an absolutist fashion. One was Miguel de la Torre, who ruled Puerto Rico from 1822 to 1837 and whose administration has been described as "the dancing, gambling and drinking administration" (in this it was not much different from others). Different governors issued such systems as the work books—the aforementioned bolitos—which had the effect of regulating labor and turning it into naked servitude. Anyone over fifteen "without profession or capital" was considered a laborer and had to register with a judge who gave him his work book. The recipient was then ordered to get a job and a master.

Then an outside event affected the islands. Pirates again appeared in the Caribbean as they had in the seventeenth century. They attacked and plundered Spanish ships in Cuban and Puerto Rican waters. Because the United States helped to put down the pirates, Spain allowed the two islands to trade with the U.S.

Though it was keeping as tight a rein as possible on the remaining two countries of its old empire, Spain was forced by necessity and the pressures of its European allies to adopt a more liberal trading policy. Puerto Rican merchants were able to become more active, and the production of the main crops, sugar, coffee and tobacco increased. This brought greater wealth to the islands, and the merchants and plantation owners profited. Puerto Rico gained too from the destruction of the Haitian sugar crop by revolutionaries. As in Cuba, there was an expansion of the Puerto Rican sugar industry. Sugar prices topped all records. But with increased prosperity, the poor became more dissatisfied with their lot, and more vocal in their discontent.

During the period when Ferdinand VII's throne had been placed in jeopardy by Napoleon, the municipal government of San Germán instructed the deputy to the Cortes of Spain that Puerto Rico "recognized the sovereignty of Ferdinand VII, but only on condition that in case the said sovereign does not prevail, the island will regain her natural right to govern herself according to her own views."[4] This was a polite declaration of independence. Unfortunately, Ferdinand was returned to the throne, but not for long. A coup in Spain toppled the Crown and restored the liberal 1812 Constitution, which had been instituted when Napoleon's troops had occupied the country.

A revolt arose in Puerto Rico in 1835, a military effort by junior officers and soldiers and some 1500 civilians, who tried to take over the government with the aim of separating the island from Spain. Three years later there was a similar rebellion in San Juan when a group of Puerto Ricans, with the help of a Granada regiment from South America, tried once more to proclaim a republic. "In 1864 an army captain was sent to Spain on suspicion of being the leader of a supposed insurrection." And once again in 1867, a military leader was shot as guilty "in an attempted revolt."[5] These were all preludes to the Grito de Lares which was to take place in 1868. Clearly, Puerto Rico was not so docile as historians have suggested.

Again movements in Spain influenced those on the islands. There was discontent with the corruption of the restored monarchy under Isabella II. At first, there were calls for the limitation of her power and for a popular monarch as in the British system. However, the moderate demands soon developed into more urgent calls for the complete overthrow of royalty. The "Glorious Revolution of Spain" had begun. In Puerto Rico, it coincided with the Grito de Lares.

The patriot Dr. Ramon Emeterio Betances issued his call for insurrection: "Puerto Ricans! An end to Spanish Domination.' Betances and Ruiz Belvis had been exiled, and escaping to New York they organized with exiled Cubans to work for revolution in both islands. In 1865, the Republican Society of Cuba and Puerto Rico was formed. Its constitution read: "Only by force of arms can we wrest from the government of the Spanish nation, the right to manage our own affairs; enjoy our liberty; insure and defend our interests; and occupy the position that is due to us among the nations of the earth."[6] Already Betances, through his revolutionary writings which were distributed throughout the island, had formed branches of the Puerto Rican Revolutionary Committee. "Revolutionary juntas were actively functioning in Lares, Mayaguez, San Sebastian, Camuy and Ponce."[7]

For some time, Betances had been purchasing military stores and weapons. Then in 1868 he launched an expeditionary force of 3,000 armed men on his ship El Telegrafo. The insurrection of Lares was meant to take place on September 29, but an indiscretion caused the conspirators to be discovered, and they were obliged to move the date to September twenty-third. Meanwhile, the Dominican Republic's dictator Báez informed the Spanish government of the expedition, and Betances who was by then in St. Thomas, ready to sail, was detained by the authorities. But for the revolutionaries in Puerto Rico, there was no turning back. The uprising included the vital support of some of the military—soldiers and artillery men from the garrisons. The leadership on the island went to a Venezuelan, Manuel Rojas, who was living in Puerto Rico and supporting its aim of independence. The rebelling forces marched to Lares and captured the town, crying "Viva Puerto Rico Libre." A provisional government was set up and the Republic of Puerto Rico declared. They forced a reluctant priest to say a Te Deum in the local church to celebrate the victory; they then moved on to San Sebastian. Without the extra men that Betances was to bring, they were defeated. However, the short-lived Republic of Puerto Rico was not without its gains.

The sense of Puerto Rican nationality, which had been growing from the beginning of the century, had a final seal stamped upon it by the Grito de Lares. For Puerto Ricans, this now was their island for which they were prepared from this time forward to fight and, if necessary, to die. In Lares "the first national symbols appeared: a hymn and a flag." This first flag was inspired by the national revolutionary movement. On one corner, on a white banner with a horizontal cross, a lone star appeared. Since the American Revolution, a star had come to symbolize independence. The lone star stood for Puerto Rico. The insurrectionists also carried a red flag "symbolizing the social nature of the struggle."[8] The hymn was written by Lola Rodriquez de Tio and called *La Borinqueña*. It is interesting that the revolutionaries in Hispaniola and in Puerto Rico should go back to the beginnings of their history and choose old Indian names. Cuba's name had never been changed from its original one.

Most important of all, the armed uprising marked the affirmation of Puerto Rican nationality and the affirmation by its people of the right to independence. That affirmation would never be withdrawn. Secondly, it marked the beginning of modern political life in the country. The ruling class had never before had the necessity to organize because its domination had been so complete that it had never had to face political opposition, particularly during the years of renewed despotism in Spain and in the islands. A young generation had now arisen, some of whose members had been educated in the universities of Europe. They called for the abolition of slavery (one of Betances' demands) and for more personal and public liberty. Two parties were formed: the conservatives and the liberals, opposing each other in Puerto Rico and opposing each other in the Cortes in Spain. The parties would change and gather new formations and new names as the years unfolded. And underneath, at times strongly, at times faintly, the Grito de Lares, the cry for independence would reverberate and be heard. Its call *Muerto O Liberdad: Viva Puerto Rico Libre* had been planted in the hearts of Puerto Ricans never to be extinguished.

There was conservatism which tended in some sections toward reactionary ideas, while the liberals deplored the "docility" of the people. But in spite of all this, the people had shown that at the apto march and to fight.

After the Grito de Lares, the independence movement was not ended. In 1873, there was the Estrallada uprising. Betances continued to spread revolutionary propaganda, now from St. Thomas, V.I. From New York in 1874, Betances again sent in more arms, but this attempt too was betrayed.

Secret societies grew up in a new period of repression, which lasted roughly from 1875 to 1885. The government imprisoned and tortured suspects. "Autonomists" were accused of being revolutionaries and were terrorized by threats and jailings.

One effect of this increased repression was to encourage reformists to support the revolutionary cause of Cuba and Puerto Rico. After Lares, Puerto Rican patriots began to call upon Spain for greater autonomy or to ask for full independence. They would remember the proclamation issued by the Revolutionary Committee, (probably the work of Betances): "Puerto Ricans . . . have conspired —and they should conspire—because one day the colonial regime on our island must end: because Puerto Rico must finally be free—like the continent, like Santo Domingo."

Alongside Betances' writings, there were now those of de Hostos and others. Eugenio Maria de Hostos (1839-1903), though Puerto Rican, was a man whose works belong to all three islands. He became a rector of the normal school in Santo Domingo. In 1884, he delivered a speech that is said to be "a masterpiece of Spanish American moral thinking." His immense output includes poetry, essays, novels and historical writings. His *La Peregrinacion de Bayoan* is a novel, but it is also a fervent and poetic summons to a West Indian Federation, "which would unite Cuba, Santo Domingo, Puerto Rico and Haiti."

In New York, de Hostos joined the Junta Revolucionaria to fight for both Puerto Rican and Cuban independence, and founded La Liga de Patriotas. When Martí led another Cuban revolt in 1895, the Puerto Ricans in New York formed a Borinquen chapter of the Cuban Revolutionary Party. With the War for Independence starting at this time, the Cuban revolutionaries made preparations also to send an expedition to Puerto Rico. General Juan Luis Rivera, a Puerto Rican who had fought with the Cubans in the Ten Years War, as well as taking part in the Grito de Lares, was to have directed it, though these plans were not carried out.

In 1897, one year before the U.S. was to send in troops, a new rebellion broke out in Yauco. It was crushed.

However, finally, Spain was forced to make some concessions if it were not to lose its remaining possessions in the New World, Cuba and Puerto Rico. With a liberal prime minister heading a new government in Spain, a pact was made with Muñoz Rivera, a leader of the autonomist party in Puerto Rico. A royal decree was passed on November 25, 1897 which gave Puerto Rico a wide measure of self-government. There was to be "universal suffrage, representation in the Cortes, power to ratify commercial treaties, to set tariffs."[9] The colony was to be guaranteed consultation in all matters pertaining to legislation that affected it.

The liberals in Cuba and particularly in Puerto Rico always hoped that by going hat in hand to the Spanish parliament they could gain some more autonomy. They expressed themselves as being faithful Spaniards, as later liberals were to express themselves as faithful Americans. But in both cases they wanted more autonomy, more measures for their own self-government. They were always deluded into believing that with the proper circumstances and with special pleading, this would be achieved. In the year 1877 which was called the "terrible year," the Spanish effected very repressive action against these liberals. They were thrown into prison and tortured, but instead of rebelling against the injustices, they endured them. From Baldoriorty de Castro to Muñoz Rivera, every political leader spent his genius in elaborate attempts to gain friends and influence people in the political arena in Madrid, much the same as Puerto Rican leaders were later to go hat in hand to Washington.

Professor Maldonado-Denis says that the grant of autonomy came to Puerto Rico due to two causes: one was the Cuban Revolution and the second, Spain's weakness in relation to the United States. It did not come due to liberal pleadings. Elections were held with everyone voting and Muñoz Rivera (father of Muñoz Marin) became governor in 1897.

But the measures of self-government given so late by the Spanish government were immediately annulled by the military government of the U.S., which landed troops in Puerto Rico on July 25, 1898. Today, after eighty years of U.S. domination, Puerto Rico has still not achieved the level of autonomy that it enjoyed during its last year as a Spanish colony. The royal decree of self-government was wiped out, and in its place the U.S. substituted the Foraker Act, which gave Puerto Rico fewer liberties than in the end had been forced from Spain.

Exiled in Paris, Betances wrote before the American occupation: "Let us not forget that Lares means something in the Hispanic-Puerto Rican battle for liberty." And dying after the occupation, he wrote: "It is the same being a Yankee colony as a Spanish one." De Hostos said sadly: "I see her [Puerto Rico] go from owner to owner without ever being her own mistress, and see her pass from sovereignty to sovereignty without ever ruling herself."

Puerto Rico would remain the only one of the Spanish colonies in the Western Hemisphere that had never obtained independence. Cuba would become independent with the turn of the century.

Meanwhile, like Puerto Rico during the period when all Latin America was in turmoil, fighting for and gaining independence, Cuba was relatively quiet. Those who did consider independence did so in terms of Bolívar's federation, as the Dominican Republic had at first done. One reason for the early lack of rebellion was that both Cuba and Puerto Rico were enjoying an economic boom. With Haiti in ruins, the sugar market shifted to the other islands.

Further, because Cuba was no longer restricted to trading only with Spain, merchants found an ever-growing market in the U.S. for Cuban sugar and tobacco. In the first half of the century, the number of sugar haciendas jumped from four to eight hundred. Cuba became at this time one of the wealthiest colonies of the world.

During the year that the British occupied Cuba, there was great increase in the import and export of slaves, and an overall increase in exports and imports. Only a dozen ships had been allowed by Spain for trading; under the British the total rose almost to 1,000. Spain allowed the trade to continue when the island was restored to her. After the Black revolution, "most of Haiti's fabulous sugar market was open to Cuba, and the United States was rapidly becoming a voracious customer of Cuban sugar."[10] Both coffee and tobacco grew as exports too.

With the relaxing of the rule restricting shipping to the motherland, the Spanish Antilles were able to develop commercial transactions with many other countries, so long as these were not active enemies of Spain. Puerto Ricos coffee, for instance, became a gourmet item in many parts of Europe, and of course Havana cigars became world famous for their flavour and excellence.

Cuba achieved further importance in this era. The archbishophric of Santo Domingo was moved to Santiago de Cuba after Santo Domingo was ceded to France in 1795. Many Dominicans fled both to Cuba and Puerto Rico after the victory of Toussaint. When Britain took over the Bahamas and Florida in return for evacuating Cuba, many Spaniards emigrated to Cuba. Similarly, when France sold Louisiana to the U.S. in 1803, many Spaniards and Frenchmen came to Cuba. These were all Spanish loyalists and reinforced the numbers of the Spanish ruling class in Cuba. As a military base, Cuba was full of troops; and this also prevented revolution from easily arising. Cuba was also important because Spain had plans to use the island to reconquer Latin America.

During the period of boom for the sugar plantations, steam-driven machinery was brought in for the sugar mills, the first railroad was started and roads were built to help in the development of the plantations. Of importance too was the fact that the growing haciendas needed more slaves. Any talk of abolition, as was happening elsewhere, meant talk against the increased prosperity of the island. The Spanish administration warned the Cuban rebels that independence against Spain would result in complete economic disaster. It was not until the second half of the century, when all Latin America and Santo Domingo were already independent, that there arose a strong movement for separation from Spain.

Here as in Puerto Rico, there had been earlier movements for independence. When in 1825 the first conspiracies against Spain were discovered, a royal decree gave the captain-general of the island authority to rule the island as if it were "a city under siege." There was the same type of aggressive governor as was ruling in Puerto Rico during this period of reaction. The captain-general of Cuba in 1834 had fought in South America against the cause of independence. In 1836, when the Spanish Constitution of 1812 was restored, he refused to honor it.

At this time, Britain in its own interest was determined to abolish the slave trade and pressed Spain into a treaty to affect this. But in Cuba the treaty was disregarded. The British consul, a man named Turnbull, attempted to inform the Negroes of the situation and was expelled. He reentered Cuba secretly and tried to foment a rebellion. The conspiracy was discovered however, and some liberals implicated in the plot were executed.

Meanwhile a right-wing conspiracy was growing; the landowners of Cuba wished to join up with the plantation owners of the southern United States. This conspiracy was led by General Marciso López, a Venezuelan who had been active in South America against the Liberators. He landed with 600 men, two thirds of them Americans. Defeated, he returned again a few years later, this time with only one-tenth of his expedition made up of Cubans or Spanish; the rest were Americans. Many American politicians supported him and wanted the annexation or purchase of the island.

López was defeated once again, but Conservative hopes were not yet abandoned.[11] Right-wing Cuban exiles in the United States persuaded William Quitman, a former governor of Mississippi and a general, to head another expedition. While he was assembling his forces, he learned that an insurrection had been prematurely started and thwarted; in this case exposing a plan for killing the captain-general as preparation for the American landing."

Soon after the quashed insurrection, in 1854, three American diplomats in Europe issued "the Ostend Manifesto, a bombastic pronouncement that Spain must sell Cuba to the United States or have it torn from her."[11] They wanted to add another slave state to the Union.

The new Cuban cultural leaders such as the priest Varela, Sacco and others were imprisoned, exiled or executed. The arrogance and intolerable authoritarianism of the new governors evoked a reaction in the Creole population. Again as in Puerto Rico, groups arose who offered different solutions of opposing viewpoints. One group wanted annexation by the U.S., and as noted above, two expeditions were launched with American backing in 1850 and 1851. Many Americans acted as White officers in these expeditions. They were mainly Southern slave owners anxious for the continuation of slavery in Cuba. The group favoring U.S. annexation was opposed by liberals who "feared the abortion of Cuba's new nationalism and culture by the voracious vitality of the United States."[12] Both of these groups were defeated: the first by the military, the second by the inflexibility of Spain.

A royal decree had convened the *Junta de Informacion,* to which representatives from both Cuba and Puerto Rico went to be given the opportunity to air their grievances. Both islands supplicated for more autonomy. Both asked for greater free trade, for more tax reforms and for a progressive abolition of slavery. The Crown turned down all appeals, dissolved the Junta, and in place of tax reform, increased taxes by ten percent.

Among the deputies to the new Cortes was Father Félix Varela, the progressive priest who was sent as a representative to Spain. He advocated autonomy for the island as well as abolition of slavery. For this he was accused of heresy in Spain and condemned to death. He escaped to die in exile during which time he contributed a number of writings on Cuba and Cuba's need for self-government. Into Valera's place at the university came another liberal, José Antonio Sacco. He spoke out not for autonomy but for independence. The Spanish governor ordered him into exile too, and like his predecessor he spent his years writing about his beloved country.

But the cries for independence could not be put down. Sacco was followed by José de la Luz y Caballero. He also called for independence and for the abolition of slavery. It has been a tradition in Cuba, as in Puerto Rico and the Dominican Republic, that the fighters were poets and the poets were fighters. And all were intensely interested in education. This is also true of Simon Bolívar, the Great Liberator. These men all wrote long prose poems on the subject of liberty and human rights for all men.

The realization that reforms would not come led increasingly to a cry for insurrection. Within a month of the Grito de Lares in Puerto Rico, came the Grito de Yara in Cuba led by José Martí and by Carlos Manuel de Céspedes, a liberal-minded landowner. José Martí had vast literary gifts. He was poet, novelist, thinker, journalist, orator, agitator and 'apostle' of independence. He appealed to what was noblest in the Cuban character. Imprisoned, he wrote *The Political Prison of Cuba*, telling of the brutalities that prisoners suffered. He had established a paper called *The Patriot* in Havana, but after his imprisonment he was exiled, so he went to the United States. In New York he established a new small journal called *Patria Libre* —the free country.

Martí sent his propaganda literature into Cuba and Puerto Rico where it was distributed underground from hand to hand. The Grito de Yara occurred in the later-famed Oriente Province. Independence was proclaimed and slavery abolished. As Bolívar said, it was madness for a revolution for liberty to maintain slavery. The insurrectionists were not so easily put down in Cuba as in Puerto Rico, and the struggle went on intermittently falling and then rising again over a ten-year period until the final armed struggle that ended in the War for Independence.

Though Betances had demanded abolition, the cry for revolution in Cuba was tied more strongly to the cry for abolition of slavery, than had been the case in Puerto Rico. When the Ten Years War began, the population of Cuba was divided in the following way: Whites, 800,000; free Mulattoes, 250,000; Black slaves, 1,370,000. In Puerto Rico around 1863 just before the rebellion, there were only 13,000 slaves, while there were four times as many free, day laborers. In

1865, the class of free workers exceeded the slaves by 56,000 men. The white population in Puerto Rico was 300,000; the 'free' Mestizo and Black population was 240,000, and the slave population including men, women and children was 41,000. Few slaves and few black 'free' men took part in the Puerto Rican rebellion, despite the fact that there had been slave uprisings earlier in the century, and despite the brutal conditions under which the slaves lived.

While in Cuba, the slaves participated in the uprising and were part of the revolutionary force. Even though illiteracy among Negroes was high, about three-quarters not knowing how to read or write, Negroes had been establishing their own newspapers. In their passionate desire for education, they had also founded their own schools. In the fight for independence, many blacks rose to the rank of general.

The insurrection grew in strength. From a hundred men under Céspedes in 1868 issuing a call for independence and abolition of slavery, by 1870 the number of rebels in the Oriente province had grown into an armed force of 40,000 men. They avoided pitched battles as far as possible, and engaged in guerilla warfare. Offering freedom to Negroes who joined them, the rebels continually enlarged their forces. The revolutionaries of each of the islands helped one another: one of the military leaders in Cuba was from the Dominican Republic.

The rebels held their part of the island for many years, but in 1873 Céspedes was betrayed, and the Spaniards garrotted him. Still the revolution continued for an additional three years, when a truce was called. The Spanish had sent continuous reinforcements to put down the rebels, and it is estimated that they lost some 80,000 men in the war. Desperate to hold her last colonies, Spain had sent more troops to hold the islands than she had sent to hold the colonies in South America.

Although Spain had been able to subdue the revolt in Puerto Rico, for all her military strength she could not suppress the Cuban revolution. For ten long years the war had continued. Negroes, Creoles, Whites, fighting together with fantastic bravery, had continued the struggle as guerillas in the mountains. Only in 1878, when Spain was ready to make concessions for greater autonomy (as she was to do in the same way some years later in Puerto Rico) did the rebels finally lay down their arms.

As with the short-lived Grito de Lares, there were gains made by the Cuban revolution. And though the gains were small for Puerto

Rico, they were necessarily greater for Cuba. In both islands, the "Gritos" had consolidated the idea of nationalism, and independence had become a national cause never again to be eradicated. Concessions were granted: the slaves were to be freed; there were to be expanded civil liberties and greater representation given to Cuba in the Spanish Cortes.

But in spite of the truce and the Spanish concessions, the Cubans were far from satisfied. The abolition of slavery did not in fact take place until 1886. Though all Spaniards were allowed to vote, less than 3 percent of the Creoles were given suffrage: a small gain. In view of this, rebellion revived, some of the revolutionaries never having accepted the truce. These continued to fight small guerilla wars, while exiles in New York raised funds and formed a party which put out revolutionary literature for *'Cuba Libre.'* They were joined by the group of exiled Puerto Rican "independentistas." As in Puerto Rico, Spain was finally prepared to offer more concessions. A governor-general was to share authority with a council of thirty: half of the members elected, half appointed. It was autonomy of a sort, but it was now insufficient, and it was less than had been offered to Puerto Rico.

Americans were moving more forcibly into the country, buying up the sugar plantations, modernizing them. At first sugar was allowed into the States with low duty. When this policy was suddenly reversed, it caused a financial depression in the island. Cuba's economic fate was already tied to that of the United States.

José Martí organized a new revolution. He had already been active in the Ten Years War. Once when caught, he had served time on a chain gang. And, when he was caught a second time, he was deported for subversion.

There were other dimensions, other effects. The oligarchy had been weakened in the long, debilitating war of ten years. The economy had also been weakened. And the United States, after the Southerners' failure to annex Cuba, moved in with greater investments and therefore greater political influence. The U.S. had control of the sugar market by 1898, and after that fateful date was to expand into all other areas of the economy.

On the island, a new group of *autonomistas* arose (parallel again to the history of Puerto Rico) who went hat in hand to the Cortes to ask for reforms. As these reforms were not forthcoming, so moderates moved to support the revolutionary cause. José Martí had in the meantime been building his independence party, and he organized within it the disillusioned break-away groups from the autonomists. The old fighters of the Ten Years War joined him, realizing that the battle must never end until its purpose was accomplished.

Martí had worked patiently for years. He issued a platform for his new party, El Partido Revolucionario Cubano (the Cuban Revolutionary Party). This was the party Puerto Rican independentistas were to join, and the goal of liberation for Cuba was linked to the goal of liberation for Puerto Rico. Two new flags were designed, the same except for the reversal in colors. The two islands were to march hand in hand towards the same appointed goal. Cuba and Puerto Rico were the "two wings of one bird."

Martí, however, planned on a short war, one that would not cause great destruction to the island, and one that by its briefness would not provoke the intervention of the United States—a possibility Martí most feared. Martí hoped "to establish a republic with justice for everyone, a government capable of abolishing social and racial inequalities," and "a republic with agricultural diversification and free from economic dependence."

Three days before the scheduled departure of the well-planned and well-equipped expedition, the United States confiscated the three ships and all their war materiel. In exactly this way had Betances' forces been detained in St. Thomas during the Grito de Lares uprising, and in both cases, it was too late for the revolutionaries to turn back.

The Cubans started their new fight badly handicapped by their lack of expected military and arms support. And tragically, three months later Martí himself was killed in one of the battles against the Spanish forces. Still the fight went on. It could no longer be a short war. It could no longer avoid destruction of the countryside. In fact, in June 1896 General Maceo instructed Brigadier José N. Aguirre to destroy every building which could offer shelter and defense to the enemy, and to destroy all tobacco and corn which could be found gathered in the territory."

This was the scorched earth policy that the Indians had used against the Spanish Conquistadores. As the cost to the Indians had been appalling, so it now was to the Cubans. Nevertheless, this time it brought Spain to her knees. She had not the financial strength to continue the war. Victory was in reach.

But at the last moment, the event that Martí had so greatly feared took place: the United States intervened. The patriotic army had fought for independence for half a century. When victory was in its hands, it was snatched from them by the United States in the Spanish-American War. The Cuban liberation army was demobilized, and a new army under conservative elements and under U.S. control, was formed. When Martí had worked in New York organizing the insurrectionary forces, he had "taught Cubans to be suspicious of the United States, the monster," he said, "in whose entrails he had lived." His well-planned expedition of three ships had been confiscated by the Americans. But the revolution had gone on. Again it was in the Oriente Province that the revolution was acclaimed and a republic proclaimed. Maceo and Gomez, now the leaders, marched towards Havana. The populace was with them, and the rebel army penetrated to the western end of the island. As the Haitians had done in their revolutions, so the Cubans, where necessary, put the sugar cane and the *centrales* to the fire, adopting the scorched earth policy against the forces of the Spanish army. Gomez had asked for recognition by the United States, but was refused it by President Cleveland. And Cleveland's successor, President William McKinley, offered secretly again to buy Cuba from Spain.

Spain offered the Cubans a new plan for autonomy, but it came too late. There were riots in Havana; the U.S. had its opportunity to move in. The battleship *Maine* arrived in the Havana harbor at the request of the U.S. ambassador "for the protection of American citizens." A week later there was an explosion on the boat. It sank and 266 U.S. sailors were killed. Commissions of the Spanish and the Americans came to diametrically opposite conclusions. The Americans claimed the ship had been blown up by an external agent. The Spanish claimed the damage was from an internal cause.

Propaganda in the yellow press in the States had been building up popular opinion for a war with Spain in the Caribbean for a long time. The necessary "incident" had happened. Again McKinley was asked to recognize the republic set up by the revolutionaries, but again he refused. The United States was going to see that American investments already at the level of $50 million were protected, and was going to fight to 'free' Cuba, whose revolutionaries had already won the fight.

10 -:- U.S. Entry and the Spanish-American War

It is not generally realized how early there was interference by North America in the affairs of the Caribbean. During the American Revolution, the French had given considerable help to the colonies in their fight against England. In fact, it is doubtful whether the revolution could have succeeded without French help. A secret treaty had been signed in 1778 by Benjamin Franklin by which the colonists agreed that for this help they would keep out of any conflict in the West Indies, where the French were battling with the British over the possession of several islands. However, once having won its independence, the newly formed republic started to build up its Navy. Eyeing the Caribbean and disregarding the treaty it had signed to secure its own existence, the U.S. began an undeclared war on French ships even before the end of the century. This 'war' began in 1789, and lasted for three years.

The French were indignant and called upon the Americans to remember the treaty and the aid the French had given them. The Americans replied that they would have to be neutral in the conflict between France and England. Secretly however, President John Adams, succeeding George Washington who had also countenanced the war, ordered the navy to engage French ships in the Caribbean. A number of battles, mostly to the American advantage, occurred during the undeclared war. The areas around Cuba and Santo Domingo were particularly involved. In one engagement, American marines landed in Cuba to help a British ship captured by the French. American marines were also landed in the Caribbean during this period at Curaçao, helping the Dutch against the French.

There was considerable division in the country between Jefferson, who wanted to help the French, and Hamilton, who wanted to help England. The Hamilton faction was successful; the treaty was disregarded. The Americans, being of British descent, may have learned lessons from "perfidious Albion." North America gained its first naval strength and experience in these adventures, and stationed its ships from Cuba right down to Trinidad and the British-held islands. As well as developing the U.S. Navy, these battles greatly helped to consolidate British power in the Caribbean.

An incidental happening: while sailing the Caribbean, U.S. Commodore David Fleet captured on the high seas a young Puerto Rican pirate named Cofresi, a sort of Robin Hood type, who was giving his gains to the Puerto Rican poor. The American navy also provided assistance and arms to Touissant L'Overture during the revolution against the French, though Touissaint and his successors were careful to pay for the arms received so that they would be under no obligation to any of the powers.

The U.S. Marines landed in Santo Domingo for the first time in the spring of 1800. But by 1806, the U.S. Congress, under pressure from France in an effort to hurt, and perhaps to bring down the Black Republic of Haiti, placed a complete embargo on trade with it.

The undeclared war with the French had been excellent training for the navy of the young republic. Even as it was fighting in the Caribbean under President Jefferson, America was engaging in another undeclared war in the Mediterranean. There also, the young nation was developing a very prosperous annual commerce of about $10 million worth of merchandise. Barbary pirates were interfering with this trade, and for 15 years, from 1801 until 1816, the U.S. made war against them, and against Morrocco, Tripoli and Algiers. President Madison continued that war.

The young republic was not sitting in quiet isolation, keeping out of the rivalries with Europeans, and concentrating on her own development. Almost from the moment of birth, the U.S. had turned from republic to empire. In particular it eyed, as Europeans had eyed, the Spanish Antilles as the most desirable possessions of the Caribbean islands.

There was almost a whole century, culminating in the Spanish-American War, when American presidents and members of Congress expressed their covetousness of the islands. By a treaty, the French had received Louisiana from the Spanish, and Louisiana remained French until the young expanding Union in North America acquired it by purchase. According to Gore Vidal in his book *Burr*, after Jefferson's purchase of Louisiana and his attempt to seize Florida, he set forth "for the west and south an imperial course as coldly and resourcefully as any Bonaparte—he was the most successful empire builder of the century." He wanted to annex Cuba. His secretary of war stated in 1824 that the island should be annexed immediately.

Presidents John Adams and James Monroe expressed similar sentiments. With the declaration of the Monroe Doctrine in 1823, the U.S. designated the whole Western Hemisphere as within its sphere of influence. No European nation was to be allowed to interfere in the area.

President John Quincy Adams wrote, concerning both Cuba and Puerto Rico: "These islands, from their local positions, are natural appendages to the North American continent; and one of them, Cuba, almost in sight of our shores—has become an object of transcendant importance to the political and commercial interests of our Union . . . it is scarcely possible to resist the conviction that the annexation of Cuba to our federal republic will be indispensable to the continuance and integrity of the Union itself."

But he felt that the best policy momentarily for the U.S. was to permit an ailing Spain to retain Cuba until it could be wrested from her without the risk of losing it later. In the interest of continuing slavery in the 1840s, the Southern states wanted to buy Cuba, and President Polk offered the large sum of $100 million for it. But President Tyler before Polk, and President Fillmore after him, both suggested taking the island by force.

At one time, the plantation owners in Cuba and Puerto Rico schemed with the planters of the Southern states to join together, so that slavery could continue in all the area. They were prepared to countenance seditiously the annexation of the islands to the slave states of America. The slave owners of the Southern states were also behind the annexation of Mexico.

Right up to the Spanish-American war, when the U.S. did take action, presidents and secretaries of state were constantly expressing their desire to take over the Spanish Antilles. In 1867, Secretary of State Seward said: "The United States has constantly cherished the belief that someday she can acquire these islands [Cuba and Puerto Rico] by just and legal means and with the consent of Spain." In 1870, President Grant wanted to take over the Dominican Republic. He felt that it had "a large promise of wealth." In 1876, Secretary of State Blaine, under President Harrison, wrote a report suggesting:

"There are three places of sufficient value to be taken: one is Hawaii and the others are Puerto Rico and Cuba." President Grover Cleveland stated: "Our actual pecuniary interest in [Cuba] is second only to that of the people and government of Spain."

Germán Arciniegas, writing of Latin America, says that "its national development can be divided into four periods: the discovery, the conquest, the colony and independence." In contrast, the history of the United States can be divided into the same four periods but in reverse order. The first step was independence" [for the Pilgrims left England originally to be free of her laws]. "Then came the colony; then from colony to conquest; and finally from conquest to discovery."

From the first the local laws in the colonies were passed by a city council or town meeting. The colonists elected their own local officials and governed themselves. The English governors were there on sufferance: the colonists fixed their salaries. The tiny theatre of war of the 13 colonies for independence "merely confirmed the already existing independence. Real conquest began with the discovery of gold in California" (the same lure as for the Spanish conquistadores). In the Mexican War, the American settlers overran Mexican territory in Texas. When Mexico moved against the usurpers, the U.S. annexed the land. In the same war, it took over half the territory of California, the richest half, where the gold was to be found.

In the beginning, as the new nation moved westward, it destroyed the original American Indian nation as the Spanish had destroyed the Indians in the Caribbean and South America. Treaties were signed with the Indians, but like the first international treaty with the French, they were always to be broken. As the gentle Tainos, Aztecs and Incas of South America, had become "savages, nonhumans" after the Spanish Conquest, so the North American Indians who had helped the first settlers to survive were now in the way of the U.S. on its path of conquest, and good only so long as they were dead.

The quick expansion of the northern territories can be seen in the following progression of the land under the U.S. flag. In 1803 Louisiana was purchased. In 1819 Florida was bought. In 1845 Texas was annexed. In the next year the Oregon territory was also annexed. A forced cession from Mexico two years later added another 500,000 square miles. Next, Mexico was forced to sell more of her land. Fifteen years were to pass before Alaska was added. With the Spanish-American War, Hawaii, Puerto Rico, Guam and the Philippines

U.S. Entry and the Spanish-American War   139

were also annexed. Cuba became as good as a colony, as did the Dominican Republic a few years later. With the lease of the Panama Canal Zone, the U.S. in the hundred years from 1803 to 1904 had added by annexation or purchase nearly three million square miles to its empire. In 1776, the original thirteen colonies had covered an area of 200,000 square miles; within a century, the Union had expanded to fifteen times that size.

In the War of Independence in Latin America, the U.S. warned Bolívar to keep out of Cuba and Puerto Rico, and not to try to liberate them. But she offered aid in cases where Spain might undertake to regain her colonies. She offered protection to Latin American and Spanish Caribbean countries, which really meant that she maintained the right to take action in the whole sphere. "In the ultimate analysis, the greatest threat to the Spanish empire came from American interests rather than European ideas [of the Enlightenment]."[1]

An example of this growing belief of the U.S. in its sovereignty in the hemisphere, was the sending in 1854 of a warship to San Juan del Norte in Nicaragua, an independent country since 1811. One American was wounded and for this President Buchanan fined Nicaragua $20,000. When it was unable to pay, the U.S. sent in its marines. It then demanded the right to intervene in Nicaraguan affairs whenever it so deemed, and insisted on its free passage throughout the country as well.

Six years later it similarly intervened in Honduras. There were many other instances of "big stick" policies. In 1895, President Cleveland supported Henry Cabot Lodge's dictum: "Today the United States is practically sovereign on this continent, and its fiat is law upon the subjects to which it confines its interposition."

In Mexico whose independence had been declared by General Iturbide in 1821, "the most feared and hated country was the North American neighbor," who between 1837 and 1849 "absorbed over a million and a half square miles of Mexican territory, including Texas, New Mexico and half of California."[2] By 1845, the United States had annexed more than half of Mexico itself. The U.S. had become the new conquistador and in the name of civilization, had restored slavery. Mexico itself was transformed into a slave colony, despite trappings of independence.

During the war "military atrocities against the Mexican civilian population were numerous."[3] There was bitter, angry dissent over the immorality of war against a country so much weaker. Thoreau expounded his belief in civil disobedience when citizens were asked to perform actions contrary to their consciences. But in general, the American people accepted the idea that it was their right and even their duty to subjugate and 'civilize an inferior people.' From its birth, the United States has been an aggressive nation—violence is as American as apple pie.

In 1861, against the lawful Mexican President Benito Juarez, France and Austria, with Spanish support, attempted to make the Hapsburg Ferdinand Maximilian emperor of Mexico. The Spanish sent six thousand of these multinational troops from Cuba to Vera Cruz. In this dangerous situation, Juarez made provisions for transferring large sums of money to his supporters in Cuba, which he could later use in a bid for his return to power should his forces be defeated. Though Maximilian was proclaimed emperor in August 1863, by a National Assembly elected at the points of French bayonets, his reign did not last long. He was shot in 1867 by President Juarez's forces. The republic was restored and the Spanish troops returned to Cuba. During this episode, President Lincoln stated that America would not stand for any infringement of the Monroe Doctrine, and that any European power who intervened in Mexican affairs would sooner or later encounter the hostility of the United States.

The Hapsburg adventure had been embarked upon partly on the advice of Guitierez D'Esfrada, a wealthy Mexican and a believer in monarchy for his country. In trying to enlist support in Europe, he wrote: "If the European Powers persist in ignoring America's aggressive policy towards her neighbors and allow it to go unchecked, still regarding this growing giant as a child, how will they be able to defend themselves in the future against America's encroachment in the field of industry and commerce. The triumph of America is only possible at the expense of Europe, who will have to pay dearly for her indifference and lack of foresight."[4]

Europeans were to find he was correct. Already, by the end of the eighteenth century, the United States had the second largest merchant fleet in the world: her commerce and industry were growing by phenomenal leaps and bounds. By 1898, the U.S. was first in the world in the value of its industry. The first economic relations between the United States and Latin America were with the islands of the Spanish Antilles. They were the gateway to the economic penetration of a whole continent.

The North American colonies had been trading with the Spanish islands since 1770. Laden with cargo, U.S. ships were anchoring in San Juan, Havana and Santo Domingo with breadstuffs from Philadelphia, and other products from New England, in exchange for farm produce, including molasses. The latter was made into rum in the States, shipped to Africa to buy more slaves, and using Cuba in particular as a way station, the slaves were then shipped to the cotton plantations of the southern states. The slave trade was for more than a century a tie between North America and the Spanish Antilles. There was also other valuable commerce, in which America was able to outstrip its European rivals in island produce: they had first access to the coffee, tobacco, sugar.

Despite all their idealistic expressions, Americans have never been motivated by ideas. As historian Charles A. Beard points out, "The matters of the Constitution were motivated to a large extent by [the signers'] own economic interests." They did not mean equality and democracy to be enjoyed by all. In the 1789 gubernatorial elections in New York State for instance, of three hundred thousand residents only twelve thousand qualified as voters.

Similarly, in many ways the American Revolution was not a real revolution. It was a transfer of power from one group to another, not an alteration of the social system as was the revolution in France. And the Civil War was one of conflicting economic interests within the country.

> "The Southern aristocracy, like that of Latin America, was primarily linked to the world market; 80 percent of the cotton spun in European mills came from the toil of Southern slaves. When abolition of slavery was added to Northern industrial protectionism, the contradiction set off the war. North and South confronted each other as two opposed worlds, two historical eras, two antagonistic philosophies of the national destiny."[5]

After the war, the South became an internal colony of Northern capitalists. The South "was all but completely stripped of power, military, economic and political."[6] The original purpose of the war which broke out in 1865 was to demolish once and for all any claim to the right to secession. The bloody battles in the Civil War were to prevent the Southern states from breaking away. It was part of the desire by Northerners for growth into a great empire.

Lincoln abolished slavery in the South in 1863, but did not abolish it in the North for another two years. He abolished slavery in the South because it was so intimately connected with secession. At one time, Lincoln thought of supporting the transfer of Negroes to Haiti as a solution of the "slave problem."

In 1858, the Haitian government issued an invitation to American Blacks to come to the island and make it their future home. The Haitians believed that American Negroes would defend Haiti against the Spanish, and help take over the whole island once again. Then Puerto Rico and Cuba could be added to a free Negro group in the Caribbean. Immigrants were promised freedom of worship, access to land, liberal political privileges, and even free passage to the island if desired. During the first months of 1861, some seven groups left for Haiti. In April of that year, however, the Civil War began and brought hope to the slaves of liberation in their own land. American Blacks also became less enthusiastic about emigration when, in May 1861, the Spanish moved to take over the Dominican end of Hispaniola, making the transfer to Haiti risky.

The Civil War safely over, the North could once again turn its attention to industrial growth and imperial expansion. First, there was the 1869 effort to annex the independent Dominican Republic. Only a land scandal in which American companies were involved made Congress decide it was an inappropriate moment to do so. Already American companies were operating in Cuba, the Dominican Republic, and Puerto Rico, and many had bought up sugar plantations in the islands. Just before the Spanish-American War, U.S. investment in Cuba was estimated at $50 million. But the Americans owned and controlled at this time mainly the sugar plantations and market. There were many other possible areas of expansion.

By the end of the century, there was also a crucial outside factor demanding the takeover of the Spanish Antilles by the Americans. The impending construction of the Panama Canal made the acquisition of the three Spanish islands immensely important.

Bolívar wrote, "If the world were to select a spot for its capital, it would seem that the Isthmus of Panama must need to be chosen for this august destiny, situated as it is in the center of the world, looking in one direction toward Asia, and the other towards Africa and Europe, and equidistant from America's two extremities."[9] The canal was originally intended to be international, and the U.S. promised that it would be neutral and not militarized. But finally under a treaty of 1850, it became a purely American interest. Though at first Colombia gave only transit rights, the U.S. carved the new country of Panama out of Colombian territory. From the inception of the Panama Canal project, the U.S. redoubled its efforts to take over

U.S. Entry and the Spanish-American War

Cuba, the Dominican Republic and Puerto Rico. Rear Admiral T. Mahan declared that Puerto Rico was to the projected Panama Canal what Malta was to the British.

The strategic importance of the islands became paramount. The trouble with annexing was that revolutionary Cubans fighting for their independence made a peaceful takeover impossible. A pretext had to be found for the U.S. to go to war over it with Spain. The yellow press did its best to drum up national support and there was an endless list of prominent people to offer the right catchwords and justifications. Moreover, from the beginning, the war was to mean more than seizing Cuba: Pacific islands, as well as Caribbean ones, were to be included.

A sanctimonious headmaster of Groton Academy considered the venture "the most righteous war that has been undertaken by this country." The U.S. minister to Hawaii, J. L. Stevens, advised the state department that "the Hawaiian pear is now fully ripe and this is the golden hour for the U.S. to pluck it." One prominent American financier, Charles Adams, thought the Filipinos would prosper under United States domination, since "many races, and, more specifically those of African descent, improve only as they come into immediate contact with Caucasians."

One strong agitator for a U.S. plunge into world politics was Josiah Strong, a militant Protestant minister. In his book, first published in 1886, he declared that "the United States was in peril of socialism and social upheavals; that the Anglo-Saxon race was chosen by God to civilize the world; and that the major responsibility for running this crusade belonged to the people of the United States." Strong differed from Hitler only in thinking that the Americans and not the Germans were the chosen race.

A great American supporter of the 'chosen people' theory, of course, was Theodore Roosevelt, who found the Spanish-American War with its booty of Puerto Rico, Guam, Hawaii, the Philippines, and, in reality, Cuba, "a splendid little war." Senator Henry Cabot Lodge of Massachusetts said in 1893 that Canada should also be annexed to the States despite its own white population which was doing its part to eliminate the Indians. Admiral Thayer Mahan was eager for the job of taking over Puerto Rico.

An economic depression in the U.S., due to a surplus of goods, also made it imperative to find outlets for these products. The time for the war of annexation, which had been building up for a number of years, had arrived.

In the yellow press, to find further popular support, were stories of atrocities committed by Spain against the Cuban rebels. Spanish spokesmen reminded the U.S. of the cruelty and abominations committed in its Civil War. On all sides, there were pleas for American aid to the "brave Cubans fighting for independence," though the brave Cubans were soon to be suppressed by their self-styled defenders. There were also "demands for help from American capitalists whose plantations and sugar mills were being destroyed in the Cuban Civil War."[7]

On April 11, 1898 President McKinley submitted his famous message to Congress declaring "in the name of humanity, in the name of civilization, in *behalf of endangered American interests* . . . the [civil] war in Cuba must stop" [emphasis added].

The Secretary of the Navy, John D. Long, said "The best and largest function of the navy is to serve commerce in its distribution of our manufactured goods." The Congress empowered the use of the U.S. Navy and Army to end Spanish rule. At the same time, it refused to recognize the independence of the Cuban rebel army, which had fought first in the Ten Years' War and then again since 1895.

Nevertheless, the famous Teller Resolution put forward and accepted by the U.S. Congress quite clearly stated "that the United States had no disposition or intention to exercise sovereignty, jurisdiction or control over the island." This U.S. Congress amendment was to placate opponents to the War, who did exist in fairly large numbers; some calling it "the political economics of barbarism."[8]

The incident of the battleship *Maine* provided the excuse for the American invasion, as many years later the Tonkin incident was to provide a pretext in the Vietnam war. Havana was blockaded as well as Santiago de Cuba, where the small Spanish Fleet was soon destroyed in its efforts to escape from the harbor.

The U.S. had had more than Cuba in mind in its "splendid little war." The U.S. wanted Puerto Rico too. Towards the end of the war, the U.S. government was afraid that Spain was going to surrender before it had time to land "in the second island," and so have a legitimate excuse for Puerto Rico's being included in the armistice treaty. A force was therefore quickly landed nineteen days before the surrender. Even then Spain was anxious to keep Puerto Rico, and offered other territories in exchange. But the U.S. refused.

Also included in the war booty were the islands of Hawaii, Guam and the Philippines. The Filipinos were the only ones who put up strenuous opposition. The fighting there under the leadership of

Aguinaldo for independence went on, in the face of the most brutal repression, for three years. Aguinaldo set up a revolutionary government and declared the Philippines independent on June 23, 1898, that is, one month after the defeat of the Spanish fleet and also six months before the Treaty of Paris. The U.S. refused to recognize that independence. The Philippines were given to the U.S. in the treaty after a payment of $20 million.

For three years the Filipinos waged war to throw out the U.S., and after the three years turned to guerilla warfare until they were overpowered and exhausted by superior strength of arms. The most cruel and sadistic practices were used to crush rebels fighting for their independence. Something close to genocide was practiced against the Philippine people.

All the islands were immediately put under military government. After all the tremendous propaganda of fighting to free the brave Cubans, justifications for staying in the island were a little difficult to find. However, it was suddenly discovered that the Cubans were "a mixed-blooded rabble interested more in stealing food and supplies than in fighting or working."[9] Thus were the Cuban patriots who had fought and died so long for their independence insulted by the new overlords. The disarming of the Cuban forces proved a painful problem. When the Cuban revolutionaries discovered that the Teller Amendment, by which Congress had sworn its unselfish intentions, was not intended to be implemented, they were not ready to lay down their arms. The U.S. Army was there, however, to take care of the situation, and it was decided that the American flag "was to float over Cuba until law and order was restored."[10] The disarmament of the people took place. The most reactionary elements of the society were put into positions of power, with the wealthy allowed to keep their fortunes and possessions.

The Treaty of Paris was signed, by which Spain gave up her colonies in the Caribbean to the United States. The U.S. had pledged to honor Cuban independence. To circumvent what was from the American point of view such an undesirable situation, the Platt Amendment was introduced in Congress. This gave the U.S. the power to preserve "law and order" and to "protect" Cuban "independence" by landing its marines at any time it was felt to be necessary. Though there was strong opposition to the Platt Amendment, only by agreeing to it was Cuba to get from under American military control. Only after it was accepted was the military occupation ended. Even then, the Americans insisted on leasing a military base at Guantánamo Bay in perpetuity for $2,000 a year. Gómez, a leader in the war against Spain, said the Platt Amendment reduced "the independence and sovereignty of the Cuban republic to a myth."

The U.S. occupied the island from 1898 to 1903 when the Republic of Cuba was formed. But the U.S. military was to be back again shortly. A new revolt brought about a second occupation from 1906 to 1908.

Of the three islands of the Spanish Antilles that Columbus had conquered at the end of the fifteenth century, by the beginning of the twentieth century only Puerto Rico remained a colony. She had passed in 1898 only from a Spanish master to an American one.

Independent in name at least, and not so completely subject to the United States, was Cuba. The same was true of the Dominican Republic that had won its final independence, after four brief earlier attempts, in 1848. Haiti, the other half of Hispaniola, became a Black republic in 1802, and though she too was to come under American domination, she too was independent.

The Spanish-American War was to usher in a new era in the islands. A new power was to be imposed: a new culture. The ties with Europe were ended. The U.S. hegemony was to be dominant. Dr. Daniel Shirmer perhaps best expresses the tremendous significance of the Spanish-American War. He says:

> Modern foreign policy is associated with the rise of large scale corporations, industrial and financial, as the dominant economic force in the country, exerting a most powerful influence upon the government of the United States. The Spanish-American War and the war to subdue Aguinaldo and the Philippine insurgents were the first foreign wars conducted as a consequence of this influence. The United States suppression of the Philippine national revolution was the progenition of the Vietnam War; it represented the beginning of counter insurgency.
>
> Turning toward interventionism in the affairs of colonial peoples and a policy of imperialism with the Spanish war, and what followed, the United States assumed for the first time the burden of militarism as a sustained feature of national life. It entered the international arms race which has continued intermittently throughout the twentieth century, and at present assumes monstrous proportions. The crisis of the Spanish war initiated the elevation of the role of the military in American society and politics which has gone so far today; it gave first impetus to those connections between the military and corporate interests which comprise what is now called the military-industrial complex.

11 -:- American Domination

The ten week war of 1898 marked the end of the Spanish-American empire. As the old world moved out of its imperial position, the U.S. moved in. Having successfully acquired power over the Spanish Antilles, the U.S. turned its attention to Panama, for which the islands were a necessary strategic component.

In 1903, the Roosevelt administration decided the canal should go through Panama, an integral part of Colombia. When the Colombian legislature objected to the terms offered by the United States for the cession of the necessary territory, "a sponsored revolution broke out in Panama. United States Marines went in and prevented Colombian troops from putting down the rebellion, and the Panamanians declared themselves an independent state. The Roosevelt administration speedily recognized the new government and the banking house of Morgan just as speedily became its financial agent (reportedly loaning that government a large sum to help pay off the bribes that eased its birth)."[1]

The Panama Canal Zone, which was to have been international, neutral and nonmilitary, was thus easily acquired on easy payments on a long-term lease by the United States. In order to discourage "disorder" in any Caribbean country, President Theodore Roosevelt in 1904 announced his celebrated corollary to the Monroe Doctrine, which implied the intention of the U.S. to exercise supervision when necessary over all Latin American countries. The theory of "guardianship" could be used whenever the U.S. decided that its criteria had been violated. What had been in its origin a prohibition of European imperialistc ventures, became transformed into a mandate for American imperialism.

The canal's protection became of great importance. "Throughout the four centuries from the Spanish conquest to American occupation of 1898, Puerto Rico was at once representative of the Caribbean and unique; representative because its history was shaped by the same concatenation of forces—war, conquest, slavery, commercial mercantilism—that were at work in the whole area; unique because the Council of the Indies treated the island not so much as a territory to be colonized as a strategic outpost of empire."[2]

It was now in the early years to fulfill the same role under American conquest.

"To [Admiral Alfred] Mahan, William McKinley, Theodore Roosevelt, and Henry Cabot Lodge, colonial possessions, as these men defined such possessions, served only as stepping stones to the two great [further] prizes: the Latin American and Asian markets. This policy much less resembled traditional colonialism than it did the new financial and industrial expansion of the 1850-1914 period. These men did not envision colonizing either Latin America or Asia. They did want to exploit these areas economically. . . . To do this, these expansionists needed strategic bases from which shipping lanes . . . could be protected."[3]

Panama, Cuba, and Puerto Rico supplied these bases. But Puerto Rico was an exception in that it was also to be colonized, though its strategic importance was always to remain paramount. In Puerto Rico, the military ruled for 21 months. At first the island was ruled by General Miles, who earlier had warred against the Indians. Then civilian governors were sent down from Washington, not chosen because they knew anything about Puerto Rico, but as part of political patronage. They knew no Spanish and few cared to learn the language. Instead, the obsession of almost all the first governors was that the populace should learn to speak English. They were to be Americanized as quickly as possible. The Puerto Rican flag was not to be displayed. When at some function in high school a boy brought one with him and hoisted it, he was told to take down "the enemy flag." American teachers were brought into the island to take the place of Puerto Rican ones. The Puerto Rican children were taught American history, learned the names and stories of American patriots, and nothing of their own. The pledge of allegiance to the United States was duly learned by the school children with hands placed over their hearts. The American national anthem was also duly learned. The Stars and Stripes was raised and flew over all official buildings. Puerto Rico was American territory by right of conquest. Naval bases were begun, as were cooling stations and provision centers. The military stayed on, and still remains, though it gave up the actual running of the island. The federal government took over all essential services; customs, tariffs, and post offices, along with the responsibility for immigration, foreign relations, the issuance of currency; all the centers of sovereign rule which put the reins of control squarely in its own hands. "Puerto Rico's first constitution under the American flag [was] drafted unilaterally by the United States with no Puerto Rican having a voice in its operation."[4]

The political gains made during the last years of Spain's ownership were obliterated. The Foraker Act passed by the new conquerors in 1900 now gave Puerto Ricans fewer rights than ever. The U.S. confirmed its unlimited power over its colony. While Puerto Rico had its own legislature, any law passed by it could be vetoed by the U.S. Congress. American laws, on the other hand, could be applicable or not, also as the U.S. Congress decided. Both these two basic factors of the Foraker Act remain in force today.

Below the governor, chosen by the U.S. president was an executive council, again chosen by the U.S. president. The majority of these officials were Americans, who more often than not did not speak Spanish. There was an elective body below the executive council, but it could be overruled in the higher chamber or in the United States Congress. Among the populace, only those who could read and write and who could make a contribution to the public treasury were given a vote. The poor, 83 percent illiterate, had no say in how their country was run. But then the poor are always excluded from 'the nation'.

American investors and speculators came down in numbers to see what profits might be gained from the new possession. They arrived two weeks after the troops. The sugar and coffee and tobacco plantations began to be taken over by Americans, who were usually absentee owners.

American goods were brought into the new market and the growth of Puerto Rican manufacture was destroyed. Puerto Rican businesses were undercut in price by American competitors, and when the Puerto Ricans had been forced out, prices rose again to higher levels. The peso was changed for the dollar and in the change the former was devalued. For his rice and beans, the peasant paid almost twice as much as he had before the war.

The *jibaro* in the hills had kept some of the philosophy of the early inhabitants. A few coffee trees and plantains, a cow and a horse, an acre of land in corn and sweet potatoes, constituted the property of what would be denominated a comfortable *jibaro*. This individual "mounted on his emaciated horse dressed in a wide sombrero, going off to a fiesta or mass, [and] considered himself a fine and lucky fellow.[5]"

Until early in the previous century, Spain had allowed commerce only between the islands and herself. With that restriction lifted, the Antilles had experienced an upsurge in prosperity. Puerto Rico had also experienced a sugar boom in the nineteenth century, so that it was relatively prosperous when taken over by the United States. Now, however, all imports and exports had to be carried in American merchant ships, making all imports, and particularly food, higher in cost.

Adding to the confusion of the new ideology and language was the greater poverty into which the majority of Puerto Ricans were plunged. The poets and writers and intellectuals fell into a commensurate despair. Betances wrote: "It is the same being a Yankee colony as being a Spanish one." Muñoz Marin described the change in the island after some years of control: "The North American flag encountered a Puerto Rico, poor but satisfied. Now it floats over a factory where slaves work who have lost their land."

Patriots still uttered their cries for liberty. But in the struggle for living, in bewilderment at new instructions in a new tongue, at new values, new mores, the people heard the cries only dimly. The United States did very little for its colony until 1917. Puerto Rico was left indeed to become 'the pesthole of the Caribbean.'

The Spaniards, since the beginning of their stay, had brought some benefits to the islands: the horse, the cart, many new crops and new types of citrus fruits, towns with magnificent buildings. They also brought to Puerto Rico a cultural heritage, customs and language shared with all Latin America, and a new stage in development. The Americans too brought some advantages. There had been no effective circulation of money in Spanish times, few roads, and a bare twenty kilometers of railroad track. In 1898, the capital city of San Juan had a population of less than 35,000. The separation between town and countryside was exacerbated by medieval communication systems, for predictably Spain restricted her construction activities in the island to the building of a road system by her military engineers. The impressive Carretera Milita linking the north and south coasts of the island across the crest of central mountain range was built by convict and imported Chinese labor. Under American rule there was an increase in the railroad lines, and an increase in good roads. However, the new road system developed in Puerto Rico after 1900 primarily catered to the transportation needs of the new American sugar company, as the main road in Spanish Puerto Rico had catered to the needs of the military. There was betterment in health services, betterment in schools (despite what amounted to an American obsession with teaching the 'natives' English), a greater modernization, and a greater industrialism. The U.S. occupation allowed a stronger middle class to grow up, whose increasing numbers were to act as surrogates for the new colonizers and to provide a foreign-dominated bourgeois class, a new strata in society that was necessary in an expanding capitalist economy.

In 1917, with war with Germany imminent, the strategic value of Puerto Rico came again to the fore. There were German submarines in Caribbean waters. The U.S. could not afford to have an island whose population might be hostile, whose patriots might take advantage of the war situation. A new patriotism must therefore be imposed. Earlier efforts had not been sufficiently effective. Puerto Ricans remained obstinately Puerto Ricans. Puerto Ricans should now be given American citizenship to forestall once and for all any idea of independence. Therefore U.S. citizenship was forced upon them. If people refused it, they were deprived forever either of voting or holding public office. They were made aliens in their own land. Further, Puerto Ricans were forced into compulsory service in the first world war, then in the second, and in all subsequent American wars in which they themselves had no national interests. They were to die for the U.S., to be wounded and disabled in U.S. military adventures. Cuba and the Dominican Republic were also to be maneuvered into fighting on the Allies' side during the world wars.

Following the Spanish-American War, the U.S. administration could only congratulate itself on its new successes. The assistant secretary of state in 1904 said, "It seems plain that no picture of our future is complete which does not contemplate and comprehend the U.S. as the dominant power in the Caribbean." When the Roosevelt Corollary was added to the Monroe Doctrine, it postulated that the U.S. "regulate the financial and other conduct of the Caribbean nations in their relations with the European powers."[6]

These doctrines allowed the U.S. to rationalize its taking over of the Customs of the Dominican Republic. Dominican Republic finances needed the guiding hands of Americans. There is no doubt that the country's presidents had woefully mismanaged its economy. Yet at least one outside observer attests that the country was not in such a poor state as U.S. politicians may have claimed. "Mr. James Redpath, a talented English American and a most acute observer, [about 1860] travelled a portion of the Haitian territory and came to the conclusion that the entire island [Hispaniola] was capable of sustaining twenty million people."[7] Its population at the time was one million.

Yet the republic seemed always in need of money. Buenaventura Báez, when president, "intrigued with various promoters and politicians to sell naval bases or special rights during the Andrew Johnson and Grant administrations."[8] He also borrowed money from a London firm at exorbitant rates, which made the repayment several times the small amount he had borrowed, and put the country into debt for years.

During the Spanish-American War, Ulises Heureux, a Negro, was president. He allowed foreign firms to buy up the sugar plantations. The Dominican Republic's main activity became sugar production for the United States with American ownership. The Dominican Republic became economically dependent and therefore politically dependent on the U.S. Heureux also borrowed money from abroad, from a Dutch company, to bolster the shaky economy. The foreign debt grew ten times during his regime. The U.S. had no desire to have European powers develop any rights in the island because of these debts. So the U.S. stepped into the breach. Roosevelt, in an agreement with a new president, Morales, assumed the rights to adjust the various claims and debts. In return, the U.S. was allowed to take over the custom houses, paying part of the receipts to the Dominican Republic and part to the foreign debtors.

The U.S. thus established control over the Dominican economy. It deposed one president in 1912 by withholding the Dominican share of customs. It also kept the marines handy, for rebellions flared from time to time. The Dominicans after all had established their republic four times, but President Wilson believed "they were incapable of self-government."

With the war with Germany on the horizon, the U.S. decided on increased measures of domination in the area. First, U.S. troops took over Haiti in 1915, remaining there until 1934. (As in the Dominican Republic, it held a customs receivership from 1905 to 1941).

This was "a good precedent," thought President Wilson, the pacifist, and should be followed on the other side of Hispaniola. Accordingly, he ordered the occupation of the Dominican Republic in

1916. He had informed the Dominican Congress that he would recognize no president who was not sympathetic to both customs controls and a constabulary directed by Americans. When no president could be found who was sufficiently compliant, the U.S. Navy took over and established a military government.

All the islands of the old Spanish Antilles were well under control of the American military when the U.S. entered the war with Germany. Haiti and the Dominican Republic were occupied. There were bases in Puerto Rico, and the people, made U.S. citizens, were also conscripted to fight. They were, however, segregated from 'whites' and usually worked in labor battalions doing the menial tasks of the army. Both Puerto Rican and Virgin Island G.I.'s met with all forms of discrimination in the camps. In American Southern cities, on buses and streetcars, they were forced to sit in the rear; in many places they were forced into sections of restaurants, etc. designated by signs which read "For Colored Patrons." As a consequence, these and similar discriminatory practices of American Southerners on occasions led to near mutiny in the Puerto Rican and Virgin Island contingents.

At the beginning of the war, Cuba was in the hands of a president, friendly to the U.S.; busy in fact putting down a new revolt with the aid of American arms. American warships were standing off Cuba's shores. "In March 1917, President Menocal's forces penetrated the rebellious areas and captured Goméz. The revolution collapsed and the revolutionaries were rounded up and put in jail. One day after the United States declared war on Germany, President Menocal did the same."[9] However, the U.S. was unsure of the Cubans and dared not draft them into the allied fighting army. Instead it reenforced its own troops in the Guantánamo Bay, and landed marines elsewhere on the island. They remained from 1917 till 1922 as an occupying force.

The Platt Amendment instituted after the Spanish-American War had given the U.S. rights to interfere in the affairs of Cuba. The Platt Amendment was followed by the Treaty of Reciprocity. "This treaty assured Cuba of 20 percent tariff preference on her sugar entering the United States. In return, Cuba granted tariff preferences to certain American products. The effect of such an apparently advantageous position was to make Cuba almost totally dependent upon the American market and the price of sugar. Cuba began to be engulfed by the American economy."[10] It became an economic "colony". In politics, "the decisive factor was American influence. After

1906, almost every major political aspirant looked to the U.S. State Department for approval."¹¹ So its politics too were dictated by Americans. In 1912, marines landed because of "increasing unrest". Cuba's freedom of protest was forcefully constrained by an outside power. Interestingly, two of the prominent leaders of the revolt in 1912 were a Dominican and a Haitian. The sense of solidarity among revolutionaries of the islands has always been strong.

After the American occupying forces left following World War I, the U.S. still took a hand in the elections. There was corruption of most officials in the government, and suppression of revolutionary movements. In Cuba there was the same postwar depression, and the same contrasts in the ostentatious wealth of the few and the extreme poverty of the many, as in the other Spanish islands. Havana grew into a modern city with skyscrapers and luxury hotels and the impressive offices of foreign investors. Gambling and prostitution and vice in all its forms were rife. Small farmers lost their land to large American companies. Mafia types from the States were bosom friends of Cuban officialdom. By 1919, American interests controlled 68 sugar mills and 51 percent of total production. Before the coming of the Americans, a similar situation existed for the peasant as in Puerto Rico.

> Twenty-five years ago the rural Cuban squatted on a piece of land which produced most of what he needed for food and shelter with perhaps something extra which he could exchange for rice and cloth. The coming of the sugar industry on a large scale has completely changed his world. He has, willy-nilly, exchanged a simple life, ignorant but virtuous, for a vassalage to a foreign colossus. His future is not his own. It is determined for him in a directors' room in New York.¹²

But the Cubans seemed irrepressible. Had they not fought Spain for thirty long years for their freedom? They did not take kindly to new foreign domination.

In October 1923, the first national congress of students was held in Havana. One hundred twenty-eight delegates from all over the country attended. They adopted the name "National Revolutionary Congress of Students," vowed to fight for the realization of Bolívar's dream of a united Latin Republic, and condemned all forms of imperialism, especially the intervention of Yankee imperialism in Cuban affairs. Anti-American fervor never died out in Cuba. With U.S.

support of the dictator "Butcher" Machado, Herbert L. Matthews in the *New York Times* quoted a headline in the Havana newspaper *La Nacion* on June 22, 1922: "Hatred of North Americans will be the religion of Cubans."

There was a boom in the islands during the World War I and immediate postwar years. When both the United States and Europe were buying sugar, great profits were made by American interests in the islands and some betterment of living was experienced by the people. But following the war, the price of sugar fell, and there were desperately hard times once again.

With their economy tied so closely to that of the States, when the depression occurred in the late twenties and early thirties all the island people suffered terribly too. In Puerto Rico, unemployment was as high as 60 percent. It was hard even for a man with a job to keep his family above starvation level.

Writing in 1931, Dr. Bailey W. and Justine Whitfield Diffie contended that Puerto Ricans were definitely worse off than they had been before the Americans took over.

> With all profits being drained off, by 1929 Puerto Rico was getting poorer by some $10 million a year—after 1930, Puerto Rico headed rapidly towards bankruptcy. Even as late as 1928, wages on the island were the same as in 1898, though the cost of living had enormously increased.

The large American sugar corporations had taken over the bulk of cane production in Cuba, Santo Domingo and Puerto Rico. By 1925, the principal sugar estates in Santo Domingo were American owned. By 1933, the first year of Batista, American sugar investment had become the basis of Cuban economy, supported by incorporation into the U.S. import system. By 1935 nearly 50 percent of all land operated by sugar companies in Puerto Rico was under the control of four big American-owned concerns.

As economic interests in the islands grew, so did political interests. The U.S. needed "stable" governments in each country, governments that would provide the appropriate ground for the financial holdings of the U.S. to grow and flourish. Since the American economic interests were not the same, but usually contrary to the interests of the islands' economies, there had to be either outright rule as in a colony, or puppet governments controlled by the U.S. And if at times the local situation became "unstable," then the U.S. needed only the flimsiest excuses to intervene militarily to restore "law and order." Each increase by private companies in their investments increased the "national" interest. Yet, in fact only the profits of a few, usually the monopolistic companies, were involved. True, jobs were created by foreign markets and foreign trade, so that some group of workers benefitted. But an important reason for having colonies (whether in name or fact), is not only to produce new markets and new sources for investments, but to provide cheap labor. There was no lack of cheap labor. In Puerto Rico, women and children, to supplement their men's wages, worked on fine embroidery and needlework, earning two dollars for a sixty-hour week.

Cuba and the Dominican Republic were ruled by a series of dictators, put in power and upheld in power by the United States in the interests of its national investors. The masses were downtrodden in all the islands.

In Puerto Rico, one incompetent or ignorant American governor followed another. The first break in the line of politically appointed blunderers came with Franklin Delano Roosevelt's appointment of Rexford Tugwell as governor. Tugwell was not only concerned with the plight of the people in "the stricken island," but was also an able administrator. At the same time, there arose in the legislature an outstanding Puerto Rican, Muñoz Marin. He was a poet, writer, eloquent orator, and his had been a strong voice among those calling for independence. He was to say then: "The only remedy for Puerto Rico is independence, not the self-government in a *dominion* status that some liberals espouse."

He worked with Tugwell and together they helped lift the island's economy out of its morass. Achieving power, Muñoz gave up his support of independence and evolved a new concept of commonwealth, by which Puerto Rico would still be under the sovereignty of the States in all essential matters, but would receive some measure of autonomy. He was the first Puerto Rican to be elected governor and he received tremendous support. Much of it came from *independentistas*, who thought that after he had helped in the amelioration of economic conditions, he would move on to obtaining political freedom. But Muñoz was walking a new path, one that led to greater industrialization of the island, that took men from the countryside to new American-type towns. The peasantry was proletarianized, and the call for independence was taken up by other voices.

The writer Tomas Blanco, called for liberation from foreign domination lest "we submit ourselves to a slow agony of death." A Nationalist Party was formed under the leadership of the brilliant, fiery Pedro Albizu Campos, a Negro, Harvard educated, and an ex-officer in the U.S. Army. Clashes between students and police occurred, in which several people were killed. Seeing in the American chief of police the symbol of their enemy, rebels shot him in the street. The police captured the two young men responsible and beat them to death. Albizu Campos and other Nationalists were accused of a conspiracy to overthrow the government of the United States by force and violence. Albizu and the others were sent to prison in Atlanta, Georgia for fifteen years; Albizu put into solitary confinement for a year.

In another incident in Ponce in 1937 on a Palm Sunday, the Nationalists had permission for a peaceful march. This was rescinded at the last moment, but the Nationalists, being already assembled, decided to proceed. They walked quietly singing the national anthem, *La Borinqueña*. The police opened fire on the unarmed group of young people, wounding more than a hundred and killing fourteen. The U.S. Civil Liberties Union termed the affair "a massacre." To bring their plight before the world, some Puerto Rican nationalists fired shots in the U.S. Congress, slightly wounding some senators. Four of these nationalists are still political prisoners in U.S. jails after more than twenty years. No political prisoners have ever been held anywhere else in the world for so long.

On the cultural front, there had been every effort made to destroy the nationalism of Puerto Rico which had grown during the last century and a half. The feeling of *Puertorriqueñismo*, the sense of the island's individuality, its own special culture and nationalism, as distinct from those of Spain, was meant to wither in the new colonial climate. The Indian and Spanish heritage was to be wiped out as far as possible, and every small Puerto Rican was to be helped to develop into a small "Yanki," or at least the best imitation of him that could be made. Values of U.S. commercialism were to be substituted for those old ideas of family worth and responsibility, of sharing with neighbors and fellow countrymen. This was to give way to the necessity of competition to get on in a "free enterprise" system. The *siesta*, the general easiness with *compañeros*, the supple bending with natural and life forces, as the palm trees bend when the winds blow; such attitudes were to give way to the rigidity of efficiency in industrial corporations. *Dignidad* was laughed at by the gringo interlopers.

"The [visiting] Latin who sees the same illiteracy he has at home, the same extremes in wealth, and the same social injustices, is also shocked by Puerto Rico's disappearing personality. Not Spanish, not American, Puerto Rico is a sort of illegitimate child."[13] The slow process over three hundred years that had produced in the nineteenth century the Puerto Rican was to be changed to form a new type. Puerto Rican identity was to be snatched away, broken, made to seem worthless. Puerto Ricans had to be made to believe in both the Almighty Dollar, and of Americans as the Greatest Race on earth. Many were gradually to lose their own special sense of identity. They were made to feel alien in their own land. That their skin was darker than that of the big, blond American executive was somehow also made to seem in their national disfavor, to make them an inferior race. The "civilization" of their new conquerors constantly drummed into Puerto Ricans the idea that they had no culture, no civilization, no worthy past of their own.

To be part of America was to be part of the only glory. The United States was the greatest power in the world. To belong to it, to receive some of the crumbs from its overflowing table, Puerto Ricans were expected to be humbly grateful. Tugwell and Muñoz Marin did institute some reforms, and tried some experiments in developing Puerto Rican industry, but these were considered "too socialistic" by Washington. A government-owned cement factory and a bottle factory were sold back to private industrialists like Luis Ferré, whose families became millionaires on the profits. (Ferré was later to become governor for a term from 1968–72 and to be a leader of a movement to make Puerto Rico a state.) There was, however, considerable economic growth under Muñoz Marin's governorship, which led to the early enthusiasms that Puerto Rico would "by pulling itself up by its bootstraps" become "the showcase of the Caribbean." Puerto Rico was allowed its own flag at last to fly side by side with the Stars and Stripes.

The effort to make Puerto Rico the showcase of the Caribbean did not last long, and its sham facade was soon exposed. One basis of the new conception was a petroleum refining industry from which were to be developed a number of "downstream" industries manufacturing consumer items for export. The petrochemical producers promised that the industry, particularly later on, would be an important source of employment for the Puerto Rican people. It failed to keep this promise. Corco (Commonwealth Oil Refinery) along with Union Carbide, Phillips Petroleum, and Pittsburgh Plate Glass, are part of this group. All the banks, such as First National City Bank, have been intertwined with the big corporations. "The Bootstrap philosophy has turned out to be a prodigious generator of profit and pollution, and scarce contributor to the Puerto Rican job market."[14]

As the country developed industrially, however, as the gross national product rose, and the average yearly income increased to $1,500—the position of the poor, those on the bottom rung, scarcely changed. Two thirds of the people lived below the poverty level; some earning only $100 a year.

In 1966, one Latin American observed: "The Virgin Islands, with their tax-free enticements to Miami and Westchester County playboys, and Puerto Rico with its lax gambling laws, both exhibit some of the most ostentatious luxury sites this side of Monte Carlo. In Puerto Rico, which seems to have become the brothel of the Carribean since Castro's puritanical squads drafted the prostitutes into the militias, one luxury hotel crowds another along San Juan beaches. Each hotel has its own casino, and in each thousands of dollars are tossed at a wheel every night. A few miles away, thousands of Puerto Ricans are jammed into waterless slums."

Puerto Rico is a colony and considered therefore stable. There has been less unrest there than in the other islands, and though this is changing and a new militancy rising, the United States has a firmer, more 'legitimate' hold. It will not relinquish it easily. In fact, as it imposed citizenship upon Puerto Ricans in 1917, so in 1981 it may impose statehood, from which secession may be impossible as it was for the Southern states in the Civil War, impossible as it would be for Mexico to regain the territory snatched from it in the nineteenth century.

For example, what attracted W. G. Grace Corporation and other firms to the island was the investment climate which Puerto Rico offered U.S. companies. "Puerto Rico's colonial status gave U.S. corporations that added degree of security in a continent which is prone to nationalization sprees. Puerto Rico [was] ideally located to serve U.S., Central and South American markets. Its deep water ports facilitated transportation. Its tax exemptions and cheap labor force made for low cost production. Its 'Operation Bootstrap' was ideally conceived to provide U.S. capitalism with a major offshore industrial subsidiary to the mainland, and U.S. companies responded by turning Puerto Rico into the largest single recipient of U.S. foreign investment in the world."[15]

In the Dominican Republic, officers of the U.S. Navy and Marines were the virtual rulers from 1916 to 1922. They were not qualified to administer the country, and they frequently abused their authority. They headed the government only to guard U.S. commercial and financial interests, and to help quell the guerrila attacks emanating from a continuing undercurrent of rebellion against the 'Yanki' oppressors. A *guardia nacional* was trained by the Americans to continue the policy of oppression. One enthusiastic recruit was Rafael Trujillo.

Though it was now peacetime, strict censorship was imposed. The prominent Dominican poet and intellectual, Fabio Fiallo, accused of violating censorship, was jailed. One deed of Fiallo's that helped to bring the ire of the authorities down upon him, was his reporting that J. H. Hollander, U.S. commissioner in Santo Domingo, had accepted a handsome private fee from the Dominican government. When a U.S. House of Representatives subcommittee discovered the bribe a decade later, Hollander was imprisoned. The scandal and the cover-up became a *cause célèbre* of Latin American freedom.

Nationalistic fervor continued to rise as American servicemen acted with racist brutality against the populace. Finally, under President Warren Harding, the Americans in 1922 agreed to evacuate the military from the country though Americans still continued supervising the customs. They had militarily occupied a supposedly sovereign state for eight years. They left behind a locally developed group of thugs.

"The creation by the U.S. Marines of a modern, unified military constabulary provided the instrument by which some future Dominican strongman could seize power and use it to dominate the country."[16] Horacio Vasquez was elected president in 1924; the U.S. market crash in 1929 ruined the Dominican economy; and a revolt was launched against Vasquez' rule. The strongman arose. The military under Rafael Trujillo took power in 1930. The dictatorship of Trujillo lasted thirty years. It was one of the longest, cruelest and most absolute dictatorships the world has ever seen.

The "anti-communist" dictator is believed to have executed 500,000 of his opponents during his rule. One mass massacre occurred in 1937 when he invited Haitians to work in the sugar plantations. When they were no longer wanted, he had his army kill between twelve and twenty-five thousand of them in one night. For three decades, the country was to endure the tyranny of this ferociously evil man's dictatorship, which was supported during the whole period by the U.S. government. During his tenure he built his own personal fortune and the fortunes of some Americans. A U.S. economist stated: "This is a government of gangsters. And anyone who did business with them knew it."[17] Yet plenty of U.S. businessmen did business with Trujillo and so did the U.S. government, giving Trujillo millions of dollars with which he supported a large lobby in Washington—to sell *his* sugar to U.S. housewives.

Finally the U.S. government found that it could no longer support Trujillo's corrupt and repressive regime. In 1961 the CIA had him assassinated. At the end of that time, in spite of all the American dollars that had flowed through the Dominican Republic, most of its people continued to live in conditions that were poor compared even with those in other Latin American countries.

A study done in 1961 found that out of 18 Latin American countries, the Dominican Republic ranked 11th in education, tenth in medical care, and eleventh in average income. Only 38 percent of the children began school at all, and only 28 percent attended for two years. There were twenty-seven hospital beds per thousand inhabitants, and one doctor for every fifty-two hundred. The average annual income was $190.

Juan Bosch in 1963 was the first democratically elected president in the island's history. He was accused by President Johnson and the state department of being a communist. He was never that. But in the military attack upon his government by the right wing, the U.S. stepped in on the side of the junta. Four thousand marines were landed. John Gerassi, a one time editor of the magazine *Newsweek*, wrote of the event that "democracy was being saved from communism by getting rid of democracy."

Balaguer, one of Trujillo's henchmen, was put in Bosch's place. The U.S., as always, sided with the right-wing reactionary forces against the forces of the people, and the revolution was suppressed. Balaguer still remains as a U.S.-supported dictator.

As always too, the American public was lied to about the happenings in the Dominican Republic. Tad Szulc, *New York Times* reporter on the spot wrote:

> As had inevitably been the case with everything concerning the Dominican crisis, once more we were faced with the fact that there was very little resemblance between the realities of Santo Domingo, and the picture that the Administration, or some members of it, were painting in Washington for the benefit of public opinion.

At one point, even a group of Boy Scouts had been arrested as rebels. Every semblance of opposition was crushed.

In the Dominican Republic, the exports of just five leading products, sugar, coffee, cocoa, bauxite, tobacco, form 91 percent of all exports. Any reduction of the world demand for any one of these commodities immediately produces a balance of payments crisis. The island never gets free of its economic and therefore political slavery to the United States.

On the other side of Hispaniola, 'Baby Doc' Duvalier's private army, ten thousand hoods previously known as Touton Macoute (bogeymen) was headed by a twenty thousand strong United States-trained militia. The son of the infamous 'Papa Doc' still has full U.S. support. Since the Spanish-American War, the United States has intervened in Haiti time after time, landing Marines who have stayed as an occupying force.

Since 1945, the new phenomenon (in the world) "is the assumption by the United States of leadership of the entire imperialistic system—U.S. military groups are located in at least 64 countries—which though officially politically independent are, in fact, enmeshed in the net of financial and diplomatic dependence." As far as the Southern Hemisphere is concerned, "small Latin American countries that produce relatively little profit are important in United States policy-making because control over all Latin America is important."[18]

In Cuba, from the beginning from 1898, U.S. presidents were always ready to send marines down to help "stabilize the political situation." American warships were constantly in Havana's harbor, and the forces at Guantánamo Bay were always ready to defend the island from outsiders or the internal revolutionary enemy. The American ambassador loomed large behind any Cuban president. Once President Zayas was foolhardy enough to suggest that there had been an understanding in the U.S. Congress originally that America would not interfere in Cuban affairs, but since he continued to welcome the financial take-over of the island by American companies, he stayed on to complete his four-year term of office. He was succeeded by the 'butcher' dictator, General Gerardo Machado, approved and applauded by American businessmen. At the end of Machado's first term of office, the U.S. ambassador favored his re-election, with President Coolidge's approval. Machado's second term was extended to six years. 'The Butcher' stated that his idols were Mussolini in Italy and Salazar in Portugal.

When the inevitable rebellion to his rule occurred, there was a small landing of revolutionaries in Pinar del Rio and a group in the Oriente Province. A period of bloody strife followed and a reign of terror ensued. It was said that Machado's men fed the defeated rebels to the sharks as one means of many forms of death. But the revolt was not overcome, despite killings and arrests, closing of the universities and suppression of the press. The building up of opposition spread through the country over a long period until revolution broke out again in 1933. Finally, Machado fled the country under the protection of the U.S. Embassy.

F. D. Roosevelt sent Sumner Wells to Cuba as ambassador to try to dampen the situation. He helped in setting up Céspedes as the new president. Céspedes was the son of the old Cuban revolutionary, and so had an honored name, though he was not himself a revolutionary. But the forces against Wells and his desire for mild reform were soon able to evict the young Céspedes. The situation was once more polarizing. Dr. Ramon Grau San Martín, a leader of left wing university students, proclaimed the beginning of the social revolution and his own presidency of its Councils. At that, 29 American warships entered Cuban waters. Meanwhile, a Cuban army sergeant, U.S.-trained Fulgencio Batista was enlisting men in a plot in an army base near Havana. He arrested the army chief of staff, named himself chief of staff and advanced on the capital. At first, he seemed to be supporting Grau. But Washington refused to recognize the Grau regime, which it termed "socialistic." Batista realized this would give him his chance.

In a bloody battle initiated by Batista, Guiteras, who had been secretary of war under Grau, and was one of the revolutionary leaders, was killed. In 1934, the Council was ousted by pressures from the U.S. State Department. However, some gains had been made. The Platt Amendment was finally withdrawn and a new treaty made between the countries, with the U.S. giving up any rights of intervention. During the years from 1938 to 1944, there were several presidencies, but all were dominated by American interests.

During this time, as in 1917, Cuba and the other islands entered World War II on the side of the Allies, fighting for a 'free world' in which they themselves were not free.

In 1944, Dr. Grau came to power again for a short time. "With him started the last stage in the policy of submission to Yankee imperialism practiced by the Cuban bourgeoisie."[19]

During this period, Batista, the sergeant of humble beginnings and supposedly populist views, was learning the political game and developing his own cadres within the Army and the parties. As Hitler called his party National Socialists, so Batista was to name his party Democratic Socialists. The peoples' desire for social justice was in both cases made use of by demagogic leaders.

Batista was a presidential candidate in the 1952 elections. When it became apparent that he would not win, he used the army to take over the government. A new dictator with American support was now enthroned. Havana glittered in an *extravagancia* of luxury hotels, gambling, expensive prostitutes, high living for American gangsters and their wealthy and new Cuban counterparts. But the irrepressible desire for liberty, and their ever-ready willingness to fight and die for it, surged again among Cubans.

Eighteen months after the Batista coup, Fidel Castro planned an attack on the Moncada Barracks with only 125 men. The attack might have succeeded, but the small force split up and, by an unfortunate circumstance, did not meet together at the right time. Castro had planned to take over the radio station and issue a call for revolution, calling on the ordinary soldiers to come over to the revolutionary side. With the failure of the plan, most of the young rebels were caught and killed. Castro and a few others escaped for a while, but were finally captured. Castro was imprisoned, and then an attempt was made on his life which was unsuccessful (as later attempts by the CIA were to be). In court on trial, he was allowed to act in his own defense and there issued his famous statement, "History will absolve me."

Expressing his surety that had he been successful, Castro said that the people would have answered his call. He spoke of the seven hundred thousand unemployed Cubans; the half-million farm workers inhabiting miserable shacks whose families starved when the four-month cane-cutting period was over; of the four hundred thousand industrial laborers, whose life was eternal work and indebtedness; of the one hundred thousand small farmers who, like feudal serfs, lived and died working on land that was not theirs; of thirty thousand teachers and professors, devoted and dedicated, but badly paid and treated; of twenty thousand small businessmen weighted down by debts; of ten thousand young professionals: doctors, engineers, lawyers, newspapermen, artists, who despite talents and degrees, found themselves at a dead end with all doors closed. These would be his supporters, he said, for the people yearned for a better, more dignified life and a more just nation. People, he said, "to attain the changes, are ready to give even the very last breath of their lives, when they believe in something or someone, especially when they believe in themselves."

In his final passages he said, "The man who abides by unjust laws and permits anybody to trample the country in which he was born, the man who so mistreats his country, is not an honorable man. . . . We were taught to cherish and defend the beloved flag of the lone star. . . . To live in chains is to live in disgrace . . . to die for one's homeland is to live forever." He was sentenced to twenty-five years imprisonment. His final defiant words were: "Condemn me. It does not matter. History will absolve me." Five years later he was in power, and he was not to be overthrown. The Cuban revolution was successful. When Castro took over, more than sixty percent of the whole economy was owned by Americans. Now Castro was to put all of it in the peoples' hands.

As a successor to Spain after 1898, America had conquered all the islands and controlled them completely: militarily, politically and economically. Nowhere were the bonds broken until Castro's valiant challenge to the northern giant. It created the most intense excitement in the whole of the Caribbean and Latin America.

America's war with Spain, its occupation of Puerto Rico as a North American colony, its successes in Panama, its Platt Amendment and the successive interventions of North Americans in the Caribbean, created a violent reaction in Latin America against the United States. "Yanqui Imperialism was from then the normal theme in Latin American politics and in the literature of its most prestigious writers."[20]

The Cuban Revolution inspired the hopes of all the oppressed in the world. There had arisen again a group of people who were convinced "that the land of Cuba should belong to the people who inhabited it; that, rationally managed in the interests of all the people, their rich island could become what Columbus saw, "the most beautiful land human eyes have ever seen. . . . In 1952, they dedicated themselves to the task of making their dream come true."[21]

12 -:- Cuba's Challenge

Before coming to power, Castro said: "Cuba could easily provide for a population three times as great as it now has, so there is no excuse for the abject poverty of a single one of the present inhabitants. . . . What is inconceivable is that anyone should go to bed hungry, that children should die for lack of medical attention; what is inconceivable is that 30 percent of our farm people cannot write their names and that 99 percent of them know nothing of Cuba's history. . . . *What is inconceivable is that the majority of our rural people are now living in worse circumstances than were the Indians Columbus discovered in the fairest land that eyes have ever seen.*"

And of Batista's barbarity after the July 26 movement he said: "Chronicles of our history down through four and a half centuries, tell us of many acts of cruelty: the slaughter of defenseless Indians by the Spaniards; the plundering and the atrocities of pirates along the coast; the barbarities of the War of Independence; the shooting of the Cuban Army by forces of Weylek; the horrors of the Machado regime, and so on to the crimes of March 1935. But never had such a sad and bloody page been written in numbers of victims and the viciousness of victimizers—as in Santiago de Cuba eleven weeks ago."

Batista's men had shot people indiscriminately in Santiago de Cuba; people who had had no connection with the rebellion; people living their everyday lives far from the scene at the Moncado Barracks. The prisoners that were taken were tortured, their testicles shattered, their eyes torn out, and then they were killed.

Batista issued an order "Ten prisoners must be killed for each dead soldier." Prisoners were taken who had had no part in the attack. "Men were compelled to dig their own graves, others were buried alive, hands tied behind their backs."

When Castro was released from prison on the Isles of Pines in May 1955, he went to Mexico. There he was joined by the few remaining survivors of the attack on the Moncada Barracks, and there he met Ché Guevara, who was to become one of the new leaders. Ché believed that when there is a revolutionary situation, the vanguard parties can "contribute to creating the conditions needed for the seizure of power, and not await a revolutionary wave that will appear from the masses."

Both he and Castro felt that it was unnecessary to wait for a spontaneous uprising of the people. So long as the proper conditions existed, which they believed did in Cuba, then the revolutionary party could initiate action in which the masses would join: and so spark a new moment in history.

The small band, therefore, underwent intensive training for 18 months in guerrilla warfare under the instruction of a Mexican fighter. Then Fidel audaciously announced his imminent arrival in Cuba to free his country.

He set forth to attack Batista with probably the smallest invasion force ever assembled. There were only 82 men aboard the yacht *Granma* that landed in Cuba. After the first encounter with the army which decimated the small group, those that remained retreated to the Sierra Maestro in Oriente Province.

From hiding places in the mountains, Fidel began to rebuild his forces; developing underground supporters in other parts of the countryside and in the towns. Living a life of extreme hardship and danger, but one shared by all, the guerrillas harried the regular army sent to wipe them out. Losing men in battle, but gaining always new recruits, they worked out and learned the best system of tactics. Yet like the leaders of the War for Independence in South America, not one of them had previously been a professional soldier. With the peasants they encountered and on whom they had to be dependent for food and information, they became on friendly terms. For where the regular army roughly requisitioned what it needed, the rebel army paid for everything it received. Soon in the towns, "men in factories and mines, and women in offices, led double lives. They worked at their jobs and they worked for the underground army. With home-made bombs they blew up theatres, buses, freight trains, government warehouses, bridges, homes and business offices of informers. On mimeograph machines in cellars they ran off leaflets urging the people to overthrow the dictator. When Ché Guevara asked for materials to set up a revolutionary newspaper, the forces received the necessary supplies of stencils, paper, and ink, and soon they were distributing *Cuba Libre* everywhere. With a dynamite explosion, they blew up the gas and electric main in Havana, cutting off all gas light, and telephone service and paralyzing the city for 54 hours."

This was warfare. "On secret presses, they printed 'freedom bonds' in denominations of $1 up and sold them in every province of Cuba, and thus added thousands of dollars each month to the revolutionary treasury."[1]

Workers wanting to join the army in the mountains were told they must bring their own weapons. Those who lacked the money for this would waylay a regular soldier, divest him of his uniform, boots, guns and ammunition, though they always left him with his papers, his money and his underwear.

Batista increased his terror, fostering more hatred and opposition. Meanwhile in the mountains, Castro and his followers were setting up a government of their own, and creating such industries as bakeries, butcher shops, and shoe factories to supply their own and local needs. They set up hospitals and schools, all the time working with the peasants. In little over a year's time, on February 24th, 1958, they had set up a radio station. From then on, every night, Castro was broadcasting on *Radio Rebelde*, counteracting the lies from the other side, making his announcements from "The Territory of Free Cuba in the Sierra Maestra." One month later, he was announcing that a general strike would soon be called. Then he called on Batista's army to rebel and join the revolutionary forces. A month further, on April 5, it was announced that Raul Castro would advance with a rebel force to invade the northern part of Oriente. At the same time, all people were called upon to stop paying taxes to Batista's government. For Fidel Castro as for Danton, it was always "l'audace, l'audace, toujours l'audace." The general strike failed. But Castro's certainty of success remained as high as ever.

Enraged, Batista decided to crush the rebellion once and for all. He organized one third of his total army: twelve thousand men, well supplied with tanks, armored cars, cannons, machine guns, which had been obtained from the United States. He had an air force, mostly U.S. trained, carrying not only ordinary bombs, but napalm bombs too. These were bought from Trujillo in the Dominican Republic, but came through him from the United States. Batista's forces outnumbered Castro's forces by forty to one. In addition, the former had an equivalent superiority in weapons. But Fidel reminded his followers and the people, of José Martí's saying: "What matters is not the quantity of weapons at hand, but the number of stars on your forehead." During battles when ordinary soldiers fighting the rebels were wounded or captured, they were given medical attention and sent home. Fidel said over the radio: "We do not wish to deprive these Cubans of the company of their loving families. Nor, for practical reasons, can we keep them, as our food, cigarettes and other commodities are in short supply. We hope the Cuban people will understand our position in this respect."

The mothers, wives, sweethearts who had their men returned to them, no longer believed the lies told against Castro, and he gathered further support among the people for his humanitarianism. Within a matter of months, Batista's soldiers began deserting, and Castro's forces, opening up other fronts, were achieving victories. The U.S. was still sending Batista military supplies and U.S. forces were still training Batista's troops.

A letter was sent to President Eisenhower to stop this outside interference in a civil war. The U.S. reply was that while governments might change, its military aid went to whichever government was in power and was for "hemispheric defense needs." This attitude changed, of course, when Fidel was in power.

With Batista's forces demoralized, Castro decided to descend from the mountains and fight a decisive campaign on the plains. Ché Guevara was given the post of top strategist. In the ensuing battles many were killed, but within four months, victory was at hand. "On Christmas Eve (1958), the people of Cuba heard a new voice on the radio: 'This is Radio Sancti Spiritus in the free territory of Cuba.' Ché Guevara's forces had taken the city."[2]

In Havana and elsewhere, army installations were blown up. The revolution spread everywhere. It was unbeatable. Recognizing the end had come, Batista fled to the protection of his fellow dictator, Trujillo, in the Dominican Republic.

By New Years Day, 1959, Fidel, a young man then of only 32, led a triumphant march through the capital to the wild enthusiasm of the populace who embraced the green-fatigue-clad heroes.

Ché believed a "new society can arise only on the ruins of the old world, the world of injustice and exploitation, oppression and lies, the world of the generals and bankers, latifundia owners and policemen, the CIA and United Fruit." When Castro took over the government of Cuba, more than 60 percent of the whole economy was owned by the U.S. A completely new order had to be instituted even though it could not be accomplished overnight. Immediately Fidel set up a new government and issued his first directives. First all rents were lowered, almost by half. By May 7, 1959, a Land Reform Act was promulgated. By this act no one was allowed to own more than one thousand acres and all the land that was expropriated was distributed into small lots for peasants or made into state farms. (By 1966, there were still one hundred twenty thousand small farms in existence.) But the large state farms could be used more efficiently, and as more land came into its hands, the government could better plan the agricultural production of the whole island. Men had been used to working as farm laborers, but the cane cutters had worked for only four months and were mainly unemployed the rest of the year. Now they were paid an annual wage. The government also gave back to each state farm the necessary money to build local schools and houses. This work was done when the harvesting was over. Each community planned for its own needs, but those plans had to fit in with the central planning.

There was no end to the task ahead, for the Revolution needed to penetrate into all social and political spheres. But the challenge created a dynamism of energy everywhere. Industries began to be expropriated with workers given some part of the control.

Nationwide, new schools and health systems were inaugurated. In one year, Castro had wiped out 90 percent of the illiteracy on the island. With free medical attention for all, those doctors who were in the profession for huge salaries realized the new Cuba was no place for them. They fled the island. The land speculators went too. The wealthy without social consicence and the gamblers evacuated the big hotels, along with the American Mafia and the prostitutes. Then there were those who had been ready to accept a modicum of reform as necessary, but were not prepared for Castro's complete restructuring of society. They fled to Florida, where they were welcomed with open arms by the U.S. government and helped as the nucleus of a counterrevolutionary force. Some were pulled into the service of the CIA. Castro briefly visited New York and stayed in Harlem for a few days. His mission was to raise funds or credits.

The International Monetary Fund, directed by the U.S., refused Castro any loans. The World Bank refused to help. The World Bank, which was dominated by the U.S., has withheld loans from countries attempting nationalization of U.S. properties. Trade with Russia in 1960 was still small. "Cuba had arranged to buy oil from the U.S.S.R., but the U.S.-owned refineries refused to process it. Cuba retaliated by taking over the refineries, and the U.S. then cancelled the Cuban sugar quota, leaving Cuba with some three million tons of unsold sugar. It was at this juncture that the Soviet Union and other socialist countries stepped in, providing a market for Cuban sugar and in general taking the place of the United States as Cuba's leading customers and suppliers. No less important, the socialist countries became a vital source of credits."[3]

The largest sugar factories had been in American hands. At first, because sugar had been the symbol of the hated old regime, there was a hurry to diversify in agriculture. At the same time, there was a hurry to develop heavy industry. Attempted was "the expansion of thermoelectric energy, the development of mineral industries based on Cuba's nickel, the development of a large chemical industry based on byproducts of the sugar-refining industry, and the substitution of Cuban-made goods for imported goods."[4]

But Cuba needed to trade to buy necessary equipment. The plans could not be implemented without going back to intensive sugar production to obtain the necessary money for exchange. As Lenin had found in the early days of the Russian Revolution, progress moved two steps forward, one step backward.

In spite of the intensification of sugar production, the plans for diversification were not neglected. There was an increase in production in the basic staples of rice and beans, of development of livestock for milk and meat, the planting of more forests, and a great increase in fishing.

In a country so fertile, so rich in natural resources, it was against all reason, as Castro had said, that the mass of the people should be poor. Yet poor they had been. In 1957, the average income was about six dollars a week, which meant that many lived on even less. In the hovels everywhere in the countryside, there were no toilets, no running water, no electric lights. They were dilapidated shacks, less well-made than the *bohios* Christopher Columbus found: those were said to be well constructed log houses. Palm trees were still being used by the rural poor for their homes with the palm leaves for thatch, but the bohios the conquistadores saw in villages were constructed by the whole group and "were ingeniously" made, were in fact often "engineering feats." The modern shacks, though the ancient model had been passed down by the generations, were miserable imitations. Those early Tainos had had the time and leisure to erect their homes and tribal centers, and leisure also to ornament and decorate them. Even the ceilings had been well-contrived, intricate plaitings of different colors, and carved stone monuments had stood outside the doors. The Tainos had fished, hunted and grown their crops, so that food was plentiful for all. They had the satisfaction of slowly making their household pots and tools. They had woven the small amounts of cloth they wished to wear, colored to suit their fancy. They had made golden jewelry for their pleasure and enjoyment, made instruments to accompany the poems and songs they composed, enjoyed as a group their ball games and dancing and fiestas. Theirs had been a communistic society, too.

There was no joy in the life of a Cuban peasant in 1957. There was only misery, hardship, poverty, hunger, sickness. From the time of the Spanish conquerors through the economic and political takeover by the Americans, the people had lived in the most dismal conditions, filled with hopelessness and despair in the hardness of their lot. From the decimation of the Indians, through the slavery of the Blacks, to the situation after abolition of near serfdom, the inhabitants of that beautiful island, "the Pearl of the Artilles" had known only man-made sorrow. Living in ignorance and squalor, those in the towns were little better off than those in the country.

So it was through the centuries until Castro and his men were both to light the torch of hope, which every man needs, and to fill the people's stomachs with food, without which hope cannot arise. Among those things that became free as Castro took over the government were "homes, hospitals, schools, school meals, telephones and transportation." The basic ills were conquered: no poverty, no unemployment, enough food, a decrease in sickness. no doctor's bills, rent free or for a very small payment, no cost of transportation for getting to work. Machines were used not to lay men off their jobs, but to make those jobs easier. "Machinery," said Fidel, "has to be the great ally of the worker. It must take the drudgery out of labor."

Sugar cutting is a particularly hard task. Castro set the technicians and engineers to solve its problems, giving an opportunity for their inventiveness. Such machinery that could be obtained abroad, as far as the economics of the country allowed, had been bought. But some necessary machinery had never been built. Cubans started inventing such machines themselves.

"Today," says Fidel, "it is possible that no single thing will have a greater effect on the future of the country than these machines—we owe debts of gratitude to the men who designed and built them. They will mean the liberation of hundreds of thousands of workers from the most back-breaking work. . . . The present pace of our development will permit our agriculture to rank among the most advanced in the world."

The Cuban's ration book may still denote certain shortages. A further meaning of it is that everything is shared. This is not the situation where abundance of food is in the stores but the poor cannot buy it. Work too is shared. The intellectual and the professor are not bypassed. It has been found that some manual labor is good physically for them. The worker is offered every opportunity to develop his capacities through education. All the arts are encouraged.

Like Puerto Rico, Cuba had been largely dependent for its imports and exports on the United States. To increase Cuba's foodstuffs so that it could as far as possible fill all the needs of the people had been the stated aim of all revolutionaries, including José Martí. Castro put this desire into practice. Within four years, the staple protein of beans had been increased by 136 percent and rice, its accompaniment in the diet of the people, increased 100 percent. Production of corn was almost doubled. The raising of beef, though showing a growth much less spectacular, increased by 25 percent. The production of eggs was a "spectacular economic success." By 1965, rationing was discontinued: in fact surplus eggs were exported.

Now six liters of milk a month at twenty cents a liter is allowed adults: children up to seven get a liter a day. Fish is mainly unrationed, particularly cod, but also lobsters and shrimp. Meat is still rationed. In the three years between 1963 and 1966, all products—textiles, shoes, milk, vegetables, butter, bread, flour, cigarettes—had all shown considerable increase.

New land was brought under cultivation and though bulldozers and tractors had to be obtained from abroad, the numbers of these being brought in was tripled. Naturally, there were some disappointments but in its short history, there was no question that despite overwhelming odds, the island quickly produced a greatly improved life for most of its inhabitants.

Agriculture had to loom large in the country's planning because one of Castro's primary goals was that Cuba must feed all its people, whatever the threats from outside. Agriculture was therefore approached scientifically to obtain maximum results.

As well as developing its cattle industry and increasing its numbers of hogs and chickens, Cuba as an island can take advantage of the seas all around it for fish, as another source of protein. So as well as the old fishermen's rowboats to bring in the catch, Cuba has developed a fishing fleet that can provide enormous quantities of excellent meals for its population.

All the progress mentioned above came in the short period from 1958 to 1962. By the latter year, the production of sugar gave the largest yield in Cuba's whole history, which had had many booms in sugar. By that time too, many new factories had been built and more were under construction all the time. At first, these were mostly in light industry, and mostly produced utensils for immediate household or farm use.

According to a United Nations report, from 1963 to 1966 Cuba doubled its production of pasteurized and natural milk, its bread and biscuits, and increased its yield of cotton by 50 percent. Most items for mass consumption had increased by nearly a half. People now had money to buy, and though there was still rationing of many items at that time, it meant there was equal distribution. The approach to manufacturing and production was now totally different from what it had been.

Postrevolutionary Cuba, out of necessity, produced certain items such as sugarcane for profit. But "most things were for use, regardless of profit. This disregard of money and profit is fundamental to the revolution."[5]

Cuba needed dairy cows for milk for the children. Some had to be imported. However, there were limiting factors such as lack of money and also limitations caused by the U.S. blockade. There was experimentation with cows that gave a high quantity of milk, but that could be mated with bulls that were of a different strain, and cheaper to buy. By 1970, Cuba had half a million dairy cattle and production of milk had increased fourfold.

The Cubans used their land rationally: rice was planted where it would grow best, the same with coffee, citrus fruits, tobacco, sugar. From many crops, particularly sugar which is the biggest, there have been developed byproducts. The bagasse from the cane can be used for paper-making and box making. More importantly, it can be turned into protein for cattle. The molasses from sugar, combined with a type of yeast, provides feed for a fast-growing pig industry. It also can be used for fuel. Thus have the imagination and inventiveness of man developed along with an increase in production. Instead of being grown merely for its own sake, as it was in the old days, sugarcane is being utilized in diverse ways to produce a number of other necessities.

At present, virtually the entire population of nine million is involved in the regime either through schools or mass organizations. No one is neglected. The inmates of a Havana insane asylum operate a chicken farm that produces eight thousand broilers a week. "That is our contribution to the Revolution," a doctor explained. "Cubans live in the only Latin American country that has no misery, no slums, no flagrant contrast between unlimited private wealth and beggars in the streets, no malaria, no polio, very little child mortality."

Fidel says: "Marx conceived of socialism as the result of development. Today for the underdeveloped world, socialism is a necessary condition for development because without employing the socialist method—placing all the natural and human resources of the country, channelling these resources in the direction necessary to achieve the desired social objectives—no underdeveloped country can pull itself out of underdevelopment."

American companies used to own most Cuban mines; that is, its natural resources belonged to others. Now Cuba owns them. Cuba mines more managanese now than any other Latin American country and all the profits go to the people. Cuba also has nickel and chromium which are being developed as part of a growing steel industry.

Now more self-sufficient, Cuba will produce surpluses, thus creating its own capital without need of borrowing. And without going into debt, it will be able to buy those items that it still needs to obtain from abroad. So the means of production have been transferred from the private to the public sector. This was a first necessary step on the road of socialism.

"Before the revolution, the basic structure and developmental tendencies of the economy and society were determined by international and domestic market forces. Now a complete and total change had to be made. The leadership in its planning had to substitute itself for the market as a guide and engine of economic and social development."[6] Since those in charge were amateurs, there had to be trial and error, mistakes made and overcome. Yet they knew the socialistic path they wished to take, the socialist goals which they had set for themselves. Since they were idealists, their goals were high; since they were dedicated, they approached their tasks with excitement. Their excitement spilled over and engulfed the populace, especially the youth. And this was their major first accomplishment, since without the trust and confidence of the people, nothing could be accomplished.

Castro's long spellbinding speeches to the crowds in which he openly explained all the difficulties, but also set forth what with the proper will could be done, were necessary tasks of the Revolution.

These were the lessons he gave the people on socialism. In a socialist system, an economic plan for the country is devised to satisfy the needs of the people and is not a plan where the question of profitability is the main factor. In the case of Cuba, it is not a question of how much profit can be made by growing rice, vegetables, fruits, raising chickens, pigs and cattle. In a socialist plan, the key factor is how much is needed to supply the wants of the people: how much can realistically be produced, without relying on foreign imports. The basic necessity of food for all families must be satisfied, whether it can be done profitably or not. Obviously things must be produced as efficiently as possible. But if there is a deficit, the socialist state makes up the deficit. The primary base for the planning is that there will be sufficient nutritious food for all, jobs for all, homes and schools and hospitals to accommodate all. This is the difference between socialist and capitalist planning or capitalist free enterprise.

Fidel said Marxism was conceived out of "a love for man, for humanity; the desire to combat misery, injustice, and all the misery suffered by the proletariat." Ché said: "One should be a 'Marxist' as naturally as one is a 'Newtonian' in physics, or a 'Pasteurian' in biology, considering that though new facts determine new concepts, these new concepts will never take away that part of the truth which the older concept had." And, "it is the people themselves who must really become the creator and leader of their history *where their own happiness will be built by their own hands.*" Both leaders thought that socialism must be more than an equitable distribution of wealth: it must produce a new morality, new values of what is worthwhile in life. The new leaders did not believe in incentives. According to Ché, "If you start trying to give individuals a desire to get rich you are back into the rotten morality of capitalism. You lead [people] away from the socialist goal: "to each according to his needs.' The fight is not only against poverty but to raise man up to his highest levels. Incentives mean putting men in competition with other men under capitalism. A man must want to do his best for the good of all."

The sense of equality, and the realization that everyone had to work for the betterment of all—these two factors provided the stimulus for the idealism that inspires young people. And the young provided the country with the volunteer labor needed to fill the many tasks to be done. By allowing people to use their own initiatives, by giving them outlets for their creativity, by giving workers a say in what should be done and how it should be done, most of the drudgery of mindless, repetitious labor was alleviated. And all the workers were at the same time learning, growing as individuals.

Castro, like Bolívar, believes in the great importance of education. And the people, deprived for centuries of literacy, went thirstily to the wells of knowledge that were now at last available to them. UNESCO, in a report published in 1965, six years after the revolution, found that almost a "miracle" in schooling had been achieved. Radio and television were used to educate the people and to carry the slogans of the educational campaign to everyone: "If you know, teach. If you don't know, learn," and, "Every Cuban a teacher; every house a school." Thousands of volunteers were sought, the so-called *alfabetizadores*. Older children would teach younger children. Children would teach their parents.

Not only were children being taught, but adults also who previously had never had the opportunity. In a period of six years, a half-a-million adults had been enrolled in the educational program. Tuition and books were all free. Further, the teaching was arranged for the best times both for the country and the pupils. In the rural areas, schooling took place when the work on the sugar crop was completed. If there was no schools available, lessons often took place in homes in outlying areas with just a few neighbors getting together. In the towns, schoolrooms were set up in offices and factories, again at times most convenient to workers. So the new revolutionary regime did not say, "We haven't enough schoolrooms, and we don't have the money to build them." Everything was adapted to what was at hand. There was no bemoaning there were not enough teachers. Amateurs and volunteers augmented the professionals. School building did take place; so did the printing of suitable reading books and the production of other learning materials. In the meantime, there was no waiting. Everything that was at hand was used. Educated people would offer their services, and the volunteers would go everywhere into the remotest villages to take part in this tremendously exciting project.

In the same way, doctors trained assistants: nurses and aides who could attend to some of the smaller ills and teach lessons of hygiene. It was exciting for everyone taking part in the tasks—the whole country was involved. There was no need for adolescents to hang around on street corners; they could feel important and useful instead of alienated.

UNESCO said in regard to the wholesale wiping out of illiteracy that it "was not a miracle, but rather a difficult conquest obtained through work, technique and organization. . . . Never in the history of education anywhere had there been so successful an achievement."[7]

In Cuba the emphasis has not alone been in seeing that everyone is literate, but on giving its students on the higher levels the finest possible training. "Within a short time—between 5 and 15 years —Cuba can have scientists of international calibre, precisely because this development has the backing of the Revolution," Castro says. The U.S., on the other hand, it cutting down on its expenditures on scientific research (except military research) and this also follows for its colony, Puerto Rico.

Ché thought: "Society as a whole must become a gigantic school, but . . . under socialism it must be a self-motivating society in which people sought self-education and in which the cultural level of all was raised." For "Marxism implies a humanist morality—humanity is the universal value." The development of man to his highest potential is the aim. But almost as gratifying is the pride of a peasant who has learned to write his own name and to read papers and books, something he could never previously have dreamt of.

In boarding schools, once only open to the wealthy boys and girls, children are taken on merit. They live a healthy life in the mountains, not only studying hard but doing all the necessary maintenance and household chores. They will not grow up believing they are an elite who must have others wait on them. University students spend part of their time studying and part of their time teaching or going out in the fields to help at harvesting time. Mothers take part in helping in nursery schools where their children are enrolled, and where school meals and school clothing are free.

Ché Guevara, in his last letter to his oldest daughter, wrote: "Try to excel as a student; excel in every sense."

Why should these young people with so much to do, filled with such high aims, become drug addicts or petty thieves? These problems, which are plaguing Puerto Rico and the Dominican Republic, do not exist in Cuba. In the former countries, they are not enough prisons in which to hold prisoners. No youngster is rehabilitated in these places, where conditions are unspeakable. He comes out a habitual criminal. Capitalist societies spend thousands of dollars on each person they cage like an animal.

As there was a remarkable achievement even in the first year in education, so too there was in medical care; this despite the number of doctors who left their country and had no desire to take part in its formidable tasks. The blockade by the U.S. had made it difficult to obtain many medicines and hospital equipment. Students were now to go into medicine not because it was a highly profitable profession, but because they could help cure illnesses and more importantly, prevent many of them. Young people, whatever their background, could become doctors if they had the ability. More nurses were trained, and para-medical help was enormously increased.

In Cuba, before the Revolution, as in Puerto Rico and the Dominican Republic, thousands had died because they were too far away from the medical centers and because they could not afford the medical help they needed. In the latter two countries, patients still have to put down money before they can enter hospitals. Even desperate cases are often turned away. In Cuba, however, the first two years of any doctor's professional life have to be spent in the rural areas. By its efforts, today Cuba has the lowest rates of child and maternal mortality in the whole of Latin America. It has lower rates than other Latin American countries in almost all other mortalities and sicknesses. The reason is that "people are treated like human beings entitled to the best care whether rich or poor."[8] According to recent United Nations figures, Cuba's health statistics are the best in the Western Hemisphere, even better than in Canada which has an excellent "socialist" health system.

In the United States during all this time, there was a deliberate attempt to distort news about Cuba. The U.S. press tried and still tries to portray Fidel Castro as a bogeyman. But there are exceptions.

Herbert L. Matthews, a leading *New York Times* correspondent, who first interviewed Castro in the Sierra Maestra in 1957 (at a time when Batista had claimed Fidel was dead), gives this profile of Castro. "He has, to an overwhelming degree, that almost religious appeal now labeled as charisma." He adds, "unlike the typical Latin dictator—Peron, Pérez, Jiminéz, Trujillo, Somoza, Batista—Fidel has no interest in money. If he is driven from power, he will have no millions salted away in Swiss banks, or like Batista, in Florida real estate. He is scrupulously honest and has given Cuba its first honest administration since Columbus discovered the island."

Further, he is no man's puppet. He does not take orders from Moscow or anywhere else. When he makes mistakes, they are his own mistakes. He loves the revolution as an artist loves his work. He has a great creative desire to provide for all his countrymen the best possible life that he can help them to achieve for themselves.

The reporter quoted above makes the accusation: "The information given out in Washington is often deliberately misleading or quite simply incorrect." For instance, one official at the U.S. State Department made a public statement that "there had been a demonstration in the streets of Havana with protestors carrying a coffin" (for Castro). The story was completely false. A foreign ambassador said he was "appalled" at so high a U.S. official making such a statement. "It showed an astonishing depth of ignorance, but unfortunately a typical one." Later Fidel asked about the incident "whether it was a case of ignorance or lying."[9]

Stories about Cuba that were sympathetic were suppressed. Herbert Matthews, who wrote sympathetically, was subject to much harrassment from the U.S. government, from American rightists and exiled Cubans. There was even a threat against his life from one Miami group. Soon his stories were not printed by the *New York Times*, or were severely cut. The untrue stories printed in Puerto Rico and the Dominican Republic, as well as the U.S., gave the public a completely erroneous idea of what was happening in Cuba, and caricatured Fidel as a communist monster under whose dictatorship Cubans suffered.

It was essential for U.S. foreign policy that audiences at home and in its satellites in the other islands heard only the lies. "Foreign news editors were content to print slanted news on Cuba," Matthews wrote, and went on to say that the editorials in the *New York Times* "were hostile" and that the same was true for all U.S. newspaper editorials.

After some years, Lee Lockwood, a photographer for *Look* magazine, was allowed to visit Cuba. He, like Matthews, was not a radical, but his book *Castro's Cuba: Cuba's Fidel* gave a true account of the revolution as Matthews' *Cuban Story* had done. Both these men were moved by the revolutionary fire they discovered in Cuba; by the tremendous social achievements made in spite of all the odds against a small island in the Caribbean; by the passionate affection and trust that the Cuban people gave their leader.

The propaganda, of course, had an aim. The U.S. was preparing to invade Cuba, and trained Cuban exiles in Guatemala for the purpose. The project had been started under President Eisenhower and was continued by President Kennedy. The U.S., in its 1961 Bay of Pigs misadventure, thought it could bring down Castro's regime when it sent armed Cuban exiles and its own marines from Puerto

Rico, and planes from Florida. It spent $200 million to learn that the Cuban people, who had fought for their independence for ninety years, would not weakly give in to this new aggression. Castro gave the people arms, formed militias, and *"Patria Muerto: Venceremos"* was the *grito* to which the whole island responded.

The U.S. government lied that it had not been involved in the invasion. But Raul Roa denounced in the General Assembly of the United Nations the North American bombings and the landing of counterrevolutionary troops on the island. "The airplanes are theirs; the bombs are theirs; the mercenaries have been trained and paid by them," he said.

All that he said was true and the countries of the world knew it was true. Instead of overthrowing the regime, the unprovoked aggression put the Cuban people more strongly than ever behind Castro and helped further radicalize them, while the U.S. press mislead its people by outlandish stories, making such make-believe statements as that Fidel's militia had deserted and that Fidel and his brother had been captured. Were those "news" items prepared in advance by such sources as the Associated Press so that the invasion, which they did not visualize could fail, would prove to the American people that Castro did not have the support of his countrymen?

Fidel recognized that the Bay of Pigs incident would not be the only invasion attempt. How could he safeguard the island against a bigger and better-prepared attempt by the United States to overthrow his regime? There have been many explanations of his reasons for allowing Russian missiles to be placed in Cuba. A rational one seems to be that Fidel realized he had to have a trump card. To have Russian missiles put on the island would fit in with Castro's general audacity. The idea behind it: If you invade again, your own territory will not come out unharmed.

Kennedy called on Kruschev to withdraw the missiles or face retaliation against the U.S.S.R. The missiles were withdrawn, but there was an obvious deal that in return the U.S. would not attack Cuba. Castro has remained ninety miles from the North American mainland, independent, cocky, a perpetual thorn in U.S. flesh.

During the Cuban missile crisis, the U.S. Senate stated that it was prepared "by whatever means necessary including the use of arms," to prevent Castro from "exporting his aggressive purposes," also to prevent harm to the security of the U.S. naval base at Guantánamo, and to work with "freedom-loving Cuban refugees to support the legitimate aspirations of the people of Cuba for a return to self-determination."[10] The self-determination was the same Cuba had enjoyed under the Platt Amendment; the same they had enjoyed since 1898 when the U.S. went to war with Spain to gain Cuba's freedom. In regard to the 1,170 prisoners taken in the Bay of Pigs combat, Castro again acted unconventionally. He traded them for medicines and drugs from the United States.

It is said that there is no democracy in Cuba because there are no free elections. Yet it is everywhere acknowledged that Castro has the full support of the people. Many of the bourgeoisie would have been ready to go with him on the path of independence, but were not ready to go further along the road to socialism.

How easily power won in an electoral process can be overthrown by a military coup d'etat is seen in the examples of Guatemala in 1954, in the Dominican Republic in 1965 and in Chile in 1973. Once in power, Castro recognized that it was necessary to see victory was not snatched away by counterrevolutionaries and by the United States. A revolution that does not go the whole hog is lost. Castro says it is a myth that modern arms render the people helpless to overthrow tyrants or the domination of a great power. Cuba, Korea, Vietnam have shown that despite its colossal might the United States can be defeated. The United States has proved to be not invincible and in Latin America, Cuba is the new star in the Western Hemisphere.

Lee Lockwood wrote, "Fidel Castro is an extraordinary man who has created an extraordinary revolution. It is time for us to accept the Cuban Revolution as a fait accompli and to deal with it in a way which does us more credit as a democratic people. At a minimum, we ought to cease our efforts to bring down the Castro regime!" Yet the U.S. has continuously and unsuccessfully tried to bring down the regime. It has been unsuccessful even in its many attempts to assassinate Castro. Finally, it has been unsuccessful in its blockade. All the Latin American and Caribbean countries, except Puerto Rico, are now trading with Cuba and have diplomatic relations with the country. This is also true for the majority of Western powers. Even the Pope has an emissary there who is a friend of Fidel's and who calls Cuba "a Christian country."

It is because Cuba has made great progress as the years have gone by that other countries of the world have started trading with it. A newspaper headline in Puerto Rico in March, 1976 read: "Cuba has clout in the Caribbean". The article said that "Cuba is developing in a big way, and this in the long run is good for all the other countries of Latin America." It predicted "there would soon be a big rush to do business with Cuba." A change of attitude was seen in the *New York Times* reporting on March 22, 1976. It states "in the last two years Cuba has gained considerable influence among the small republics of the Caribbean—the principal friends—are Guyana and Jamaica. In addition, [U.S.] officials believe that the younger generation of political leaders throughout the Caribbean view Cuba as the most successful model of social and economic development in their experience." For a while it seemed that the United States might begin a new relationship with the island. Several senators visited Cuba and urged a modification of attitude. This changed again with Cuba's help to the revolutionary forces in Angola. But there is again a new friendlier direction of policy under President Carter.

After only seventeen years of struggle against great handicaps, there is no gainsaying the success of the island's socialist experiment. Before he died recently, the Chilean Nobel Prize-winning poet, Pablo Neruda wrote: "In the midst of the arena of America's struggles, I saw that my human task was none other than to join the extensive forces of the organized masses of the people, to join with life and soul, with suffering and hope, because it is only from this great popular stream that the necessary changes can arise for writers and for nations."

A young Cuban interviewed by Paul M. Sweezey expressed his views on what is happening in his country in this way: "I still choke a little. Before the revolution, I never stopped thinking of my career, aching, groaning—[now] all around me in Cuba things are being done that answer my dreams. You say that sounds like happiness. All right."

This is Cuba's challenge.

13 -:- The Social and Economic Situation

The differences between Cuba and Puerto Rico today can perhaps best be gauged by the inaugural speech of ex-Puerto Rican Governor Hernández Colón in 1973. Undoubtedly he would have liked to paint a rosier picture of the situation of the majority of his people, for he is both a believer in capitalism and in the "permanent union" with the U.S.

But he said,

> While some segments of our society enjoy growing progress, thousands upon thousands of Puerto Ricans languish in seemingly unending poverty. Hundreds of thousands are deprived of their fair share of the resources available to us in our country. Their present circumstances deny them the opportunity to move ahead in life and to find meaning in their lives. Rising costs of living reduce their real salaries. Hopelessness pervades the countryside. The products of our soil no longer sustain our rural population. For them there is lack of opportunity to enjoy the advantages they see others obtain. The poor in our cities, as well as in the country, still hope for a better life, but so far their hopes are unfulfilled.
>
> "Our economy has not yet been able to develop sufficiently to create enough jobs and to provide work for all Puerto Ricans who need it. Thousands have had to emigrate, to abandon their homes, to uproot themselves from their communities in search of new opportunities outside of Puerto Rico. And many times, instead of finding the opportunities they sought [in the U.S.], they have been obliged to rely upon public welfare; instead of being able to hold up their heads in the pride of their identity, they have encountered prejudice and incomprehension. The unemployed and the

migrants still hope for new opportunities here in Puerto Rico; but so far their hopes have remained unfulfilled.

One third of our families live in housing unfit for human habitation. Thousands are crowded in flimsy shacks, squatting on land that is not their own, without sanitation and many are without potable water. Most of the poor live in wretched urban slums. Their children play in filth and in mud; they must bathe in contaminated water; they breathe polluted air; and they sleep huddled on the floor. The families and children in our slums and rural backwaters still hope, but so far their hopes have remained unfulfilled. Our sick suffer for days, for weeks, and even for months before they receive treatment. Many die without receiving it. There are not enough doctors, not enough nurses, and sometimes not even enough medicine to relieve the suffering of the poor. Those who can afford to pay receive a higher quality of medicine. Our sick people still hope, but so far their hopes of receiving the same quality of medical care regardless of their economic limitations, have remained unfulfilled.[1]

Hernández Colón is thus shown to be a compassionate man, but within the present framework he was unable to help his countrymen. For Puerto Rico is a colony. Hernández Colón during his term 1972-1976 was subservient to American big business and American financial interests, as well to the wealthy citizens of the island, whose interests are intertwined with those of big business. He rejects socialism and independence, the only solutions to Puerto Rico's problems.

The governor talked of the hopelessness of the poor in 1973. Five years later, with the recession in the U.S. affecting Puerto Rico, the conditions have worsened. Unemployment is up since then. Schools are becoming more dilapidated. There is a large and rising number of drug addicts. Crime has increased enormously. Health services have deteriorated even more. Within the present situation, only superficial improvements can be made. The one action taken that has curbed what could become a serious revolt in Puerto Rico is the distribution of food stamps to the poor, but this does not provide the hope that Hernández Colón so eloquently showed people needed. The food stamps do provide an edge against rioting and deep unrest.

The situation for the mass of the people in the Dominican Republic is several degrees worse than that outlined by Hernández

Colón in Puerto Rico. The Dominican Republic is rural to a greater extent and the poverty of the people is greater. In the Dominican Republic, 85 percent of the active population lives in the countryside. In 1971, the sugarcane workers were getting less than $30 a month; they are not getting any more today. "The average annual wage is $180; that of an industrial worker $478; that of a rural laborer $92." (The latter was the same figure as existed in Cuba before the Revolution.) 87 percent of the peasants have neither electricity nor water. After Balaguer came to power "for more than five years, water in Santo Domingo had the status of a luxury. Only 11 percent of the peasants drink milk; and only 4 percent eat meat; 2 percent eat eggs and less than 1 percent eat fish."[2] The last figure is incredible for an island. But as Marx wrote, "Under capitalism, the greatest majority is always poor and must remain poor."

Let us take the lowest annual income in Puerto Rico of $100, the more widespread low of $92 in the Dominican Republic, and compare these sums with the incomes of the wealthy in both countries. Puerto Rico has a relatively high average income of $1,800 a year, but this high average is made up of two-thirds of the people who live below the poverty level, and only one-tenth on the high level of wealth. The magnitude of the wealth of upper-class Puerto Ricans compared with that of their indigent countrymen is on the order of 50 to 1. Between Americans visiting or in residence, and the poor, sometimes a differential of two hundred to one. The gap is enormous between the rich—riding cars worth the price of a modest house, gambling thousands at night in the casinos, paying $185 a day in hotels—and the poor living in hovels without running water, and needing food stamps to survive.

In Cuba, "there is at most a two-to-one differential in wages, a condition very close to absolute equality."[3] The wealth of the island is distributed fairly evenly among all. Fidel Castro and his administration live very little better than the rest of their countrymen and undoubtedly work twice as hard as the average person.

In Puerto Rico, everyone puts a large share of the blame for the island's ills on overpopulation. "The fertility rate of women in Puerto Rico must be reduced by a third as soon as possible if the island is to avoid a 'cataclysm of overpopulation' " according to Health Secretary José Alvarez de Choudens. Teodoro Moscosco, Formento Administrator, who arranges for U.S. firms to operate in Puerto Rico, calls growing population "the worst woe."

Ruben Berrios, one of the *independentista* leaders, says Moscosco talks like a modern Herod wanting to get rid of Puerto Rican babies. Cuba, once similarly considered overpopulated, is now desperately short of people to develop the country.

Two Puerto Rican professors, Sanchez and Guitierrez, have found in a careful, computerized, demographic study of the island that Puerto Rico is not overpopulated. "Before I began this study, I believed what was said about Puerto Rico's overpopulation problem," Sanchez said. "Now I see it is the reverse. There has been a steady decline in the birth rate." Professor Fuat M. Audic of the University of Puerto Rico writes that what seems to be a soaring birth rate among the poor of the less developed countries is often an illusion. The problems that accompany 'overpopulation' can be solved by better income distribution, improved health and educational facilities, and most important of all, more income.

Despite all the fanfare about American industry's solving Puerto Rico's unemployment problem, it has, in fact, aggravated it. At the close of 1966, Puerto Rico had a total of 2,431 manufacturing establishments with a total employment of 118,000 persons in manufacturing industries. In 1976, ten years later, the figures were much the same.

The United Methodist Church has been urged by one of its Board members to support independence for Puerto Rico. He underscored the failure of American industry:

> The population is primarily destitute, with 81.8 percent of the households having incomes of $1,367 or less. Unemployment is estimated at 33 percent but this figure is kept by exporting workers to the United States where they mostly live under inhuman conditions.
>
> Operation Bootstrap, an economic development program launched in 1947, lured over two thousand firms to the island by offering 10-25 year tax holidays and a cheap labor force. Unemployment nevertheless is now [1976] higher than it was when the program began.[4]

Unemployment pay in Puerto Rico is $55 weekly. In January, 1976, the number of persons obtaining unemployment compensation was 138,107. This represented 21.9 percent of the labor force, and did not include those unemployed who were not receiving unemployment pay.

It is therefore not the Puerto Rican people who benefit from the presence of American industries on the island: it is the industries themselves. The island provides such a favorable climate for business, in fact, that most manufacturers starting in Puerto Rico arrive at a bottom-line profit in just six-to-nine months.

Nor are tax breaks and cheap labor the only benefits that industries receive. Utility rates are adjusted so that private citizens subsidize manufacturers. "Thanks to Public Law 82, industries of the size of Union Carbide and P.P.G. receive a governmental subsidy of no less than $3,250,000 annually to help cover their energy costs. P.P.G. consumed an amount of electrical energy in 1972, equal to that spent in all of Puerto Rico in 1950. As well as receiving the subsidies, the big companies pay a rate one-third less than the ordinary consumer. An agreement between the water authorities and the companies, in total in one year cost the people of Puerto Rico more than $10 million."[5] The companies use 35 percent of the electricity produced in the islands.

The question of oil has now entered the picture of U.S. relations with Puerto Rico. Geologists and geophysicists of Mobil have estimated there is an 85 percent chance of finding oil off the north coast. The Industrial Mission now feels more strongly than ever that Puerto Rico will be shortchanged on the oil revenues. Professor Tomas Morales Cardona of UPR says Puerto Rico could achieve full economic benefits if it paid just for exploratory drilling. There is production possibility of two hundred thousand barrels a day. The U.S. Interior and Justice Departments have taken the position that Puerto Rico has no jurisdiction over the oil deposits. The islands could acquire jurisdiction by an act of Congress, but only up to three miles. Puerto Rico says it has jurisdiction up to ten miles.

The Puerto Rican government has an agreement with Mobil, Shell, Exxon, and Continental Oil, authorizing those companies to extract 200,000 barrels of oil per day for a period of 30 years at an investment of $400 million.

U.S. companies have also shown interest in Puerto Rican copper, but many sections of the populace have resisted attempts to mine it. There is now a proposal to form a Puerto Rican Mining Corporation, which would invest in the total mining operation with two U.S. companies, Kennecott and American Metal Corp Each company would receive a third of the profits from the copper.

"The Dominican Republic is one of the most attractive Latin American nations for investment," according to a U.S. Embassy report in November 1974. "Some of the most important opportunities for U.S. investment lie in the fields of construction and mining." The report praised the fiscal policies of President Joaquín Balaguer and suggested these would be even more improved when Balaguer began his third consecutive four-year term in office.

U.S. influences reach into all spheres of Dominican life; such companies as Esso, Texaco, Alcoa and the U.S.-owned South Puerto Rican Sugar Company exercise considerable influence. U.S. involvement in the Dominican Republic is so extensive that it raises the question, just how extensive is Dominican sovereignty over its own affairs? At times it is difficult to determine whether the U.S. Embassy or Dominican officials are actually formulating policy. It is the same way with military policy. The U.S. is largely responsible for the training, equipment, army, clothing, and instruction of the Dominican Armed Forces.

Ex-Fomento (Industrial Development) Administrator Teodoro Moscosco is quoted in a *New York Times* advertisement as praising the high productivity of Puerto Rican labor as well as its relatively low costs.

> "The latest U.S. Census of Manufacturers found that a worker in Puerto Rico returns an average of $4.03 in value for every dollar of wages earned." In the States, it is roughly three dollars. According to the Planning Board, "the island's manufacturing sector rose [in labor productivity] at twice the rate of U.S. manufacturing during the 1967 to 1972 period."

The Puerto Rican worker then is a hard worker, not lazy as is so often claimed by those who exploit him.

The minimum wage in the States is around $2.75 an hour. Only a few industries in Puerto Rico, such as hotels and restaurants, pay this rate, and then not to all their employees. About 40 percent of industries pay less than $2.40 an hour. In manufacturing industries, the average hourly wage is 48 percent of that paid in similar U.S. industries.

The Commonwealth Labor Department's Census of the Puerto Rican Manufacturing Industry shows that though the nominal average wage of factory workers rose from $1.50 to $2.59 between October 1968 and October 1975, the real average wage rose only by one penny during the same seven-year period. Marx said workers sell their labor at a minimum price, and buy the goods they themselves produce at a maximum price. The difference is the profit that goes into the pocket of the capitalist. And Lenin pointed out that "surplus capital is never used to raise the living standard of the masses."

"Why Puerto Rico is Unique as a Place for Manufacturers to Make More Profits," was the headline of an advertisement written by Malcolm S. Forbes, president and editor-in-chief of *Forbes Magazine*. He told how the unique relationship between Puerto Rico and the U.S. provides manufacturers with advantages for profits *they will not find anywhere else in the world*. He points out that purchases from the U.S. in millions were $101 in 1940 and $2,676 in 1974. Bank deposits of $76 million jumped to $4,137 million in the same period: motor vehicles from 26,847 to 851,615. Further there are no federal taxes; 100 percent exemption from local taxes; and over one hundred thousand workers (the unemployed) available, at low wages.

In regard to the tax exemption, U.S. firms produced $500 million worth of drugs in Puerto Rico in 1973. A study of the top seven firms showed they saved more than $66 million because of their tax exempt status. Lilly and Searle alone saved over $33 million. These figures were given in a Chase Manhattan report.

In Puerto Rico, there is little that is not in North American hands: "the large domestic transport companies, air and marine transport, communications, petroleum refining and distribution, cement, petrochemicals and pharmaceutical production, the subsidiaries of *Fortune's* 500; all the blue chip companies, most of the banks, and investment houses, real estate, hotels, chemical, textile, and garment industries, electronics. Under an independent socialist government, able to utilize the island's wealth, Puerto Rico could become a major international supplier of manufactured and intermediate goods. She is sufficiently developed, but at the present time, industry in Puerto Rico is a valve appendage of U.S. industry. Industrial colonialism has built factories that are only one part of a technical process that begins and ends abroad. [The] island has been converted into a sweatshop of cheap labor, where [U.S.] capitalists enjoy unparalleled political and economic privileges, use of the air, water, and electric energy, and exorbitant tax exemptions."[6]

In 1974, Puerto Rico bought $3 billion worth of goods from the United States: that is an average of $1000 per person in a country that has an average annual income of $1,800. More than half of this was spent on food that could mostly be grown on the island. In the American supermarkets all over Puerto Rico, it is almost impossible to get any Puerto Rican produce. About $400 million was spent on U.S.-made clothing, most of which could have been manufactured on the island.

Puerto Rico is the fifth largest consumer in all the world of U.S. goods. It generated $2.5 billion in gross income in 1974 and $3 billion during the fiscal year 1974 to 1975, and created thus the equivalent of one hundred forthy thousand jobs in the U.S. All these figures have increased in the succeeding years. In 1974, U.S. corporate profits from direct investment in Puerto Rico amounted to more than the total profit from U.S. direct investments in all the European countries combined, according to both the *Manchester Guardian* of Enggland and *Le Monde* of Paris. U.S. profits from Puerto Rico were four times more than from Japan, twenty times more than from Argentina, and about half as much as of all the U.S. profits derived from Latin America.

As to the food stamp program, Puerto Rico imports approximately 80 percent of all the food it uses. If the program reaches a top level of $600 million in 1978, against which the beneficiaries will be paying approximately $150 million (food stamps are not yet free) this means that much of this will return to the United States—a healthy boost to the stateside economy.

Both Puerto Rico and the Dominican Republic are markets for U.S. goods, and sources of raw material, investment and cheap labor. Instead of bringing cheap labor from Europe as was done in the beginning of the century, manufacturers now find cheap labor outside the U.S. and bring their plants there; in this case into the two islands. Wages in recent years have been higher in Puerto Rico than in the Dominican Republic, so smaller American factories are moving to the latter island. American companies in Puerto Rico constantly threaten that if the workers demand increases in wages, they will move out to find cheaper sources of labor, and so increase the present unemployment levels. Formento paid more than $10 million extra in special incentives over a three-year period to four U.S. companies to get them to stay in Puerto Rico.

The availability of cheap labor is particularly obvious in the case of the garment industry, where it is easy to move equipment and machinery to the next island. ILGWU statistics for average hourly earnings for apparel workers in the U.S. and abroad show United States $2.99, Japan $1.35, Hong Kong 57¢, Mexico 56¢, Columbia 45¢, *and the Dominican Republic at 38¢ per hour.*

Slavery actually exists in the Dominican Republic today, though it is mainly imported labor. "Sugar is the Dominicans' oil, the radio reminds the nation every hour. But it is the Haitians who do the bulk of sugarcane cutting, for three pesos a day—and of the three pesos, they are lucky to see one, for they have to tip the "boxers," who load the cane, and the man who weighs it. This is modern slavery."

This condition is now taking on even worse forms. Haitians in the Dominican Republic are said to number three hundred thousand to five hundred thousand. Supposedly an agreement was reached between 'Papa Doc' Duvalier and President Joaquín Balaguer in 1966, by which Haiti would supply the Dominican Republic with fifteen thousand laborers a year to cut cane; the latter country paying for them at $10 a head. But recently with the fall of sugar prices, Balaguer is trying to get Dominicans to take over this hard, poor-paying labor. A drive is on by which three thousand Haitians are being deported each month. The Haitians, wishing to escape deportation, pay $50 to stay; this despite the terrible conditions under which they work. A well-known journalist, Ramon Antonio Veras, writing in *El Nacional de Ahora,* says when this happens "the person who buys a Haitian has the right to put him to work without pay; he need only furnish the slave with basic needs; that is, take care of him so that he can cut sugarcane. The master has the right to kick him and even kill him if the slave refuses to cut cane. . . . It is unbelievable that in the twentieth century human beings are still being sold."

This is a liberal columnist writing. Mostly the propaganda is predominantly anti-Haitian, with strong racial overtones: the Black Haitian is degrading the 'White' Dominican. As the refugees are herded over the border in army trucks under the glare of soldiers toting bayoneted automatic rifles, one is reminded of Trujillo's massacre of 20,000 Haitian cane cutters in one night in 1936, when the dictator had no further use for them. Also there is now the threat that Dominicans themselves will be herded into slave labor camps to do the cane cutting, saving the owners and the government money. "Most Dominicans have incomes close to zero: they buy little, sell little and subsist on the verge of starvation and death. The sheer poverty of the bulk of the people is the single most striking feature of the Dominican economy. . . . The country suffers, then, from the paradox of being inherently rich agriculturally but not having enough food to feed its own population."[7]

Of the Dominican Republic's labor force of eight hundred thousand, three hundred thousand are unemployed. U.S. interests have dismantled every independent union. The other unions are U.S. unions and are infiltrated and controlled by the CIA. Large amounts of money have been poured into the Dominican labor movement by the U.S. to keep it in the hands of leaders whom the U.S. can control.

Before the revolution, there were half a million unemployed in Cuba. Now there are none. The figures for the Puerto Rican unemployed are given only for the island. They do not include the figures for the third of the people who have emigrated to the States to find work. The figures in both places are equally high. At least 40 percent of the Puerto Rican youths in New York can find no work. And if they find no work, how can they live, except by petty crime for men or by prostitution for women?

> "In order genuinely to solve the crime problems, it is necessary either to put lower-class neighborhoods under military occupation, which would surely produce new uprisings in the cities, or to eliminate poverty in the United States."[8]

In one of his preelection speeches, Jimmy Carter said, "The poor are the only ones who serve jail sentences." In Cuba, prisoners work outside in socially useful jobs, such as construction, and are paid an hourly wage. Compare Cuba's penal systems with New York's Attica prison, where in the riots of 1971, men said they would prefer to die than live in such conditions, but where in 1978 the conditions remain the same. Compare Cuba's penal system with the prisons in the Dominican Republic where torture is said to be used, or to the abominable La Princessa jail in Old San Juan, or to other prisons in Puerto Rico, where police officers beat up prisoners, and where even beating a young boy to death over "a traffic violation," goes unpunished. A country's prison system is a good reflection of its basic values.

According to the Puerto Rican secretary of agriculture, the island could double its agricultural production in the next ten years, generating an additional $354 million a year at the farm level. Experiments conducted through the University of Puerto Rico's agricultural experiment station over a period of a year and a half, show that rice could be grown cheaper in Puerto Rico than it can be bought from the United States. Such a move would increase farmers' profits and put many people to work.

Puerto Rico has the capacity to grow all the rice it needs, but unfortunately the island is too good a market for the excess produce of American growers. Giant U.S. agribusiness is unlikely to look on kindly while its $40 million yearly market evaporates. Through selective cutting of prices, American growers are able to destroy their Puerto Rican competitors. At one point, the price of American rice plummeted below that of native rice, and through a similar maneuver, American poultry industries were able to undercut and wipe out Puerto Rican farmers.

Consumers in Puerto Rico pay between $30 and $60 million more a year than they would pay for the same products in the States. Also, food brought from the States is often of inferior quality: some of it rotten or damaged in transport. A one-day survey by the Consumer Affairs Department found that 45 percent of the fruit and vegetable packages surveyed in six metropolitan area supermarkets had one or more items damaged, and the damage itself was over 40 percent.

Pueblo supermarkets (U.S. owned) has 75 percent of its total sales on the mainland and 25 percent in Puerto Rico, yet fully half its earnings come from sales on the island.

During 1975 in Puerto Rico there was some effort made towards bettering agriculture, which had been allowed a smaller and smaller place as industrialization by American firms superseded it. Immediately illustrating the possibilities of its growth, agriculture rose 14.7 percent. Even allowing for inflation, its real growth was 7 percent, the highest in any sector of the economy. Increases were in the production of milk, sugar, plantains, eggs, truck crop and some fish. The money generated by agricultural production in 1975 was $875 million, and this has a multiplying factor since the money remains in the island, and every dollar of direct agricultural production becomes two dollars in its indirect effect on the economy.

Clearly, Puerto Rico should be using more of its land for agriculture. However, less and less land is available for this purpose. Agricultural land is being reduced at the annual rate of three percent. Also the U.S. military uses thirteen percent of Puerto Rico's best land.

Just 150 acres of intensively grown tomatoes could supply Puerto Rico's entire annual need of twenty-five million pounds. There is at present no structure that either permits or motivates the farmer to produce. Until ten years ago, Puerto Rico exported its excellent coffee. Today it must import coffee. Puerto Rico imports 80 percent of its food from Iowa, Idaho, Florida and California among other states. But even twenty-six years ago in 1952, Puerto Rico was still producing sixty percent of the foodstuffs it consumed.

Castro says that Cuba has the potential to produce enough food for three times its population. So too the Dominican Republic could supply all its people with sufficient food; in fact, it could create an excess. The simple fact is that although the food is already there, the people cannot afford to buy it. One authority, Professor Crassweller, writes: "The Dominican Republic has by Caribbean standards an enormous potential as an exporter of food stuffs" while "Puerto Rico has a great capacity as an exporter of petrochemicals, capital goods and relatively sophisticated manufactured products." The Dominican Republic now grows sufficient rice for its own needs. Puerto Rico could do the same but instead buys dearly from California.

The U.S. suggested a formal trade alliance between the two countries, since a very rational exchange could be made between them. The Dominican Republic protested, however, that it would be forever held down to an agricultural role. A socialist alliance between the two countries would be beneficial to both. In the present situation however, all the benefits would go to the American monpolists who hold control in both islands. The poor would still remain hungry.

The big industries have ruined the agricultural sector of Puerto Rico's economy so that a great deal of the food the island could grow for its own needs has to be imported at high cost. Further, hundreds of small fishermen around the coast have had their daily living denied them by pollution. Farmers have been forced from their land, while speculation in land and real estate has been rampant.

Especially with its high population, Puerto Rico should devote a considerable part of its economy to agriculture. The shrinkage in that sector has meant tremendous unemployment for farm workers. With a change of emphasis away from heavy industry, which should play little part on a small island, Puerto Rico could supply its own food instead of importing it from America, or relying on U.S. food stamps. These stamps are given grudgingly, and can be reduced or eliminated at the will of the U.S. Congress. Federal aid is always given as U.S. charity, but this is a simplistic way to look at it. The expenses of food stamps, or of army bases, are really part of the cost of administering a colony. In the end, these expenses work to the advantage of the industries in Puerto Rico, not the people.

Of Cuba, The World Health Organizations says, "the thing that must be stressed is the tremendous progress which has occurred in Cuba in the last 15 years as regards all health parameters." Four Puerto Rican professors from the Medical School at the University of Puerto Rico, wrote after a visit to Cuba in April, 1976:

> The availability of health facilities is exemplified by the fact that Cuba had 56 rural hospitals in 1974 as compared to one in 1958. The entire country has 255 hospitals and 336 "policlinicos" or out-patient dispensaries. The total number of beds in 1974 was 44,379 of which 57.8% are located outside of Havana. This compares with the 28,536 beds available in 1958, of which 61.7% were located in Havana. Cuba has created three new medical schools since 1959 (in Oriente, Las Villas and Camaguey) and the number of health personnel in the Health Ministry today exceed 12,000 as compared to 2,973 in 1958. This is most amazing when one considers that Cuba lost one half of its physicians (3,000 out of 6,000) between 1959 and 1969. Eight-thousand physicians have been trained between 1959 and 1974. Thirty-four schools of nursing are operating with a three-year curriculum, a huge increment from the six schools open in 1958.
>
> The availability of free health services in Cuba today is a living reality for all citizens, making the conservation of health an achievable objective for all Cubans.

Beside ordinary illnesses, Puerto Ricans are also subjected to many health hazards due to American industry on the island. There has been much well-substantiated evidence of serious ill effects of mercury poisoning on workers and of deformation of fetuses in pregnant women. Institute of Legal Medicine director, Rafael Criado, said the death of a former employee of Becton, Dickinson and Co.'s Juncos thermometer plant was definitely the result of mercury poisoning. The cause of death was also recognized by the State Insurance Fund.

In Yabucoa, the effluents from Sun Oil and Union Carbide are making the town unlivable. The smell is intolerable and, respiratory ailments, especially among children, have risen considerably. People vomit in the streets, and some families have moved away because they cannot stand the stench. Industry is responsible for more than 40 percent of the sulphur dioxide in the air, not counting other pollutants. In Guayanilla, there was a leakage of chlorine gas at the PPG Industries plant. More than three hundred people were hospitalized. "Chlorine is one of the most dangerous gases around . . . it is so potent that a standard gas mask offers no protection against it," said Cruz Matos, who was executive director of the Environmental Board. When he attempted to enforce standards of safety on industries that were responsible for pollution, he was fired on a flimsy pretext.

The air, land, beaches, rivers and oceans are all being polluted. Some of the worst has come from the oil companies. "The day to day seepage can be called 'death by the installment plan'" the *New York Times* reported. Usually the industries get away with high pollution levels and the dumping of their waste in the rivers.

Due to pharmaceutical industries, the situation in the Barceloneta-Manatí area is an incredible threat to the lives of the inhabitants. Factories discharge toxic wastes into the river and into the ocean near the shore. Death in this area caused by asthma since the establishment of the pharmaceutical companies in 1967 has increased from 5000 deaths per 100,000 inhabitants to 55,000 deaths per 100,000 in 1972. As well as creating health hazards, air pollution costs Puerto Rico about $70 million annually according to Dr. Tomas Morales Cardon, Professor of Pharmacology at the University of Puerto Rico.

Life in twenty-nine island towns was called "almost a disaster" in a study made by the University of Puerto Rico Graduate School of Planning. Indications were in the number of homicides, in health conditions, in the number of doctors per population, in the death rate by accident, cancer, diarrhea-enteritis, infant mortality, venereal disease. Yet Puerto Rican conditions are better than those in the Dominican Republic.

Dr. Fernando Pico, a Jesuit priest teaching at the University of Puerto Rico, has a small, graphic story of health care today in the Dominican Republic. 'We were walking through one of the poorer sections of Santo Domingo followed by a crowd of barefoot children. One of them cut his foot on a piece of glass. 'Don't worry,' the other kids told me, 'his mother will tie a dead cockroach on the wound, and he will stop bleeding.'"

In an interview, Nov. 16, 1974, Dr. H. Jack Seiger, a physician and professor of community medicine at the State University of New York at Stony Brook, attests after a visit to Cuba with 17 American delegates that "health care is truly a right under Castro." Every Cuban can obtain "totally free of charge, with no fees, no insurance, no deductibles, or costs of any kind, medical care for everything from simple infection through prolonged cancer treatment." The health system is a complex of "polyclinics" in the city and "outposts" in rural areas. Complicated illnesses are cared for in the larger hospitals where there are modern intensive care units and coronary care units as in American hospitals. They are staffed by the nation's top medical specialists. Infant mortality is the lowest in Latin America, 247 per 1,000 births, roughly the same as in the U.S. Polio, malaria and venereal disease have all been eradicated. Doctors' salaries are set by the government. They are somewhat higher than the salaries of average workers. Doctors are honored and respected members of the society for the work they perform for all in the national service. In fact, the health service in Cuba has been acclaimed by the United Nations as the finest in the hemisphere.

In Puerto Rico and the Dominican Republic if people are sick and poor, they can get attention—hurried attention by harried doctors, after hours of long waiting in the public clinics. It is impossible to get into hospitals without some prepayment. The statistics on doctors and hospital beds in the Dominican Republic indicate how difficult it is for the poor to get adequate health care. There are only 2.7 beds per thousand inhabitants, and only one doctor for every 5,000 inhabitants. Of every 1000 one-year-olds, 38 die before they reach the age of two. Infant mortality is 34 percent. A peasant's life expectancy is only forty years. Differences in education are striking between the people in Cuba and those in her sister islands. In the Dominican Republic, most citizens have only two years of schooling. An Education Department study in Puerto Rico showed that in 1974 high school enrollment in rural areas was only 27 percent of what it should have been: nearly three quarters of the children had dropped out. In urban areas only 57 percent were still in school; an over 40 percent dropout rate. Even at the elementary level, in both urban and rural areas, there was an almost 20 percent dropout rate. The study also found a disparity between town and country schools, both in facilities, buildings and teaching programs. The percentage of the budget assigned to education was 28.5 percent in 1970; it had dropped to 23.6 percent in 1976. Fifteen hundred school jobs could not be filled in 1976 because of loss of funds. School construction in 1973 was $32 million. School construction in 1975 was $6 million.

In the realm of education, Cuba has worked miracles, again attested to by the United Nations. For Castro deeply believes that 'a free man is a well-educated man.' He wiped out illiteracy in three years. In the Dominican Republic, on the other hand, only 38 percent of eligible children even begin school, and 10 percent of these are dropouts after the first year. Since Trujillo's times some vocational schools have been opened. One of them, run by the armed forces, suggests the "vocation" students are training for.

In Puerto Rico, the situation is better, but the dropout rate of students is so high that a majority do not have more than four years of schooling. Many of the schoolhouses, especially in the rural areas, are a complete disgrace—broken down, disreputable buildings without even a decent place to play.

In Cuba, there are free summer camps for children as well as good playgrounds for year-round use. Frank Ramos, the managing editor of the English-language *San Juan Star,* is no radical, but is, like most Puerto Ricans, a man of compassion. Here is how he describes the present school situation in Puerto Rico.

> Whether we want to admit it or not, Puerto Rico is very much a segregated society. The middle and upperclass families live in their urbanizations and send their children to private schools attended by children from similar backgrounds. The poor families remain in their slums and public housing projects, attending public schools that have pretty much the same problems as Pales Matos. While the division is primarily social rather than racial, who would deny that the percentage of dark-skinned persons is much greater among the lowest fifth of the population than it is among the top fifth?
>
> The young people attending schools like Pales Matos are trapped in a labyrinth from which most of them will never escape. Lacking a solid education, most of them will never go to college or learn a trade. Whatever jobs they finally do obtain will probably be low-paying since they lack marketable skills. Ironically, in such a situation a life of crime offers the quickest route of escape from poverty—provided, of course, they aren't caught and sent to jail. . . .
>
> And what about the social implications of our neglect of the public school system? The end result will be an increase in the gap between the "haves" and the "have nots" and a deepening of the divisions that exist in our society. These divisions will be reflected in a rising crime rate and growing friction between the classes. We are sitting on a powderkeg that could explode at any moment.
>
> At one time, I was puzzled by the fences that have been built around some public housing projects, such as Llorens Torres. But it doesn't seem so far-fetched when one takes a deeper look at our society. In a divided and segregated society such as ours, building fences around the neighborhoods of the poor is our way of telling them to keep in their place, inside their ghetto, and leave the rest of society alone. If we have built fences and not walls, its only because we don't want to be too obvious.

14 -:- The Political Situation

The natural resources of the Dominican Republic are controlled in one of two ways. Either foreign investors control them directly, or foreign investors share the control with the Dominican government.

In the first instance, American companies such as Falcon Bridge Nickel Mines and Alcoa exploit vast, extractive concessions of copper, nickel and bauxite. These companies *"have converted [some areas] into autonomous interior states, with police, administration, laws, and ports of their own."*[1] Other resources are government owned. Since Trujillo took over for himself and his family, most industrial corporations have recognized that "whoever runs the state administration and exercises political power controls the economy." But Trujillo's successor controls the country's economy and resources "only to the degree he coordinates his efforts with the second largest investors, the U.S. monopolies, and allows the extreme degree of economic, political and military control which is exercised in Washington." In fact, Washington is said to be "a parallel government" to that of the Dominican Republic.[2]

The U.S. gives help through AID finances to programs "in education, public works, roads, [plumbing, construction of houses,] and electrical energy—for their maintenance as well as their execution." The U.S. Government's method of domination "is to intervene in all processes of government which fall under these headings by means of its right to verify the use of the funds."[3]

U.S. business also has its way of intervening in the affairs of foreign governments. The essence of bourgeois democracy is the belief that governments exist to protect business, so nobody in the U.S. thinks it strange that businessmen finance presidential campaigns.

It is stated by *Claridad*, the 'independence' newspaper, that ITT gave Puerto Rico's Governor Romero Barcelo great financial support, in the same way that it had used its money to affect elections in Chile. During the year before the elections, Barcelo was said to have been coached in Washington for the position. When Secretary of Agriculture Earl Butz was on the island, months preceding the election, he rudely stayed away from a cocktail party given in his honor by then Governor Hernández Colón, and went instead to a party given by Barcelo, in which Butz toasted him as the next governor. There was no doubt which candidate the U.S. was supporting.

The Government Development Bank allowed Puerto Rico to sell bonds at a new low rate once Barcelo was in power. Bank President Mariano Mier said the bond market's growing confidence in the Puerto Rican economy has been evident since immediately after the November elections when Barcelo won. Barcelo had had financial and propaganda support in the newspapers and television from American Big Business, as well as from anti-Castro Cubans. The latter were asking for cabinet posts or other acknowledgements of the part they played in his victory.

Romero Barcelo will try as quickly as possible to take Puerto Rico into statehood. Statehood may be imposed on Puerto Rico, as American citizenship was on its people in 1917. Puerto Rico as a state would be quickly all-Americanized. The island may be rushed into statehood to combat a rising tide of militancy. The *independentistas* are gaining ground among working people, in particular in the labor movement, and U.S. corporations have too much invested in Puerto Rico to allow this trend to continue. Puerto Rico and the Dominican Republic are excellent places for capital investment and are today of great importance in the U.S. economy.

Today, the two principal parties for independence and socialism are the Partido Independentista Puertoriqueña (P.I.P.) and the Partido Socialista Puertorriqueño (P.S.P.). Reuben Berrios, the leader of the P.I.P., believes that independence can be won peacefully, and he is beginning to receive support from sections of the middle class, though the party's slogan is *"Arriba Los Abajos"* (Up With The Downtrodden). Marí Bras, leader of the P.S.P. believes that there can be only a revolutionary solution. He believes with Ché Guevara that "the oppressors themselves impel us to this struggle," and that it is a fight against the institutionalized violence of those who exploit the poor masses of mankind. The P.S.P. general declaration also states: "It is obvious that the national liberation to which we aspire is set within Puerto Rican national territory, the seat of our nation. Yet this liberation cannot be complete until it encompasses the enormous sector of our people living in the United States." The P.S.P. looks to Cuba as its model.

Yet, because at this moment Puerto Rican independentistas do not have sufficient support, the likelihood is they will be ruthlessly crushed, and the island may become the fifty-first state. "Now it looks as if we are on our way to statehood, and this brings a feeling of anxiety to a vast majority of the population, who, I think, do not want statehood," says Attorney Graciano Miranda Marchand, president of the Puerto Rican Bar Association. He believes that *individual* violence on the island which is increasing alarmingly today, is due to this anxiety.

The individual violence can continue without its leading to the organized or even spontaneous mass violence of an insurrection. However, his diagnosis of a general uneasiness on the island is true: an uneasiness accompanying a fatalistic sense of being maneuvered into statehood. Graciano Mirando also notes the presence of police brutality and repression. "I could not say at the present [whether] police brutality responds to the persecution of political minorities or if they tend to persecute those who belong to the subculture of poverty."

The *San Juan Star* gave its endorsement to the present chief of police because he had been a chief for many years in the National Guard, and this made him suitable because "the police are a paramilitary force." Recent findings also showed that a bomb manufactured in police headquarters was found on the following day in the house of an independentista, who was being charged for possessing it.

Ruben Berrios says President Carter is a hypocrite because he preaches human rights to the world while his own government is guilty of some of the greatest violations of these rights. Berrios says further that he favors United Nations supervisors when a plebiscite on Puerto Rico's status is held, not to supervise Puerto Ricans but to "supervise the Americans who are here as an intervention power."

The U.S. boasts that there are free elections in the Dominican Republic. Yet the U.S. Attorney General's Department has been investigating a continuing payoff to the Reformist Party by a subsidiary of the Philip Morris Company: the checks were made out to Balaguer as president of the party. By frustrating Bosch, who came to power to attempt to alleviate conditions, the U.S. is directly responsible for the poverty, starvation, and death of a great number of people in the Dominican Republic.

University of Puerto Rico's Fernando Pico reports: "One of the greatest landholders in a coffee-producing province was campaigning for reelection to the Dominican Senate last May. Before each harvest (he is the major source of credit, at usurious rates, for the local peasants and small farmers), his successful campaign speech was 'Vote for whomever you please. Just bear this in mind. If I'm not re-elected, I'll not lend a cent to anybody in this place for the next ten years. I'm rich enough not to have to do anything for the rest of my life." In that province, whenever the attempt is made to form a credit cooperative, the national police find occasion to shoot at the organizers' homes.

"Alongside the frontier with Haiti the military are kings. An officer summons a campesino to the barracks: 'You are under arrest.' 'But I haven't done anything, sir.' 'Yes, you have; we are just finding an illegal weapon in your possession.' The officer opens his desk drawer, picks up a knife and places it in the campesino's hand. That night the officer forces his attentions on his prisoner's wife."

Although newspapers, including the leftist *La Noticia*, publish daily without any prior censorship, from time to time they are reminded none too subtly that there are limits to the government's tolerance. This was the case when *La Noticia* was shut down for several weeks after publishing a series of articles that displeased Balaguer. Four newsmen in the Dominican Republic were arrested on trumped-up charges, and held virtually incommunicado twelve days. Their lawyer was not even shown details of the charges against them. It is still the case with the radio stations, which are not allowed to interview certain politicians, including José Francisco Pena Gómez of the Dominican Revolutionary Party, or even to read the statements which these politicians give the newspapers. In a country with an appallingly high rate of illiteracy, the newspapers reach only an elite. Radio, however, reaches the masses, so the radio is more controlled.

Juan Bosch says that his Dominican Liberation Party, formed in 1973, participated in the 1978 elections, but only as a means of strengthening the party and making its point of view known. No one had any illusions of winning against Balaguer.

Like the citizens of the Dominican Republic, Puerto Ricans suffer under U.S. domination. But Puerto Rico's case seems especially sad because this island, unlike the Dominican Republic, is not free even in name. Under the long history of U.S. rule, Puerto Ricans have been denied their own language, their own flag, the control of their own flag, the control of their own natural resources. They have received insufficient education and health care, and have been forced to suffer the social and environmental problems of industrialization without receiving any of its benefits.

Puerto Rico's commonwealth status—neither free nor state—invites comparison with its neighbors in the British Commonwealth. Long ago, the smallest islands of the West Indies entered into a free and voluntary association with Britain, as "associated states." By this agreement, Britain took over the defense and foreign policy of these islands, and gave grant aid in return. The larger of these islands later chose to be independent. If Trinidad and Tobago, and the Bahamas can claim independence without fear, surely Puerto Rico, double the size of any of them, and already well industrialized, could do the same.

President Osvaldo Dorticos of Cuba considers Puerto Rico "a Latin American nation subject to U.S. colonial domination and not as an U.S. internal matter." *Claridad,* the daily newspaper of the Puerto Rican Socialist party, predicts that the Third World forces in the United Nations will support the motion for independence for Puero Rico with increasing vigor.

As the former colonies of Britain have obtained independence and seats in the United Nations and in the Organization of American States, they are gaining power in the Western Hemisphere. With unity, they can have effect in these bodies where there has traditionally been a one-nation, one-vote rule. Even tiny Grenada with only one hundred thousand inhabitants can make its voice heard, if its vote is pooled in a Caribbean united front. Only Puerto Rico, despite its size, is not heard in these community forums. The United States speaks for it, although North American interests and Puerto Rican interests are opposed to each other rather than coinciding.

"The law of the British Parliament applies locally with the consent of the specific associated states," Dr. Calderon Cruz of the University of Puerto Rico writes. He emphasizes that "British policy allows the . . . overseas associated areas—St. Kitts-Nevis, Dominica and St. Lucia, to accept or reject London-created legislature." Puerto Rico has no such freedom or privilege.

Puerto Rico is beginning to have some notice taken of its condition by outside countries, often in places where previously the island was completely unknown. Paris' *Le Monde,* for instance, carried two long articles on the island, mentioning the tourists' sumptuous hotels less than a stone's throw from the misery and the poverty of the Puerto Rican slums. Despite election results that seem to prove the opposite, *Le Monde* notes, the desire to remain Puerto Rican is strong throughout the whole populace. "It is not by accident," *Le Monde* says, "that ex-Governor Hernández Colón once said, 'All things taken into account, he would prefer independence to assimilation.' " The magazine also comments that there is "fear and reservation" in the U.S. towards "a distinct ethnic community, more volatile and less sure of assimilation than the others."

An international conference on Puerto Rico held in September 1975 in Cuba had seventy-five countries participating through three hundred delegates. It was presided over by Beatrix Allende, widow of the late Chilean President, and unanimously called for independence for the island. The representatives literally came from all over the world: from Latin America, Europe, Asia and Africa. Former Secretary of State Kissinger called the conference "an unfriendly act" and totally unwarranted interference in U.S. domestic affairs.

Antonio Fernos Lopez-Cepero, a former director of the Civil Rights Commission and a professor of law, dissented from the view of Ford, Kissinger, William Rogers and Patrick Moynihan who in 1976 were orchestrating the theme that the status of Puerto Rico is an "internal," a "domestic" affair. He pointed out that the Treaty of Paris of 1898 is an international contract, not a domestic document. He further pointed out that Canada and India while still colonies of Great Britain had become members of the League of Nations. All were colonies of colonial powers: none were domestic territories of those powers in the international sense. Another point he made is that the U.N. Charter is a treaty, signed by the United States, and as such part of the supreme law of the land, according to the Constitution of the United States. Under U.N. law until 1953, the U.S. had to submit an annual report on Puerto Rico—Puerto Rico was a subject of international law. Though the U.S. no longer makes that submission, the U.N. in 1953 recognized Puerto Rico as an autonomous state. But an autonomous status of one country as regards another is not in international law a domestic relationship. In Cuba's 1967 plebiscite the opinion of Puerto Rico's integration into the U.S. was defeated. The U.N. constantly reaffirms that the question of Puerto Rico's status is an international one, not a domestic concern of the U.S.

The U.S. was jubilant that the question on Puerto Rican status in the U.N. in 1976 was postponed for a year. But it was only a postponement. "There is no question but that Puerto Rico is a colony under international law," says former North-South Director, Roland Perusse.

Though militancy is growing in Puerto Rico, there is not a pre-revolutionary situation. In the Dominican Republic, on the other hand, there is widespread unrest and a smoldering anger among large sections of the population. Even the clergy has been affected. In an open letter, young seminarians of the Colegio Santo Tomás de Aquinas wrote with bitterness: "The Church cannot declare a system like capitalism holy—God is the father of all men including the communists—Dr. Balaguer may do [something] in the name of the unjust and anti-Evangelical imperialism of money, officially defended by the United States, but never in the name of the God of the Gospel." They refer to a statement of the Second Vatican Council:
"Whatever offends human dignity such as subhuman living conditions, arbitrary arrests, deportation, slavery, prostitution, or degrading working conditions which reduce the laborer to the rank of a mere instrument of profit, with no respect for the freedom and responsibility of the human person; all these practices and others like them are in themselves insulting. They degrade human civilization, dishonor their authors more than their victims, and are totally contrary to the honor owed their Creator."

The heads of the Catholic Church in the Dominican Republic also lambast both the government and the private sectors of society for the widespread corruption, which they say has reached unspeakable levels. The authors of a pastoral letter included the archbishop of Santo Domingo and the country's six other bishops. They cited as part of the pervading corruption, the business of prostitution, illegal sale of drugs and blackmail. The document stated "corruption invades private and public life; the administration of justice and politics; commerce, services and industry; the professional sector and the state administrative sector and the lower, middle and upper classes."

This corruption is directly linked to U.S. financial and political domination of the island. The revolution was defeated twelve years ago, but the causes of it and the feelings beneath the surface remain.

With the United States, private business has inextricable involvements with foreign policy. In foreign policy, the members of Congress essentially stand together and operate in the interests of big business in the country's overseas ventures. Today "empire" means more than the holding of colonies as it did in the nineteenth century. It means the holding of economic and political power by supernational conglomerates and multi-national corporations. Their power center is within the major country of their operation—the country of their headquarters—in this case the U.S. Like a giant octopus, they reach their tentacles out in many directions; reaching out ever further in capitalism's need for increasing expansion.

In the colonial country (Puerto Rico) or the country subjected to their trade and economic expansion and investment (the Dominican Republic), the multinational corporations and their home governments, who represent their interests, have need of a national upper and middle class who will provide law and order, that is provide security for foreign properties and investments. The local bourgeoisie is forced out of any competition with American companies. Their role is limited solely to that of surrogates, clerks. In this way, they have no interests hostile to their masters. They exist only to carry out U.S. desires. The only sections then of Puerto Ricans and Dominicans to oppose the foreign power are the working people in the city, the rural workers, and the intellectuals. There is constant propaganda, however, to fool the people into thinking that existing conditions are in their interests. When propaganda fails, repression comes into play. The national guards and the police in each country are specially trained to fulfil this role.

In Puerto Rico, when the Nationalist party revolted, the local national guard was able to take care of the situation. In recent strikes, it has been called upon to do the same. The CIA and the FBI are also there always to help the police play a similar part in harassing or imprisoning the present Puerto Rican independentistas, especially the Partido Socialista Puertorriqueña (P.S.P.), the present revolutionary party. Anti-Castro Cubans are also being used, as in the case of the recent assassination of the son of Marti Bras, leader of the P.S.P., and they have been used in the numerous bombings of the party's headquarters and homes of party members.

In the Dominican Republic in 1965, when local forces were insufficient to control the revolutionary situation, the U.S. used its own armed forces from bases in the States and Puerto Rico. The revolution was crushed and Balaguer put into power. "In the background of the Dominican picture, behind the political divisions and changing foreground is the U.S. presence, implacably opposed to abandoning its domination."[4]

Carlos Mariá Gutierrez suggests:

> If the model of the Puerto Rican Free Associated State was the answer of Rooseveltian liberalism to the threat of decolonization, the military-industrial complex which runs U.S. society today intends to convert Santo Domingo into a model of the only type of ally the new foreign policy will tolerate in Latin America . . . the juridicial fiction of sovereignty, total economic occupation, complete U.S. control over the centers of military and political power . . . the drastic elimination of every possible social change by means of the direct and bloody suppression of any and every revolutionary outbreak."

The U.S. will allow no more Cubas in the Caribbean, if it can prevent them. "Trujilloism" survives and is gaining ground. It has changed names—but Trujillo's conception remains as a political idea, as a system of exploiting the people, and as an instrument of a U.S. domination that is not afraid to show its presence. The CIA is ubiquitous; and fascist bands operate everywhere with government and CIA support. 'Terror, but efficient terror,' U.S. controlled, seems to be the motto.

In 1961, when the regime found itself headless, Balaguer was provisionally confirmed in the presidency by the CIA and the U.S. ambassador. He was elected president in 1966 under an electoral system marked by fraud and the coercion of police and CIA. In 1970, he had himself reelected with U.S. approval for another four years. He is still in power, and will remain so as long as he does Washington's bidding or is not overthrown by revolution. Juan Bosch says, "Here there are no elections, only masquerades."

Under Trujillo, there were half-a-million of his opponents executed during his regime of thirty-two years. Under Balaguer, there have been by conservative estimates "more than 2 000 political prisoners assassinated in the past five years." The Policia Nacional controlled by the CIA has instigated a White terror. The terror functions with an efficiency of technology perfected by the United States. The U.S. wants no possibility that a revolutionary movement will be able to raise again. "In reality," one Dominican leader says, "we are under the strict control of the Pentagon. . . . It has complete control over all Dominican armed forces." The Pentagon has also seen that the army has been purged of all elements that might become subversive. They do not want another situation like that in Portugal. More than one half of the Dominican budget is expended by the army. Even one of the few technical schools built in recent years is run by the army.

A council set up after Trujillo, but before Balaguer was put in power, set up an investment guarantee which gave the U.S. the right to impose policies in regard to those investments. "The council," writes John Gerrasi in his book *The Great Fear in Latin America*, "gave orders that all 'disturbing' Leftists be rounded up; literally hundreds were deported." Then the jails were immediately filled with new inmates and again the Dominican Republic was clamped under a rigid, vicious, repressive dictatorship—all in the glorious name of saving the country from Communism. A new fascist U.S.-controlled dictatorship was set up.

The Dominican experience is duplicated in almost all of the old Spanish empire. "Everywhere in Latin America a large, powerful segment of the bourgeoisie lives from imperialism. Think of those in the export and import houses, the lawyers and the accountants working for the foreign mines and factories, the hotel and restaurant owners (or managers) dependent on tourism, the storekeepers selling foreign goods, [the executives working for U.S. firms]. And everywhere, the bourgeoisie is threatened from below and could not maintain its position without imperialism." These managers and professionals support not their own country, but the United States. They are quite ready for the CIA or the U.S. military to help them keep their positions of affluence. They are the anti-Cuban exiles. They are the upper and middle classes who helped overthrow the elected governments of Juan Bosch in Santo Domingo and Allende in Chile. Nationalists [in Latin America] now know that winning power through elections is useless. They have had the example of Guatemala in 1954, of Brazil in 1964, of the Dominican Republic in 1967, and of Chile in 1975. The American government supporting the multinationals, and with the expenditure of millions of dollars, or with marines, has overturned democratically elected presidents and their governments in the recent past and is ready to do so again.

Since Columbus' time, Puerto Rico has always had military value. Puerto Ricans were used to fight Spain's battles in Latin America; and the United States' battles in Europe, Japan, Korea, and Vietnam. U.S. bases are now concentrated at Roosevelt Roads on the island. These are as vital to the United States in any confrontation with Russia as they were in previous wars. Even without any direct confrontation, Puerto Ricans could be used as pawns. There is now a stepped-up recruitment of Puerto Ricans into the armed services. In a period of high unemployment, it is being effective. In fact, the U.S. Armed Forces are the largest employers in Puerto Rico today.

Strategically too, Puerto Rico is as important today as it was in Spanish times. Professor Crassweller, in a recent book, says: "America has a crucial need for continued use of Caribbean waters and certain adjacent land and island areas for defense purposes." Further, he points out their value in regard to the Panama Canal. Its "military significance, although altered and diminished by modern developments, still remains." The present uneasy situation in Panama, where the old treaty of 1903 has been changed, could well affect the Spanish Antilles. Ten thousand soldiers are stationed there, and since the canal cannot be defended against nuclear attack or Panamanian guerilla warfare, "the only explanation for so many U.S. troops is that they constitute a strike force for intervention in some Latin American country."

When this force is considered together with the force at Roosevelt Roads in Puerto Rico, the base at Guantánamo, and the army under Pentagon control in the Dominican Republic, it can be seen how strong the area is militarily, and what strength Puerto Rico or the Dominican Republic would have to face in the event of a revolution, or Cuba in the event of an invasion. In fact, Crassweller writes, "In the Caribbean area . . . the port facilities . . . would assume particular significance if possible future diplomatic moves vis-à-vis Cuba should affect the status of Guantánamo, and the nature of the security interests can be simply stated: no part of the Caribbean may safely be permitted, through conquest or subversion, *or even through orderly process** to serve as a military power base hostile to the United States." No more Cubas are to be allowed. Puerto Rico would not be permitted to be independent even if the majority voted for it except under strictly controlled conditions. After Angola, it is possible to imagine Cuban and U.S. troops fighting on Puerto Rican soil, the former to help a revolutionary movement; the latter to crush it.

"There are also other dimensions to the strategic value of the islands today as part of a U.S. undersea surveillance. The entire area must be judged of considerable importance for space programs of the United States."[5]

The Spanish Antilles are therefore of great military value to the U.S., though when the term "common defense" is used in regard to

*Author's emphasis

Puerto Rico, it is only the "crucial need" of America that is involved. Nevertheless, Puerto Ricans have to give up part of their land for American military bases, and give up their lives in wars in which they themselves have no commitments.

The Dominican Republic is equally important as Puerto Rico in this overall strategy of the United States: to keep free the shipping lanes for its commerce; to prevent the penetration of any other power in the area; and to suppress the rise of revolutionary forces. This strategy applies not only to the Caribbean but also to all of Latin America. "Latin America's social and economic structure is decadent, corrupt, immoral, and generally unsalvageable. That a change is coming is obvious. That it will come about through revolution is certain. That revolution entails the possibility of violence is unavoidable."[6] The U.S. is preparing for this eventuality. But from Latin American peons is heard the cry: "Some day we too will get our Castro."

A South American said, "Cuba is developing in a big way, and this in the long run is good for all the other countries of Latin America." He predicted "there would soon be a big rush to do business with Cuba." A change of attitude was seen in the *New York Times* reporting on March 22, 1976. It stated "in the last two years Cuba has gained considerable influence among the small Republics of the Caribbean. . . . The principal friends . . . are Guyana and Jamaica. In addition, administration officials believe that the younger generation of political leaders throughout the Caribbean view Cuba as the most successful model of social and economic development in their experience." For a while it seemed that the United States might begin a new relationship with the island. Several senators visited Cuba and urged a modification of attitude. This changed again with Cuba's help to the revolutionary forces in Angola. It is changing again under President Carter's leadership, though the thaw is likely to be gradual.

Guantánamo Naval Base was originally justified on the basis of common friendship and common defense. Neither of these two reasons any longer exists. It is difficult to know by what right the United States still keeps a large base there. Castro spurns the bargain rent of $4000 a year the U.S. pays for Guantánamo. He has never accepted the rental check. The base is there against the will of its people, and the United States is not paying one cent for it.

Americans believe they have free elections. What they have is a choice between a Tweedledum Republican and a Tweedledee Democrat who both have the backing of big financial interests and are therefore beholden to them. U.S. officials work in the interests not of the people but of multinational corporations. Americans say there are no "free" elections in Cuba, and so no democracy. Yet Castro carefully explains to the people what he and the government are attempting to do; what the goals are. The American people have been taught by Watergate and by Dr. Kissinger's diplomacy that they are kept in ignorance or lied to in all matters of policy, matters which nevertheless vitally affect their daily lives.

No one who has ever been to Cuba doubts the people's support of Fidel and the Revolution. It is still only 20 years old but has accomplished wonders. Castro's long dialogues took place in the beginning. Now his speeches are shorter, less necessary. Meanwhile local elections are taking place and the people are being represented. A new Constitution has been instituted after four months in which the whole population had been involved in discussions of its points.

In replies to statements that Puerto Rico is a colony of the United States, the U.S. avers that Cuba is a colony of the USSR. Though dependency on the USSR is of great importance, however, it does not make Cuba a colony of the USSR, as Puerto Rico is a colony of the U.S. Cuba can trade freely with other countries. She is not forced to use Russian ships. Every law promulgated by the Cuban legislature cannot be reversed or overthrown by Russian edict. Russian statesmen cannot arrive and announce, "We own you by right of conquest. Your island is our war booty," as Senator Henry Jackson has done in Puerto Rico. Cuban economic interests have not given place to those of Russia, as American interests have supplanted those of Puerto Rico and the Dominican Republic. There is no overriding Soviet court in Cuba, where all cases are tried in Russian and not Spanish. (In San Juan, English is the official language in the Federal Court.) Cuban children are not forced to learn Russian, and berated that they will not get good jobs unless they do so. Cubans are not subject to arrest by Russian secret police, but the FBI and CIA make arrests in Puerto Rico. Cubans have their own currency. They have their own stamps. The factories and industries in Cuba are not Russian-owned. The Russian influence is not all-pervasive in Cuba, as is American influence in Puerto Rico and the Dominican Republic. Neither does it put Cuba back into a position similar to that of pre-revolutionary days with the USSR taking the place of Americans. No Russians own any part of the island of Cuba. No Russians own its industries or its banks.

Cuba has had to undertake a debt, but the debt is not such that just paying the interest on it will stand in the way of Cuba's self-development. Despite the hardships, despite the incredible odds against it, Cuba made its own way, went its own path, held its national head high. Cuba is represented in the United Nations and has her own representatives in other international bodies. She is not represented in other international bodies or regional bodies by the USSR. Fidel says: "The Russians don't own an acre of Cuba. The Yankees used to own Cuba."

Cuba could not look to Russia or China or the European communist countries for a model. For what she is, an island in the Caribbean with a history and development like none of the above mentioned countries, she has had to make a new Cuban society adapted to her special individual needs. "There can be no model for the construction of socialism which can merely be transferred from one country to another, but each experiment in socialism is, however, a source of very valuable lessons for other countries that are also setting out on the road to socialism."[7] This is especially applicable to Puerto Rico and to the Dominican Republic. For the situation before the revolution in Cuba was in many respects similar to those in her sister islands: poverty, hunger, sickness, lack of schooling and housing, unemployment, vice, repression, one justice for the rich and one for the poor, exploitation and overall American domination. The Antilles' peoples are similar, with a common language and common roots, centuries old. They have similarities of common heritage: Indian, Spanish and Negro. Perhaps they will achieve a common future.

15 -:- Future Possibilities

What is the possibility that Puerto Rico and the Dominican Republic will follow Cuba's road? At the moment Puerto Rico seems to be headed toward statehood—forced on her by the U.S. and probably unwittingly accepted by her people. It would be national suicide. In the Dominican Republic, on the other hand, the fact that the people are more severely repressed than in Puerto Rico indicates that they have a greater revolutionary fervor.

If Puerto Rico does choose statehood, the choice will be made through the electoral process, and will seem an acceptance by the people of permanent union with the United States. It is impossible to imagine any Latin American country willingly choosing to become part of the United States. In fact, other Latin American countries already look down on Puerto Rico because of her dependence upon the U.S. The tragedy is that only when the move is irreversible will the people of Puerto Rico realize what becoming the fifty-first state will mean. At the moment they are gulled by so many false enticements, such as food stamps, that large numbers might be grievously misled.

There is now an excellent possibility that oil and natural gas will be found off the north coast of Puerto Rico. The large oil companies are already bidding for rights to explore. But an unexpected factor has entered the picture: Article 36 of the proposed "Convention of the Law of the Sea." By this article, the rights "to the resources of a territory whose people have not yet attained either full independence or some other self-governing status recognized by the United Nations, or a territory under foreign or colonial domination" —belong to the people who live there. The U.S. considers this article as now drafted unacceptable, for it obviously gives Puerto Rico full rights to the offshore oil. The U.S. wants that oil, so the article is likely to be another factor for hurrying Puerto Rico into statehood.

A State Department official writes, "We really cannot leave this matter [of status] entirely to a process of the Puerto Ricans' 'figuring out what they want'. . . . There are also strategic interests. . . . It is clear that the island's political status must be consonant with the Defense Department's legitimate requirements." The above writer "confess[es] to being impressed with the logic and clarity of the arguments presented by Puerto Rican supporters of statehood," but he does note that "a visitor to Puerto Rico is constantly struck by the Hispanic nature of the island and its inhabitants. It is more than a question of speaking Spanish." He disagrees with the view of Romero Barcelo "that the U.S. needs a Spanish-speaking state." The State Department writers says: "It would clearly require a generous measure of vision and non-dogmatism on the part of the U.S. Congress to acknowledge the uniqueness of Puerto Rico and be willing to provide for the preservation of its cultural outcome if it were to become a state."[1] Such an attitude is not only unlikely, but certain not to prevail. Romero Barcelo and ex-Governor Luis Ferré are therefore duping their supporters when they say Puerto Rico would be a *jibaro* state. Senator Henry Jackson categorically denies the possibility of Puerto Rico being allowed to be other than an English-speaking state or allowed any special cultural rights. In the U.S. Congress, both Democratic and Republican members are almost totally committed to statehood for the island.

In the United Nations, Cuba has averred that Puerto Rico is a colony of the U.S., and has found support for that viewpoint in the General Assembly. This worldwide feeling will undoubtedly hasten the United States' disposition to make the island safely into a state. Senator Jackson is prepared to proceed if an election, which would include American residents and anti-Castro Cubans, gives Romero Barcelo even 51 percent of the votes in a referendum on statehood. This means he and many of his colleagues are prepared to make Puerto Rico a state, even if half the population is against it, if those who vote for it are foreigners and the wealthy, and if its support is heavily financed by American business. In fact, statehood would never find support by more than a minority of Puerto Ricans, whatever an American-supported election might suggest. 'Commonwealthers' and independentistas constitute a majority. But unfortunately, it is greatly in the U.S.'s advantage to make Puerto Rico a state. That move would end discussion of the problem in the U.N.

It would also preclude later secession, according to the precedent established in the Civil War.

At the moment, American residents in Puerto Rico cannot help but feel they are foreigners. Their malice, even their hatred of Puerto Ricans, is shown in their constant letters of complaint in the *San Juan Star*. With the island a state, they would feel secure, as they feel secure in Arizona and Texas, California and New Mexico, which the U.S. took from the Mexicans. With fear gone and the sense of being foreigners gone, thousands of Americans would flock to the lovely island to live, as they now flock to Florida. In their place, thousands more Puerto Ricans would be forced to migrate to the States to live in slums. Puerto Ricans would find their Congress being filled by Americans. Puerto Ricans would be barred from places in their own country, as Blacks are barred in the South, as Mexicans are barred in country that once belonged to them in the Southwest.

Puerto Ricans are now encouraged to believe they would all be much richer if the island were a state. Romero Barcelo has a booklet entitled "Statehood is for the Poor." His theme is that the well-to-do would have to pay federal taxes, which they do not now do, while the poor would obtain far greater federal aid. The question then is why are all the rich for statehood? As for the poor being better off, they are not told of the great poverty that exists today in the U.S. Congressman Michael Harrington writes: "A crucial contemporary misunderstanding is that the America of 1970s has given an adequate standard of living to the majority of its people. . . . That is simply not the case." Paul M. Sweezy, editor of the *Monthly Review,* writes: "You don't see much [malnutrition and hunger] in the United States today, but plenty of congressional and other hearings have brought out in the last couple of years, that it exists, and it exists on a national scale." Robert Sherrill, a free-lance journalist, writes: "It isn't true that nobody starves in America."

With statehood, Puerto Ricans would only join their brothers in the states, at the bottom of the economic ladder with Negroes and Chicanos, poverty-stricken in ghettos, living in rat-infested houses, suffering unemployment that is high and social acceptance that is low. Their condition, bad as it is now, would worsen. And most heartbreakingly of all, they would be treated as third-class citizens in their own land. Even now, all the top jobs in Puerto Rico go to Americans, and this tendency would be greatly increased. The people's hopelessness that Hernández Colón so eloquently described would also increase. Though they would speak their own language at home, as Spanish is spoken in Mexican houses in the Southwest, they would have to speak English in schools, in the courts, in the offices. Children would be handicapped in their own schools where they would have to learn a foreign tongue. The people's sense of Hispanic identity would be shattered, their *dignidad* made a matter of mockery. Puerto Ricans living in the States and Mexicans living in what was their country (as well as Blacks and American Indians) can testify to the sort of treatment the poor Puerto Rican will receive if the island becomes the fiifty-first state. Yet that is the present danger.

Romero Barcelo is governor of San Juan owing to the support he obtained in the last election from Americans living on the island. (One year's residency is all that is required for voting, even if the American is then planning to return to the United States and never see Puerto Rico again.) He also received the support of all the anti-Castro Cubans whom Puerto Rico was obliged by the U.S. to take in.

Maurice Ferré, a Puerto Rican Mayor of Miami, and brother of ex-governor of Puerto Rico Luis Ferré, attended the inauguration of Romero Barcelo, as the representative of President Carter. A few months earlier he had attended the Congress of the Bay of Pigs Fighters Association Assault Brigade 2505, veterans of the Cuban invasion of 1961. This group has been heavily financed by the CIA, according to *The Nation,* March 19, 1977, and been trained as an army of gunmen and explosives technicians. With CIA funds curtailed, many of these men are now unemployed, and are creating a reign of terror in Miami unprecedented even in comparison with that of the Chicago gangsters of the '30s. These trained gunmen are openly supported by Maurice Ferré.

They and their friends also operate outside the U.S., and independentistas in Puerto Rico claim that the anti-Castro Cubans are responsible for the terrorism directed against their members on the island. These Cubans, almost universally disliked by Puerto Ricans, claimed in the English-language newspaper that their support had given Romero Barcelo his victory, and that they should therefore be given positions of power within the government. They already exercise considerable influence in high positions in the television and radio industry as well as in the advertising agencies on the island. They are all 'statehooders.' Their power, money and numbers in any plebiscite could easily be the deciding factor in Puerto Rico's future. Certainly, they, together with American residents, gave Romero Barcelo his victory. Thus Puerto Rico's status may finally be decided by non-Puerto Ricans used by the United States to achieve its end of imposing statehood on the island. Puerto Rico has no say in the number of exile Cubans allowed into Puerto Rico. This is decided by the U.S. immigration authorities.

Muñoz Marin says, "I identify as a Puerto Rican. You [a woman reporter for the Star] as an 'Americano'." But that identification with the island is not the significant factor it should be in the voting booth.

Romero Barcelo, when campaigning, assured the people that the question of statehood was not an issue, and that he would deal with Puerto Rico's social and economic problems. However, President Ford, before leaving office, introduced the question for the new governor. It was a well-orchestrated action, though Ford forgot to include the necessary political statement that Puerto Rican wishes would be taken into account. He similarly forgot to take Puerto Rican sensibilities into account when he arranged for a summit meeting of heads of states in Puerto Rico without informing Hernàndez Colón, the governor at the time, that he had done so. Romero Barcelo hastened to cover Ford's mistake by assuring the Puerto Rican people that statehood would only come after they had expressed the desire for it. In the meantime, he said, he would 'educate' them on its benefits.

A "Statehood Never" group has been formed to counter a new "Forward Statehood" group. Statehood Never hopes to bring together all those opposed to statehood. The organizer, attorney Francisco Hernandez Vargas, says his group is vitally necessary since "the annexionist forces, well-organized and well-led, are determined to bring Puerto Rico in any way possible to Statehood, cost what it may." He says of the present administration, "Every government office is a center of indoctrination and propaganda."

Governor Carlos Romero Barcelo took up a joint position with the United States in the United Nations in 1977. Romero's claim, that Puerto Rico can have "self-determination" any time it wishes, counters the General Assembly's claim that Puerto Rico is a colony. Romero's statement will hasten the time for calling for a new plebiscite on the status question of the island.

Puerto Rico will hold a status plebiscite before 1980 if Congress passes a bill offering the island statehood, former Governor Louis Ferré says. Romero Barcelo stated that "if the U.N. should rule the current status unacceptable then we may have to go for a plebiscite between statehood and independence." He considers a majority vote plus one for statehood sufficient. There is plenty of U.S. money and U.S. and Cuban support on the island to see this vote is attained.

But American public opinion also has to be taken into account. According to a Gallup Poll taken after Ford's statement 59 percent of Americans are in favor of Puerto Rican statehood, 21 perecnt against, and 20 percent do not know. A *Daily Mirror* poll showed the percentage in favor to be much less, and seems more plausible given the general discriminatory attitudes against Puerto Ricans.

Statehood seems the solution which the United Staes will adopt for Puerto Rico, despite opposition in the island, and of both the right and left in the States. The U.S. also has the alternative of giving independence to Puerto Rico, but only under the leadership of such a man as Romero Barcelo. The situation would then be the same as in the Dominican Republic under Balaguer. This would leave the United States military and the U.S. corporations in control as they are now. The precondition would be that independence would be tied to 'free enterprise' and the 'free world', and not to socialism and the Third World.

President Carter might consider endorsing Puerto Rico's independence under a dictator, were the U.N. to designate Puerto Rico as a colony. Such a move would satisfy liberals in the States as well as conservatives who would otherwise decry "a beggar state," the state of an alien people, that would be added to the Union. All the U.S. investments on the island would be secure. To many islanders, this option would seem better than the irrevocability of statehood. If the granting of statehood runs into strong opposition from racist, conservative forces in the Congress, as was the case over the Panama Canal Treaty, then Puerto Rico might be allowed to become a Republic, but only under the same conditions as now exist in the Dominican Republic. The U.S. would then still control the island economically and politically. The U.S. will never willingly allow a socialist republic.

Romero Barcelo downplays the effects of statehood by saying it would not represent a major change for Puerto Rico except to give Puerto Ricans full voting rights as U.S. citizens. The Puerto Rican culture and Spanish language would remain. He acknowledges that "there is always a possibility of political violence if Puerto Rico becomes a state" but says "we cannot allow the will of the majority to be thwarted."

A tense political situation has existed in Puerto Rico since December 1975, when Castro at the First Congress of the Cuban Communist Party reaffirmed the closeness of the two islands. "The flags of Cuba and Puerto Rico are one and the same—we will continue to help Puerto Ricans fight for liberation". Two months later, a resolution put forward by Cuba recommended that the case of Puerto Rico's colonialism be put before the U.N. President Ford replied by stating that Cuba must stop fomenting revolution in Puerto Rico. At the same time, the CIA and FBI stepped up their recruiting of Puerto Ricans, and the National Guard also opened a new recruiting drive on the island. In *El Mundo*, the government-supporting daily newspaper, an editorial read, "Regarding Puerto Rico, if armed revolt were to occur here, as threatened by different radicalized, proindependence elements, there is a possibility that those dissidents could invoke the aid of the Cuban dictator." (This was after the Cuban troops had helped Angola to victory.) Juan M. Garcia Pascalaqua, a lawyer, and former Forteleza aide, writes the "spectre of civil war, fought on Puerto Rican soil by U.S. and Cuban troops, hung over the island like a somber shroud."

If an attempt to thrust statehood on the island is made, the militants will fight both in Puerto Rico and the States to prevent it, and Cuba will help. Help is also likely to come from revolutionaries in Latin America and the Dominican Republic and from non-Puerto Rican militants in the U.S.: countries of the Third World might give aid too .

Speaking before the Foreign Relations Committee, José A. Cabaranes, ex-administrator of the Office of the Commonwealth in Washington, D.C., and a supporter of the present commonwealth status, was nevertheless forced to utter this warning about the dangers the U.S. might encounter in trying to make Puerto Rico a state.

> "In Puerto Rico there will always be a very substantial minority, perhaps ultimately a majority, who will resist to the utmost the idea of complete political assimilation to the United States. We have only recently seen some of the unfortunate and regrettable repercussions of the Puerto Rican political dilemma with bombings in this city and New York City. You may rest assured the problems that the United States will confront when the Congress receives a petition for statehood will be very much more serious than those we have already faced."

The petition could lead on the one hand to the loss of the semblance of democracy, to repression such as today exists in the Dominican Republic. Or it could lead on the other hand to a quickening revolutionary movement and perhaps to civil war.

For the Dominican Republic, the situation, though worse physically at the moment, offers greater hope for the future. Given an opportunity for revolution, the discontented forces, which are widespread under the surface, could suitably respond. And the Dominican Republic is not a colony; it is an independent republic that has fought again and again over a hundred years for its independence. There is wider support of the revolutionary movement there than in Puerto Rico. On the other hand, repressive regimes are not easily overthrown, as the long years of Batista and Trujillo show.

"The Balaguer administration's . . . failure to find approval among more liberal and radical younger elements of the public [and its absence of reform have] resulted not only in a wide degree of radicalization among a significant segment of the public, but also in a growing disenchantment with representative democracy."[2]

Juan Bosch, disillusioned about any electoral solution says: "Without the least doubt, all of us who have honestly fought to organize the Dominican people by democratic means have been crazy or deluded."

All the several parties of the left—The Partido Communista Dominica, the Moviemiento Popular Dominico, the Partido Revolutionario Dominica—all are convinced as the Partido Socialista Puertorriqueño that the way for each of the islands to solve its problems is the revolutionary, socialist way, the Cuban way. All completely distrust their own bourgeoisie who are not even nationalistic but are prepared to play a subservient role to the United States, as they did to Spain. One Dominican leader says: "Throughout its history, our bourgeoisie has always been ready to do so. It is more collaborative now than ever before, obliged by political as well as economic factors. I believe the same is true throughout Latin America."[3]

Recently, Trujillo's son was living in an apartment just above that of the Dominican Consolate in San Juan, where it was supposed that he was gathering supporters for a come-back. Possibly he is being groomed to take over the government when Balaguer retires. But even in the present situation the Dominican Republic is still basically Trujilloist. It is governed by terror, with groups of administration thugs roaming the streets without restraint, to wreak havoc where they will, and create a pervasive atmosphere of fear among the populace. Since the people, especially the young, no longer believe in the democratic system, knowing the elections are fraudulent, a revolutionary situation can be said to exist. The U.S. is regarded as the enemy as well as its supported dictators. Professor Crassweller says, "No one likes to have the troops of another country come in, and in this sense the 1965 intervention was unpopular." But he says it prevented the revolution from succeeding in 1965.

According to Tad Szulc, "The dispatch of U.S. troops and their interposition between Dominican forces represented an interruption of the 1965 revolution, but not its resolution. Next time it will be more violent and more anti-American than in 1965."

In regard to the press, the situation in the Dominican Republic is similar to that in Cuba prior to the Revolution. There is either little news reported in the U.S.,, or the news is completely distorted. Juan Bosch, in an interview with Carlos Mariá Gutierrez said that "the isolation was part United States' plan that the world should not know what is happening in the Dominican Republic. . . . We all know that the A.P. and U.P.I. news services are servants of U.S. policy." Recent findings by a House Committee have disclosed that many correspondents are in fact not journalists at all, but CIA agents.

A successful revolution in the Dominican Republic would have in its first years of adjustment, an easier task than Castro had in Cuba.

> "There is an economic problem unique to the Dominican Republic. When Trujillo was killed in 1961 he owned, directly or through others, a preponderant share of the entire Dominican economy. The Dominican Republic has the highest proportion of government [ownership] in the hemisphere, except for Cuba."[4]

Many of the country's assets, therefore, are still in government hands, so that in this way new economic planning would be easier. The socialist government would immediately own a great part of the country's productive forces.

65 percent of Dominican Republic's commercial activities are tied to the U.S., as was the case with Cuba before the revolution. Nevertheless Trujillo took into his own hands for his own personal gain a great number of industries. These mostly still belong to the state. They could have been easily taken over in the 1965 revolution, as they were in a sense already nationalized. They could be taken over in the same way in an overthrow of the present regime and a socialist government's coming to power.

Outside events could change the situation in both islands overnight. There is an inflammable situation continuing in Panama. Dictatorships could be overthrown in almost any one of the South American countries. The situation in Europe is changing and could quickly affect political conditions in the States and in the Caribbean. Cuba is feeling sufficiently strong to go to the aid of comrades in Angola and elsewhere in Africa, and it is leading the fight in the United Nations against the colonization of Puerto Rico. The Third World is giving its support. And the situation in the Third World is volatile. Before accepting statehood, the Puerto Rican Socialist Party will use all means in its power, despite repression, to fight for independence. Cuba, the other wing of the same bird, will give its support.

Cuba itself may be invaded. There could be a new invasion, especially if there should be any weakening in the Russian position in an effort to appease the U.S. on détente. The *London Economist* News Service, April 18, 1976, suggests that the U.S. might act against Cuba by "the mining of Cuba's main ports. Mines could be planted by aircraft, as they were off Haiphong in 1972." And in such a blockade, the news service continued "the United States could probably count on fairly wide support by the Western powers if it decided to take limited military action against Cuba in retaliation against another intervention in Africa." Here is a ready-made suggestion of how the U.S. might at this time move against Cuba.

But if the Western powers did give support, there would likely be an outcry from Latin America. The Soviet Union could airlift supplies to the island. Within the United States itself there would be great opposition as there was against the Vietnam war. The thousands of Puerto Ricans living along the Eastern seaboard might show solidarity by various forms of sabotage. Furthermore, action against Cuba by the U.S. could spark revolution throughout Latin America. There is no doubt that a revolution will again occur in the Dominican Republic. The country has had too long a history of revolt to believe otherwise; but how soon or how late is unknown.

The next time, if the U.S. lands troops, Cuba may do the same as it has done in Angola. This would make an entirely new situation. Ford said, in a campaign speech in 1976 to Cuban exiles in Miami that he would "take appropriate action against Castro if he intervenes anywhere in the Western Hemisphere." In particular, this probably meant in the Dominican Republic or Puerto Rico. It also meant giving the green light to Cuban counterrevolutionaries in any action they might take. They had been resentful of earlier moves towards the rapprochement with Cuba. President Carter, on the other hand, appears to want to normalize the relationship with Cuba.

The revolutionary movements in all three islands have been intertwined since Spanish colonial times, and they are still connected today. There would undoubtedly be repercussions in the three islands if the U.S. were to move against any one of them. Cuba might actually land military forces to counteract the U.S. attack—it has the best military forces in Latin America. If Cuba itself is attacked, there would be measures of help by the revolutionaries in the other islands. Undoubtedly there would be a heightened war of sabotage and bombings conducted against U.S. installations and other U.S. property. There would be repercussions also in Latin America, both from the right and the left.

What happens in the U.S. itself in the coming period will have widespread effect. The antiwar movement is over; the students seem to have calmed down. The workers, despite inflation and unemployment, show no particular militancy. There is no more rioting in Black districts. But this could be the quiet before the storm

U.S. power seems in decline. Middle class youth is alienated by the commercial ethic, "getting and spending," and the accompanying way of life. There is corruption throughout the fabric of society. Youth in particular needs purpose in life, a goal for living, for its energies and idealism. The classic situation for the demise of a class seems already apparent. Stanley Sporkin, chief of enforcement of the Securities and Exchange Commission, says: "What concerns me, is the tremendous corruption of our young people in the prime of their lives. They are being trained to be crooks, trained to falsify records, trained to pay bribes, trained to file fraudulent tax returns. Where do they learn this? Harvard Business School doesn't have a course in Bribery I and Bribery II. It is the environment they enter into."

When the ruling class has doubts about the young with whom its future lies, then its fall may be imminent. James Boggs, the Black writer, believes a revolutionary situation is arising. "What you have is no longer just the unemployed and the castaways, but a revolutionary force or array of outsiders and rejects who are totally alienated from this society." Of course, they could form the basis for fascist bands, but Boggs believes not. He believes it is the Negroes (and with them the Puerto Ricans, Chicanos and Indians) who will spark the new American revolution. Certainly if Puerto Ricc becomes a state in the Union, it will provide a core of violent dissent within the U.S. itself. It is bound to be a core that would ally itself with the Black struggle. And of that Boggs says, "Most Americans, including most radicals, see the Negro question only as a race question, not as a social question. They do not understand that the Negro struggle has its deepest roots in the most fundamental contradiction of the American social order and that it can achieve its aims only by eliminating these contradictions, which means by transforming the social order itself." Revolution in the U.S. would have the profoundest repercussions throughout the whole world. The Caribbean would be only one area where its force would be felt.

"For over a century, under cover of the Monroe Doctrine, the United States has ruled its Latin American domain as Chicago gangsters rule a certain territory, warning all others to keep out." Boggs prophesies in his book *The American Revolution* that the rule is coming to an end. Vietnam and Cuba have shown that the giant United States can be challenged. Against that might, great as it is, those who are willing to fight can win, if as Martí said, "they carry stars on their heads."

Professor Richard E. Rubenstein, a graduate of Harvard and a Rhodes scholar predicts "The 1970s . . . will be an era of class struggle in America. In the course of this struggle . . . which has already begun in earnest, working people will recall that government was instituted to serve human beings and not vice versa."

Marxism is a human doctrine. Man, to fulfill his potential, must be a social being, caring and compassionate. For Puerto Rico and the Dominican Republic, the only hope of solving the problems of poverty, hunger, unemployment, sickness, misery, drug addiction and crime, must come through independence and socialism and the overthrow of American domination.

Unlike the Nixons and Agnews of the U.S., "Ché Guevara was one of those people who bolster a man's faith in the value of the human race."[3] Fidel Castro is a man of limitless courage, intelligence, imagination and audacity. Together they built a society whose people can envision a time when poverty, ill health, ignorance and shoddy possessions are left behind. In their Cuba, the people dream the dreams of unfettered minds, the dreams of men and women who see a future in which all can live their lives as human lives should be lived. Emerging from the isolation of the past years, they seek to share their dreams. This is their greatest wealth: their shared satisfaction in creating a country where all people are compañeros, and their shared hope for the future of that country. Castro now considers his soldiers the "standard bearers of the Third World."

When the Spanish Antilles were discovered by Columbus, there was a high standard of ethics. An old Indian, who recognized the evil intent of the Spanish conquerors, told Columbus, "The soul, when it quits the body, follows one of two courses: the first is dark and dreadful and is reserved for the enemies and tyrants of the human race; joyous and delectable is the second, which is reserved for those who during their lives have promoted peace and the tranquility of others."

In the Spanish Antilles, named Islands of Paradise by Columbus on their discovery, there are those who in memory of their past heritage—Indian, Spanish, Negro—and the savage cruelties and heavy burdens to which they were subjected and are still subjected, are bent on carving a new and challenging road for their countrymen and the coming generations.

On September 12, 1978, the United Nations Decolonization Committee approved an amended Cuban resolution that states there must be "a complete transfer of powers" by the United States to Puerto Rico before the island chooses its final political status. It declares that any form of "free association" between Puerto Rico and the United States "must be in terms of political equality."

BIBLIOGRAPHY

Aquilar, Alonso, *Pan Americanism From Monroe to the Present*, Monthly Review Press, New York, 1973.

Aquilar, Luis E., *The American Revolution*, Monthly Review Press, New York, 1963.

———, *Prologue to A Revolution*, Cornell University Press, Ithaca, New York, 1972.

Aitkin Thomas, Jr., *Poet In The Fortress, The Story of Luis Munoz Marin*, The New American Library, New York, 1964.

Albá, Victor, *Nationalists Without Nations. The Oligarchy Versus the People in Latin America*, Praeger Publishing Co., New York, 1968.

Albizu Campos, Laura de, *Dr. Pedro Alibizu Campos y La Independencia de Puerto Rico*, Partido Nacionalista, 1961.

Albores Historicos del Capitalismo en Puerto Rico, Editional Universitana, 1972.

Alegriá Ricardo, *Describrimento, Conquista y Colonizacón de Puerto Rico*, Colleción de Estudios Puertorriquenos, 1969.

———, *Santos de Puerto Rico*, Instituto de Cultura.

Alexander, Robert. *The Bolivian National Revolution*, Rutgers University Press, New Brunswick, 1958.

Arciniegas, Germán, *Biografia de Caribe*, Edicion Sudamericana, Buenos Aires, 1963.

———, *Latin America, A Cultural History*, Alfred Knopf, New York, 1969.

———, *Caribbean Sea of the World*, Cresset Press, New York, 1968.

Balogh, Thomas, *The Economics of Poverty*, Macmillan Co., New York, 1955.

Barnet, Clifford, *Cuba: Its People, Its Society, Its Culture*, Yale University Press, New Haven, 1962.

Beard, Charles A., *A History of the United States*.

Blanco, Enrique T., *Los Tres Ataques Britanicos*, Centero Fernandez y Co., San Juan, Puerto Rico, 1947.
Blanco Tomas, *Prontuario Histórico de Puerto Rico*, Biblioteca de Autores Puertorriquenos, San Juan, 1947.
Boggs, James, *The American Revolution, Pages From a Negro Worker's Notebook*, Monthly Review Press, New York, 1963.
——————, *Racism and the Class Struggle*, Monthly Review Press, New York, 1970.
Boorstein, Edward, *The Economic Transformation of Cuba*, Monthly Review Press, New York, 1968.
Bosch, Juan, *Causas de Una Dictadura Sin Exemplo*, CEDS, Mexico, 1965.
——————, *Substitute for Imperialism*, Grove Press, New York, 1968.
——————, *De Cristobal Colon à Fidel Castro*, Alfaquara, Madrid, 1970.
Braverman, Harry, *Labor and Monopoly Capital*, Monthly Review Press, New York, 1974.
Brinton, Daniel G., *The Myths of the New World* (The Gold of Ophir), E. P. Dutton, New York, 1972.
Camon, Arturo Morgles, *Albores Historicos del Capitalismo in Puerto Rico*, Editorial Universitaria, 1972.
Carr, E. H., *Studies in Revolution*, Grosset & Dunlap, New York, 1964.
Castedo, Leopoldo, *A History of Latin American Art and Architecture from Pre-Columbian Times to the Present*, Praeger, New York, 1969.
Castro, Fidel, *History Will Absolve Me*, Book Institute, Havana, 1967.
Cesaire, Aimé, *Discourse on Colonialism*, Monthly Review Press, 1972.
Chase, Stuart, *Operation Bootstrap, A Report on Progress, 1951*. Planning Pamphlets, National Planning Association, Washington, D.C. 1951.
Coe, Michael, *America's First Civilization*, Yale University Press, New Haven, 1965.
Coletti, Lucio, *From Rousseau to Lenin*, Monthly Review Press, New York, 1972.
Crasweller, Robert D., *The Life and Times of the Caribbean Dictator*, Macmillan, New York, 1966.
——————, *The Caribbean Community*, Frederick Praeger, New York, 1972.
Creque, Darwin D., *The U.S. Virgins and The Eastern Caribbean*, Whitmore Publishing Co., Philadelphia, 1968.

Cripps, L. L., *Puerto Rico: The Case For Independence*, Alfred Schenkman Co., Cambridge, Mass., 1974.
Cruxent, José M. and Ruose, Irving, *The Entry of Man Into The West Indies*, Yale University, New Haven, 1960.
Cruz, Monclava, Lidio, *Historia de Puerto Rico*, Editorial University, Rio Piedras, 1965.
Dahlberg, Edward, *The Gold of Ophir*, E. P. Dutton & Co., New York, 1972.
Darlington, C. D., *The Evolution of Man and Society*, Simon and Schuster, New York, 1969.
Davies, H. P., *Black Democracy: The Story of Haiti*.
de Boyrie, Moya, *Monumento Megalitico y Petroglipos de Chacues*. Republica Dominica, Santo Domingo 1970.
De Diego, José, *Neuvas Campanas y El Plebiscita*, Obros Completas.
de Las Casas, Bartolomé, *The Spanish Colonie*, Readex Microprint from William Brome edition, London, 1583. Christopher Columbus kept a diary and Bartolomé de las Casas uses much of this material for his book, as well as his own experiences. Also see his *La Historia de Los Indies* and *The Devastation of the Indies*, Seabury Press, New York, 1974.
de Jesus Galvan, Manuel, *Enriquello*, An Account of the Last Indian Cacique in Hispaniola to revolt.
de Hostos, Eugenio, *Forjando el Porven Americano*, Obras Completas Cultural, SA, La Habana, 1939.
de Besault, Lawrence, *President Trijillo. His Work and the Dominican Republic*, Washington Pub. Co., Washington, D.C., 1936. (This book is dedicated to all those who love liberty, order, peace, progress and work.)
de Onis, Juan, *The America of Jose Martí. Selected writings*, Minerva Press, New York, 1954.
de Pablo, Azcarala, *La Guerra de '98*, Alianza Editorial, Madrid, 1968.
Diaz Soler, Luis M., *Historia de La Esclavitud Negra en Puerto Rico*, Editorial Universitora, Rio Piedras, 1865.
Diffie, Bailey W. and Justine: *Porto Rico: A Broken Pledge*, The Vanguard Press, New York, 1931.
Dobzhansky, Theodosius, *Mankind Evolving*, Yale University Press, New Haven, 1962.
Draper Theodore, *Castro's Revolution Myths and Realities*, New York, 1962.
Dumont, Rene, *Socialisms and Development*, Frederick Praeger, New York, 1973.
Durant Will and Ariel, *Rousseau and Revolution*, Simon & Schuster, 1967.

Dupey, Col. Ernest and Major Gen. Wm. H. Bauer, *The Little Wars of the U.S.*, Hawthorne Books, 1968.
Egli, Emil, Bronowski, Jacob, *The Ascent of Man*, Little, Brown & Co., Boston, Mass., 1975.
Fagg, John Edwin: *Cuba, Haiti and the Dominican Republic*, Prentice-Hall, New Jersey, 1965.
Fanon, Franz, *The Wretched of the Earth, The Handbook of the Black Revolution that is Changing the Shape of the World*, Grove Press, New York, 1968.
Floyd, Troy S., *The Anglo-Spanish Struggle for Mosquitia*, University of New Mexico Press, 1967.
Foner, Philip S., *The Spanish-Cuban American War and the Birth of American Imperialism, 1895-1902*. Monthly Review Press, New York, 1973.
Freyne, Gilberto, *New World in Tropics*, Alfred Knopf, New York, 1959.
Fromm, Eric, *May Man Prevail. An Enquiry Into the Facts and Fictions of Foreign Policy*, A Doubleday Anchor Book, New York, 1961.
Fulbright, J. William, *The Crippled Giant, American Foreign Policy and Its Domestic Consequences*, Vintage, New York, 1972.
Gale Addison, Jr., *The Cultural Hegemony*, Vintage Press, New York, 1972.
Galeano Eduardo, *Open Veins of Latin America. Five Centuries of the Pillage of a Continent*, Monthly Review Press, New York, 1973.
Galindez, J., *Iberia-America*, Las Americas Pub. Co., New York, 1954.
Galindez Juavez, Jesus de, *La Era de Trujillo* (Buenos Aires, 1956).
Garcia, Martinez Alfonso, *Local Regulations of the Sugar Industry*.
Geydin, Philip, *Lyndon Johnson and the World: An Interview with George Bundy*, Praeger Co., New York, 1966.
Gevassi, John, *The Great Fear in Latin America*, Collier-Macmillan, New York, 1966.
Gerard, Pierre Charles, *The Haitian Economy*.
Gimbernard, Jacinto, *Historia de Santo Domingo*, Cuarto Edicion Refomado, 1969. La Portada esta basada en un antiguo grabado de Samuel Hazard en 1873.
Godelier, Maurice, *Rationality and Irrationality in Economics*, Monthly Review Press, New York, 1972.
Goff, Fred and Locker, Michael, *The Violence of Domination: U.S. Power and the Dominican Republic*, Random House, New York, 1969.

Goodsell, Charles T., *Administration of a Revolution*, Editorial Univerania, San Juan, 1967.
Gorenstein, Shirley; Forbes, Peebard R.; Tolstoy, Paul; Lansing, Edward, *Pre-Historic America*. St. Martin Press, New York, 1974.
Gutierrez, Carlos Mana, *The Dominican Republic: Rebellion and Repression*, Monthly Review Press, New York, 1972.
Gueverra, Ernesto Ché, *Reminiscences of the Cuban Revolutionary War*, Monthly Review Press, New York, 1972.
Guerra, R y Sanchez, *Manuel de Historia de Cuba*, Havana, 1938.
Haddad, Jamil Almansur, *Revolucao Cubana e Revolucao Brasiliera*, Editora Curilizacao Brazileira, 1961.
Halperin, Maurice, *Des amoldo ecónomico y civico America Latina*, Ediciones de La Universidad Obrera, 1961.
Hanson, Earl Park, *Puerto Rico: Ally for Progress*, D. Van Nostrand, New Jersey, 1962.
Hanson, S. Y., *Economic Development in Latin America*, Inter-American Affairs Press, Washington, 1951.
Harding, Vincent, *Black History*, Amistad, 1970.
Harnig, C. H., *The Buccaneers of the West Indies in the 17th Century*, Lardix, 1910.
Harrington, Michael, *The Other America: Poverty in the United States*, Penguin Books, Baltimore, 1963.
Heilbroner, R., *El Gran Ascenso* (trans.), Fondo de Cultura Economica, Mexico, 1964.
History of the Indians of Puerto Rico, Coleccion de Estudios Puertomiguenos, San Juan, 1970.
Historia de la Nacion Cubana, Editional Historia, La Habana, 1942.
Holly, James Theodore and Hams, J. Dennis, *Black Separatism and the Caribbean*, University of Michigan Press, Ann Arbor, 1970.
Huberman, Leo and Sweezy, Paul M., *Cuba: Anatomy of a Revolution*, Monthly Review Press, 1960.
———, *Socialism in Cuba*, 1969.
Humboldt, Alexander Von, *Political Essay on the Island of Cuba*, Paris, 1828.
Jalee, Pierre, *The Third World in World Economy*, Monthly Review Press, New York, 1969.
James, C. L. R., *The Black Jacobins*, Random House, New York, 1963.
———, *The Atlantic Slave Trade and Slavery*, Amistad T. Penguin, New York.
———, *A History of Negro Revolt*, London, 1953, reprint edition, Haskell House, 1970.
Jane, C, (trans), *The Journal of Christopher Columbus*, Potter & Co., New York, 1960.

Jolly, Richard and Seers, Dudley, *Cuba: The Educational and Social Revolution*, New York, 1972.
Johnson, Gerald W., *The Imperial Republic*, Liveright Co., New York, 1972.
July, Robert W., *A History of African People*, Charles Scribner, New York, 1970.
Kirchen, Helen, Edited by, *The Educated African*, Praeger & Co., New York, 1962.
Konig, Hans, *Columbus: His Enterprise*, Monthly Review Press, 1973.
Kropotkin, P. A., *The Great French Revolution*, New York, 1909.
Krickeberg, Walter; Triborn, Herman; Muller, Werner; Zerries, Otto, *Pre-Columbian American Religions*, Weidenfeld and Nicholson, London, 1961.
Kurzman, Dan, Santo Domingo: *Revolt of the Damned*, G. N. Putnam, New York, 1965.
Lenin, *Imperialism*, Selected Works, International Publishers, New York, 1971.
Lewis, Gordon K., *Puerto Rico: Freedom and Power in the Caribbean*, Monthly Review Press, New York, 1963.
The Caribbean: A Spectrum Book, New York, 1971.
Lewis, Gordon K., *Notes On the Puerto Rican Revolution*, Monthly Review Press, New York, 1974.
Lewis, Oscar, *La Vida: A Puerto Rican Family in the Culture of Poverty*, San Juan and New York, 1965.
Lockwood, Lee, *Castro's Cuba: Cuba's Fidel*, Macmillan, New York, 1976.
Lopez, Tarmes Roman: *El Estado Libhre*, Publicaciones del Instituto de Estudios Juridicos, 1965.
Loven, S., *Origins of Tainans Culture*, West Indies, Goteberg, 1935.
Lowenthal, Abraham F., *The Dominican Intervention*, Harvard University Press, Cambridge, Mass., 1972.
Lowry, Michael, *The Marxism of Ché Guevarra*, Monthly Review Press, 1973.
Lynch, John, *The Spanish American Revolutions. A unified account of the revolutions that swept over South and Central America in the early 19th century*, W. W. Norton & Co., New York, 1973.
Magdoff, Harvey, *The Age of Imperialism: The Economics of U.S. Foreign Policy*, Monthly Review Press, 1969.
Maldonado-Denis, Manuel, *Puerto Rico: A Socio-Historic Interpretation*, Random House, New York, 1972.
Mauncy, Albert and Torres Reyes, Ricardo, *The Forts of Old San Juan*, The Chatham Press, Riverside, Connecticut, 1973.
Marigot, Anthony P., *Social Life in the Caribbean*, The American Assembly, A Spectrum Book, New York, 1971.

Martí, José, *Inside the Monster: Writings on the United States and American Imperialism*, Monthly Review Press, New York, 1975.
Martyr, D'Anghera, Peter, *De Orbe Novo* (The Gold of Ophir), E. P. Dutton & Co., New York, 1972.
Marques, René, *Essays*, Editional Antillana, San Juan, 1966.
Mathews, Thomas, *Puerto Rico: Politics and the New Deal*, University of Florida Press, Gainsville, 1960.
———, *Fidel Castro*, Simon & Schuster, New York, 1969.
Matthews, Herbert, *The Cuban Story*, Charles Scribner & Sons, 1967.
———, *A World in Revolution*, Charles Scribner & Sons, 1967.
Marx, Karl, *Capital*, Vol. I, International Press, New York, 1967.
Metgars, Betty J., American Anthropologist, May, 1975.
Mills, C. Wright, *The Marxists*, Dell Pub. Co., New York, 1962.
Mintz, Sidney, *The Culture and History of a Puerto Rican Plantation, 1876-1969*, Hispanic American Review, 1953,
———, *Worker In The Cane*, Yale University Press, New Haven, 1964.
Miranda, Quintero Carmen, *On the Development of the People of Puerto Rico*, Libro Libre, New York, 1976.
Muñoz, Marin, *Breakthrough From Nationalism*, Harvard Godkin Lectures, Harvad University, 1959.
Moore, Ernest O., *Haiti, Its Stagnant Society and Shackled Economy*, Exposition Press, New York, 1922.
Puerto Rico and the Non-Hispanic Caribbean, University of Puerto Rico Press, Rio Piedras, 1952.
Morales, Otero Pablo, *El Tibaro Americano*, Biblioteca de Autores Puertorriquenos, San Juan, 1947.
Morrison, Samuel Eliot, *Admiral of the Western Seas*, Oxford University Press, New York, 1942.
———, *The European Discovery of America. The Southern Voyages, 1492-1616*. Oxford University Press, New York, 1974.
Perez, Morris, José, *Historia de la Insurreccion de Lares*, Varcelona, 1872.
B. Mydal, Gunnar, *Teonia Economica y Regiones Subdesarrolladas*, Mexico, Fondo de Cultura Economica, 1964.
Negron, Aida de Montilla, *Americanization in Puerto Rico and the Public School System, 1900-1930*, Editional Edil, Rio Piedras, Puerto Rico, 1971.
Nerudo, Pablo, *Towards The Splendid City*, Farrar, Strauss and Giroux, New York, 1972.
Northredge, F. S. and Grieve, M. J., *A Hundred Years of International Relations*, Frederick Praeger, New York, 1971.
Ortiz, Fernando, *Humboldt y Cuba*, Revista de Habana, 1936.
Pagan, Ferraras J., Bibliograpfia de la Riquesas de Puerto Rico, San Juan, 1948.

Parry, H. H. and Sherlock, Philip, *A Short History of the West Indies,* Macmillan Co., New York, 1956.
Pares, R., *War and Trade In the West Indies,* Oxford University Press, 1936.
Pedreira, Antonio S., *Insularismo,* Editorial Edil, Rio Piedras, 1934 and 1973.
Pere, P.T.X. Charlevoix, *Histoire de l'Isle Espanole on de Saint Dominique,* Pons, 1970.
Pertusse, Dexter, *The United States and the Caribbean,* Cambridge, Mass., 1947.
Playa Givon, *Derrola de Imperialismo,* La Habana, Cuba, 1961.
Preto, Luis B., *Simon Bolivar: Educator,* Doubleday, New York, 1970.
Reckford, Barry, *Does Fidel Eat More Than Your Father?* Frederick Praeger Co., New York, 1971.
Redding, Saunders, *They Came in Chains,* Lippincott & Co., 1973.
Reichel, Dolmatoff, *San Augustin—A Culture of Columbia,* Praeger Publishers, New York, 1972.
Ribes Tovar, Frederico, *A Chronological History of Puerto Rico,* Plus Ultra Publishers, New York, 1973.
Rivera, Angel, *La Cronica de La Guerra Hispano Americana en Puerto Rico,* Editional Edil, Rio Piedros, 1961.
Robinson, A.N.R., *The Mechanics of Independence,* M.I.T. Press, Cambridge, Mass., 1972.
Rodman, Seldon, Quisqueya. *A History of the Dominican Republic,* University of Washington Press, Seattle, 1964.
———, *Haiti,: The Black Republic,* New York, 1954.
Romero, Barcelo, Carlos, *La Estadidad Es Para Los Pobres,* San Juan, 1973.
Rouse, Irving, *Pre-History of the West Indies,* Yale University Press, New Haven, 1964.
———, *Dating of Caribbean Cultures,* Yale University Press, New Haven, 1960.
Rowden, Maurice, *The Spanish Terror—Spanish Imperialism in the 16th Century,* St. Martins Press, New York, 1974.
Rubinstein, Richard E., *Left Turn Origins of the Next American Revolution,* Little Brown & Co., Boston, 1973.
Stead, William A. Fomento, *The Economic Development of Puerto Rico,* National Planning Association, Washington, D.C., 1958.
Safa, Helen Iaken, *The Urban Poor of Puerto Rico, A Study in Development and Inequality,* Holt, Rinehart & Winston, New York, 1974.
Saco, J. A., *Historia de la Esclavidad de la Raza Africana en el Neuvo Monde y en especial in los Paises Hispano,* Havana, 1938.

Sanchez, Tarriella, Andres, *Neuvo Enfoque Sobre El Desarrollo Politico de Puerto Rico*, Editorial Edil, San Juan, 1970.
Schirmer, Daniel B., *Republic or Empire*, Alfred Schenkman Co., Cambridge, Mass., 1972.
Seers, Dudley, *Cuba, The Economic and Social Revolution*, University of N. Carolina, Chapel Hill, 1964.
Seldon Rodman, *Quisqueya. A History of the Dominican Republic*, University of Washington Press, Seattle, 1964.
Severin, R., *The Golden Antilles*, Harriet Hamilton, New York, 1970.
Silen, Juan Angel, *We, The Puerto Rican People*, Monthly Review Press, New York, 1971.
Slater, Jerome, *Intervention and Negotiation. The U.S. and the Dominican Revolution*, Harper & Row, New York, 1967.
Smith, Winston George and Judah, Charles, *The U.S. Army and the Mexican War, 1846-1848*, University of New Mexico, 1968.
Stephany, Ben S., *The United States and the Caribbean*, Prentice-Hall, New Jersey, 1971.
———, *Puerto Rico in the American Assembly*, Spectrum Book, 1973.
Stewart, Julian et al, *The People of Puerto Rico, A Study in Social Anthropology*, University of Illinois, Urbana, 1966.
Stuart, *Status of Puerto Rico* (3 vols.) United States and Puerto Rico Commission. U.S. Government Printing Office, Washington, D.C., 1966.
Szulc, Tad, *Dominican Diary*, Dell, New York, 1966.
de Terra, Helmut, *Humbold, The Life and Times of Alexander von Humboldt*, 1769-1859, Alfred Knopf, New York 1955.
Thomas Piri, *Down These Mean Streets*, Alfred Knopf, New York, 1967.
Tugwell, Rexford, *Puerto Rico—The Stricken Land*, Greenwood Press, Westport, Conn., 1968.
Volsky, George, *Cuba. The United States and the Caribbean*, Prentice-Hall, New Jersey, 1971.
Von Humboldt, *The Island of Cuba*, New York, 1856. Translation by J. S. Thrasher, New York, 1951.
Weisman, Steve, *The Trojan Horse. The Strange Politics of Foreign Aid*, Monthly Review Press, New York, 1974.
Wagenheim, Kal, *Puerto Rico, A Profile*, Frederick Praeger & Co., New York, 1971.
Wakefield, Dan, *Island in the City, Puerto Ricans in New York*, Corwith Books, New York, 1960.
Washington, Joseph P. Jr., *Black Sects and Cults*, Doubleday & Co., New York, 1972.

Wells, Sumner, *Naboth's Vineyard. The Dominican Republic—1844-1924.* Payson and Clarke, New York, 1928.
Wessman, James W., *Anthropology, Historical Materialism and Population Growth in Puerto Rico,* Dept. of Anthropology, University of North Carolina, Chapel Hill, N.C., 1976. (Doctoral Thesis).
Wilcynski, J., *The Economics of Socialism,* Aldine Pub., Chicago, 1970. Allen & Unwin, 1972.
Williams, E., *Capitalism and Slavery from Columbus to Castro,* Chapel Hill, N. Carolina, 1944.
Wright, I., *The Early History of Cuba,* New York, 1916.
Zapatero, Juan Manuel, *La Guerra del Caribe en el Siglo XVIII,* Instituto de Cultura Puertorriquenca, 1964.
Zerries, Otto, *Primitive South America and the West Indies.*

PAMPHLETS AND PERIODICALS

The First Party Congress: Institutalization of the Cuban Revolution, Center for Cuban Studies, New York, June, 1976.
Cuba's Foreign Policy: Center for Cuban Studies, New York, Winter, 1976.
Cuban Family Code. Center for Cuban Studies, New York.
    Signed into Law by Osvaldo Dorticos Torrado, President and Fidel Castro Ruz, Prime Minister, February 14, 1975.
Porto Rico—La Lutte pour L'Independance. Base militaire de l'empire americain, vitrine d'un colonialisme "moderne," l'ile connait a la fois, la croissance et une misere que l'emigration ne resolve pas. Pierre Dommergues. Le Monde Diplomatic, January, 1976.
Political Thesis of the Puerto Rican Socialist Party, The Socialist Alternative. North American Congress on Latin America, New York, February, 1975.
Colonialism. The Puerto Rico Statehood Act of 1977, introduced into Congress at the request of Presdent Ford by Michigan Republican Phillip Ruppe on January 6th, 1977. Bulletin of the Puerto Rican Solidarity Committee, February, 1977.
    Staff Reports of the Select Committee to Study Governmental Operations with respect to Intelligence Activities. United States Senate, U.S. Government Printing Office, Washington, D.C., 1975.
El Ajusticiamiento del Coronel Riggs, Claridad Supplement, 20th March, 1976. San Juan, Puerto Rico.

ARTICLES

Update on a Revolution (Cuba), L. S. Stravarionas, The Nation, New York, March, 1977.

Cuba's Daring in Angola. International Bulletin, Jan. 28, 1978.

—————— Betty J. Metgars, Scientific American, reproduced from American Anthropologist, 1975.

The Rise of a Maya Merchant Class, Professors Jeremy A. Saboff and William L. Daltrye, Scientific American, October, 1975.

The Archeological Findings in San Augustin, Dr. Peter Weaver, Bulletin of the National History Society of Puerto Rico, August, 1955.

History of the Discovery of Florida, Bimini, and Yucatan by Aurelio Tio. Condensed and translated by Alicia O. Roe from the Boletin de la Academia Puertorriqueno de la Historia, June, 1972, published in La Reviste, Inter-Americane, Spring, 175.

Independence For Puerto Rico, by Ruben Berrios, Foreign Affairs, Spring, 1977.

APPENDIX I

TEXT OF U.N. RESOLUTION

Following is the text of the resolution approved September 12, 1978 by the United Nations Decolonization Committee. Ten nations voted for the resolution which was introduced by Cuba and Iraq; none voted against, but 12 abstained and two were absent for the voting.

The Special Committee

Having heard and considered the statements of the petitioners, which reflect the views of major trends of political opinion in Puerto Rico,

Recalling its resolution of 28 August 1972 and 30 August 1973, as well as its decision of 7 September 1976, concerning Puerto Rico.

Bearing in mind the decision on Puerto Rico adopted by the Conference of Foreign Ministers of the Co-ordinating Bureau of non-aligned Countries held in Belgrade in 1978 and by the Fifth Conference of Heads of State of Government of Non-Aligned Countries held at Colombo in 1976,

Conscious of the right of the people of Puerto Rico to modify the present status of Puerto Rico and aware that proposals for such modification have been made in the past by official organs of Puerto Rico,

Bearing in mind the Declaration on the Granting of Independence to Colonial Countries and Peoples contained in General Assembly resolution 1514 (XV) of 14 December 1960,

Conscious also that all peoples have the inalienable right to self-determination and independence, to the exercise of their national sovereignty, to respect for integrity of their national territory and to the exercise of complete control over their natural wealth and resources in the interest of their development and well-being,

Recalling the statement on Puerto Rico made on behalf of the United States of America by the permanent representative of the United States to the United Nations to the 8th session of the General Assembly on 27 November 1953,

Noting the public statement on Puerto Rico made by the President of the United States on 25 July 1978 and by the permanent representative of the United States on 28 August 1978.

Bearing in mind the fact that in their statements the petitioners have demonstrated that the major parties in Puerto Rico favor a change in the present status of Puerto Rico or modification of aspects thereof.

1. *Reaffirms* the inalienable right of the people of Puerto Rico to self-determination and independence in accordance with General Assembly resolution 1514 (XV);

2. *Reaffirms* that by virtue of that right the people of Puerto Rico should freely determine their future political status and pursue their further economic, social and cultural development;
3. *Affirms* that self-determination by the people of Puerto Rico in a democratic process should be exercised through mechanisms freely selected by the Puerto Rican people in complete full sovereignty in accordance with General Assembly Resolution 1514 (XV), which, inter alia, establishes the complete transfer of all powers to the people of the territory and that all determinations concerning status should have the approval of the Puerto Rican people,
4. *Considers* that the persecutions, harassments and repressive measures to which the oganizations and persons struggling for independence have been continuously subjected constitute violations of the national rights of the Puerto Rican people to self-determination and independence;
5. *Deems* that in the event the Puerto Rican people decide to form an independent republic, they have the right to recover the totality of their territory including all lands now used by the authorities of the Government of the United States.
6. *Deems* also that any form of free association between Puerto Rico and the United States must be in terms of political equality in order to comply fully with the provisions of the relevant resolutions and decisions of the General Assembly and of applicable international law, and must recognize the sovereignty of the people of Puerto Rico;
7. *Urges* the Government of the United States to release unconditionally the four Puerto Rican political personalities who have been incarcerated for more than 24 years;
8. *Urges* the Government of the United States to abide by the principles of resolution 1514 (XV) with respect to Puerto Rico;
9. *Decides* to keep under review the question of Puerto Rico and requests the Rapporteur, with the assistance of the Secretariat, to update information on this question in order to facilitate consideration of appropriate follow-up steps by the Special Committee in 1979.

APPENDIX II

The following excerpt from *Scientific American,* September, 1978, throws new light on the pretext under which *The Spanish American War* in 1898 was fought, and of the basis on which Puerto Rico became a colony, and Cuba put under American economic and political domination for three-quarters of a century.

WHITEWASHING THE MAINE

Eighty years ago the battleship U.S.S. *Maine* was in Cuban waters to protect U.S. interests in that insurrectionist Spanish colony. At 9:40 a.m. on February 15, 1898, the *Maine*, anchored in Havana harbor, exploded and sank with the loss of 260 men. A quickly convened naval court of inquiry absolved the navy of any blame for the disaster, coming to the conclusion that the explosion had been caused by another explosion outside the ship's hull.

Assertions that the trigger was a Spanish mine were widely made in the U.S., notably in Joseph Pultizer's New York *World* and William Randolph Hearst's New York *American,* which were then engaged in a bitter struggle for circulation. A slogan was coined: "Remember the *Maine,* to hell with Spain." Before the end of April, *in spite of repeated Spanish denials of any involvement,* the Spanish-American War had begun.

Appendix 243

In 1911 the hulk of the *Maine* was raised, numerous photographs were made of the damage to the battleship's hull and a second naval court of inquiry was convened. It too reached the conclusion that the explosion had been caused by another outside the hull.

Writing for the history division of the U.S. Navy, Admiral Hyman G. Rickover has now presented the results of a modern reinvestigation of the incident, undertaken on his behalf by two civilian experts on the effects of underwater explosions, Ib S. Hansen and Robert S. Price. Their conclusion, summarized by Rickover, is that "there is no evidence that a mine destroyed the *Maine*." The explosion appears to have originated with spontaneous combustion in one of the ship's coal bunkers that set off ammunition in an adjacent magazine. Actually in later years it was never widely believed a Spanish mine had caused the explosion. Nevertheless, there was some doubt, and the episode was seen as something of an example of how an ambiguous event in a tense atmosphere can precipitate (or can be exploited to precipitate) irreversible decisions. Now Admiral Rickover and his colleagues have made it possible also to see it as an example of another phenomenon in a complex society: the tendency for large institutions not to accept responsibility for errors of their own making.

NOTES

Chapter One: Pre-Columbian History

1. Walter Krickeberg, Herman Triborn, Werner Muller, Otto Zerries, *Pre-Columbian American Religions* (London: Weidenfeld and Nicholson, 1961).
2. Otto Zerries, *Primitive South America and the West Indies* (London: Weidenfeld and Nicholson, 1963).
3. Ibid
4. Leopoldo Castedo, *A History of Latin American Art and Architecture from Pre-Columbian Times to the Present* (New York: Praeger, 1969).
5. Ibid
6. Ibid
7. Ibid
8. Ibid
9. Ibid
10. Germán Arciniegas, *Latin America, A Cultural History* (New York: Alfred Knopf, 1969).

Chapter Two: How the Tainos Lived

1. Quintero Carmen, *On the Development of the People of Puerto Rico* (New York: Libro Libre, 1976).
2. Peter Martyr D'Anghera, *De Orbe Novo, The Gold of Ophir* (New York: E. P. Dutton & Co., 1972).
3. Ibid
4. Ibid
5. Irving Rouse, *Pre-History of the West Indies* (New Haven: Yale University Press, 1964).
6. Ibid
7. Germán Arciniegas, *Latin America, A Cultural History* (New York: Alfred Knopf, 1969).
8. Eduardo Galeamo, *Open Veins of Latin America, Five Centuries of the Pillage of a Continent* (New York: Monthly Review Press, 1973).
9. Arciniegas, *Latin America, A Cultural History*.
10. Martyr D'Anghera, *De Orbe Novo*.
11. Leopoldo Castedo, *A History of Latin American Art and Architecture from Pre-Columbian Times to the Present* (New York: Praeger, 1969).
12. Ibid
13. Martyr D'Anghera, *De Orbe Novo*.
14. Ibid
15. Ibid
16. Ibid

17. Martyr D'Anghera, *De Orbe Novo.*
18. Ibid
19. Arciniegas, *Latin America, A Cultural History.*
20. Ibid
21. Ibid
22. Martyr D'Anghera, *De Orbe Novo.*
23. Arciniegas, *Latin America, A Cultural History.*
24. Ibid

Chapter Three: The Spanish Conquest

1. Peter Martyr D'Anghera, *De Orbe Novo, The Gold of Ophir* (New York: E. P. Dutton & Co., 1972).
2. Ibid
3. Ibid
4. Bartolomé de Las Casas, *The Spanish Colonie* (London, Readex Microprint from William Brome edition, 1583).
5. Ibid
6. de Las Casas, *The Spanish Colonie.*
7. Ibid
8. Ibid
9. Ibid
10. de Las Casas, *The Spanish Colonie.*
11. Ibid
12. de Las Casas, *The Spanish Colonie.*
13. Jesus de Galindez, *Iberia-America* (New York: Las Americas Publishing Co., 1954).
14. Galeano, *Open Veins of Latin America, Five Centuries of the Pillage of a Continent* (New York: Monthly Review Press, 1973).
15. Germán Arciniegas, *Latin America, A Cultural History* (New York: Alfred Knopf, 1969).
16. Galeano, *Open Veins of Latin America.*
17. Ibid
18. de Las Casas, *The Spanish Colonie.*
19. Galeano, *Open Veins of Latin America.*
20. **Ibid**
21. Ibid

Chapter Four: The Settlements

1. Peter Martyr D'Anghera, *De Orbe Novo,* The Gold of Ophir (New York: E. P. Dutton & Co., 1972).
2. Leopoldo Castedo, *A History of Latin American Art and Architecture from Pre-Columbian Times to the Present* (New York: Praeger, 1969).
3. Eduardo Galeano, *Open Veins of Latin America, Five Centuries of the Pillage of a Continent* (New York: Monthly Review Press, 1973).
4. Germán Arciniegas, *Latin America, A Cultural History* (New York: Alfred Knopf, 1969).
5. C. D. Darlington, *The Evolution of Man and Society* (New York: Simon & Schuster, 1969).
6. Jesus de Galindez, *Iberia-America* (New York: Las Americas Publishing Co., 1954).

7. Arciniegas, *Latin America, A Cultural History*.
8. Ibid
9. Ibid
10. Kal Waggenheim, *Puerto Rico, A Profile* (New York: Praeger, 1971).
11. Ibid
12. Castedo, *A History of Latin American Art and Architecture from Pre-Columbian Times to the Present*.
13. Ibid
14. Ibid
15. Ibid
16. Darlington, *The Evolution of Man and Society*.
17. Ibid
18. Ibid
19. Ibid

Chapter Five: The Indians

1. Robert D. Crassweller, *The Caribbean Community* (New York: Praeger, 1972).
2. Vincent Harding, *Black History* Armistad (New York: Vintage Books, 1970).
3. Saunders Redding, *They Came in Chains* (Philadelphia: Lippincott & Co., 1973).
4. Ibid
5. C. L. R. James, *The Black Jacobins* (New York: Random House, 1963).
6. Ibid
7. Ibid
8. Ibid
9. Ibid
10. Redding, *They Came in Chains*.
11. Ibid
12. Ibid
13. Redding, *They Came in Chains*.
14. Ibid
15. C. L. R. James, *The Atlantic Slave Trade and Slavery* (New York: Vintage Books, 1970).
16. Ibid
17. Ibid
18. Redding, *They Came in Chains*.
19. Ibid
20. Ibid
21. Manuel Maldonado-Denis, *Puerto Rico: A Socio-Historical Interpretation* (New York: Random House, 1972).
22. Eduardo Galeano, *Open Veins of Latin America, Five Centuries of the Pillage of a Continent* (New York: Monthly Review Press, 1973).
23. James, *The Atlantic Slave Trade*.

Chapter Six: Entry of the Foreign Powers

1. Manuel Maldonado-Denis, *Puerto Rico: A Socio-Historical Interpretation* (New York: Random House, 1972).
2. Eduardo Galeano, *Open Veins of Latin America, Five Centuries of the Pillage of a Continent* (New York: Monthly Review Press, 1973).

3. Ibid
4. Ibid
5. Ibid
6. Ibid
7. Troy S. Floyd, *The Anglo-Spanish Struggle for Mosquitia* (Albuquerque: University of New Mexico Press, 1967).
8. Maldonado-Denis, *Puerto Rico: A Socio-Historical Interpretation.*
9. Ibid
10. Galeano, *Open Veins of Latin America.*
11. H. G. Wells, *Outline of History* (New York: Doubleday, 1971).
12. Gordon K. Lewis, *Puerto Rico: Freedom and Power in the Caribbean* (New York: Monthly Review Press, 1963).
13. Galeano, *Open Veins of Latin America.*
14. Ibid
15. Juan Angel Silen, *We, The Puerto Rican People* (New York: Monthly Review Press, 1971).
16. Floyd, *The Anglo-Spanish Struggle for Mosquitia.*

Chapter Seven: The Revolutionary Era

1. Jean-Jacques Rousseau, *Emile* (New York: E. P. Dutton & Co., 1974).
2. Ibid
3. Walter and Ariel Durrant, *Rousseau and the Revolution* (New York: Simon & Schuster, 1967).
4. Ibid
5. Louis Gottschalk and Donald Lach, *Toward the French Revolution: Europe and America in the Eighteenth-Century World* (New York: Scribner, 1973).
6. Gordon K. Lewis, *Puerto Rico: Freedom and Power in the Caribbean* (New York: Monthly Review Press, 1963).
7. Darwin D. Creque, *The U.S. Virgins and The Eastern Caribbean* (Philadelphia: Whitmore Publishing Co., 1968).
8. Gottschalk and Lach, *Towards the French Revolution.*
9. John Lynch, *The Spanish American Revolutions. A Unified Account of the Revolutions that swept over South and Central America in the early Nineteenth Century* (New York: W. W. Norton, 1973).
10. Ibid
11. Durrant, *Rousseau and the Revolution.*
12. Lynch, *The Spanish American Revolutions.*
13. Ibid
14. C. L. R. James, *The Black Jacobins* (New York: Random House, 1963).
15. Seldon Rodman, Haiti: The Black Republic (New York: 1954).
16. James, *The Black Jacobins.*
17. Lynch, *The Spanish-American Revolutions.*

Chapter Eight: The Age of Independence, Part One: The First Half of the Nineteenth Century

1. José Yglesias, *The Young Lords,* Article in New York Times, Sunday Magazine, April, 1973.
2. Leopoldo Castedo, *A History of Latin American Art and Architecture From Pre-Colombian Times to the Present* (Praeger, New York, 1969).

Notes 249

3. Germán Arciniegas, *Latin America: A Cultural History* (New York: Alfred Knopf, 1969).
4. Ibid
5. John Lynch: *The Spanish American Revolutions. A unified account of the revolutions that swept over South and Central America in the early 19th century* (New York: W. W. Norton & Co., 1973).
6. Arciniegas, *Latin America: A Cultural History*.
7. Ibid
8. Ibid
9. Ibid
10. Luis B. Prieto, *Simon Bolivar: Educator* (New York: Doubleday, 1970).
11. Victor Albá, *Nationalists Without Nations: The Oligarchy Versus the People in Latin America* (New York: Praeger, 1968).
12. Eduardo Galeano, *Open Veins of Latin America: Five Centuries of the Pillage of a Continent* (New York: Monthly Review Press, 1973).
13. Ibid

Chapter Nine: The Age of Independence, Part Two: The Late 19th Century

1. Gordon K. Lewis, *Puerto Rico: Freedom and Power in the Caribbean* (New York: Monthly Review Press, 1963).
2. Joan Haslip, *The Crown of Mexico* (New York: Holt, Rinehart & Winston, 1971).
3. Juan Angel Silen, *We, The Puerto Rican People* (New York: Monthly Review Press, 1971).
4. Ibid
5. Kal Waggenheim, *Puerto Rico: A Profile* (New York: Praeger, 1971).
6. Manuel Maldonado-Denis, *Puerto Rico: A Socio-Historical Interpretation* (New York: Random House, 1972).
7. Ibid
8. Ibid
9. John Edwin Fagg, *Cuba, Haiti and the Dominican Republic* (New Jersey: Prentice-Hall, 1965).
10. Ibid
11. Ibid
12. Luis E. Aquilar, *Cuba 1933: Prelude to a Revolution* (Ithaca, New York: Cornell University Press, 1972).

Chapter Ten: U.S. Entry and The Spanish American War

1. John Lynch, *The Spanish American Revolutions. A unified account of the revolutions that swept over South and Central America in the early 19th century* (New York: W. W. Norton & Co., 1973).
2. John Gerassi, *The Great Fear in Latin America* (New York: Collier-Macmillan, 1966).
3. George Winston Smith and Charles Judah, *Chronicles of the Gringos* (Albuquerque: University of New Mexico Press, 1968).
5. Eduardo Galeano, *Open Veins of Latin America: Five Centuries of the Pillage of a Continent* (New York: Monthly Review Press, 1973).
6. Gerald W. Johnson, *The Imperial Republic* (New York: Liveright Co., 1972).
7. Luis E. Aquilar, *Cuba 1933: Prelude to a Revolution* (New York: Cornell University Press, 1972).

8. Daniel B. Schirmer, *Republic or Empire: American Resistance to the Philippine War* (Cambridge, Ma.: Schenkman, 1972).
9. Edwin John Fagg, *Cuba, Haiti and the Dominican Republic* (New Jersey: Prentice-Hall, 1965).
10. Aquilar, *Cuba 1933: Prelude to a Revolution*.

Chapter Eleven: American Domination

1. Daniel B. Schirmer, *Republic or Empire: American Resistance to the Philippine War* (Cambridge, Ma.: Schenkman, 1972).
2. Gordon K. Lewis, *Puerto Rico: Freedom and Power in the Caribbean* (New York: Monthly Review Press, 1963).
3. Manuel Maldonado-Denis, *Puerto Rico: A Socio-Historical Interpretation* (New York: Random House, 1972).
4. Earl Parker Hanson, *Puerto Rico: Ally for Progress* (New Jersey: D. Van Nostard, 1962).
5. L. L. Cripps, *Puerto Rico: The Case of Independence* (Cambridge, Ma.: Schenkman, 1974).
9. Edwin John Fagg, *Cuba, Haiti and the Dominican Republic* (New Jersey: Praeger, 1972).
7. James Theodore Holly and J. Dennis Harris, *Black Separatism and the Caribbean* (Ann Arbor: University of Michigan Press, 1970).
8. Edwin John Fagg, *Cuba, Haiti and the Dominican Republic* (New Jersey: Prentice-Hall, 1965).
9. Ibid
10. Ibid
11. Leo Huberman and Paul M. Sweezey, *Cuba: Anatomy of a Revolution* (New York: Monthly Review Press, 1960).
12. *Political Thesis of the Puerto Rican Socialist Party, The Socialist Alternative*, North American Congress on Latin America (New York: February, 1975).
13. John Gerassi, *The Great Fear in Latin America* (New York: Collier-Macmillan, 1966).
14. *Political Thesis of the Puerto Rican Socialist Party*, North American Congress on Latin America (New York: 1977).
15. Ibid
16. Gerassi, *The Great Fear in Latin America*.
17. Crassweller, *The Caribbean Community*.
18. Ibid
19. Gerassi, *The Great Fear in Latin America*.
20. Huberman and Sweezey, *Cuba: An Anatomy of a Revolution*.
21. Ibid

Chapter Twelve: Cuba's Challenge

1. Leo Huberman and Paul M. Sweezy, *Socialism in Cuba* (New York: Monthly Review Press, 1969).
2. Ibid
3. Leo Huberman and Paul M. Sweezy, *Cuba: An Anatomy of a Revolution* New York: Monthly Review Press, 1960).
4. H. H. Parry and Philip Sherlock, *A Short History of the West Indies* (New York: Macmillan & Co., 1956).
5. Huberman and Sweezy, *Cuba: An Anatomy of a Revolution*.

6. Barry Reckford, *Does Fidel Eat More Than Your Father?* (New York: Praeger, 1971).
7. Huberman and Sweezey, *Socialism in Cuba.*
8. Ibid
9. Herbert L. Matthews, *The Cuban Story* (New York: Charles Scribner and Sons, 1967).
10. Ibid

Chapter Thirteen: The Social and Economic Situation

1. L. L. Cripps, *Puerto Rico: The Case for Independence* (Cambridge, Mass.: Schenkman Publishing Co., 1974).
2. Carlos Maria Gutierrez, *The Dominican Republic: Rebellion and Repression* (New York: Monthly Review Press, 1972).
3. Barry Reckford, *Does Fidel Eat More Than Your Father?* (New York: Praeger, 1971).
4. Cripps, *Puerto Rico: The Case for Independence.*
5. Gutierrez, *The Dominican Republic: Rebellion and Repression.*
6. Cripps, *Puerto Rico: The Case for Independence.*
7. James Boggs, *The American Revolution, Pages From A Negro Worker's Notebook* (New York: Monthly Review Press, 1963).
8. John Gerassi, *The Great Fear in Latin America* (New York: Collier, 1966).

Chapter Fourteen: The Political Situation

1. Carlos Maria Gutierrez, *The Dominican Republic: Rebellion and Repression* (New York: Monthly Review Press, 1972).
2. Ibid
3. Ibid
4. John Gerassi, *The Great Fear in Latin America* (New York: Collier-Macmillan, 1966).
5. Ibid
6. Robert D. Crassweller, *The Caribbean Community* (New York: Praeger, 1972).
7. Leo Huberman and Paul M. Sweezy, *Socialism in Cuba* (New York: Monthly Review Press, 1969).

Chapter Fifteen: Future Possibilities

1. *Staff Reports of the Select Committee to Study Governmental Operations with respect to Intelligence Activities.* United States Senate (Washington, D.C.: U.S. Government Printing Office, 1975).
2. Carlos Maria Gutierrez, *The Dominican Republic: Rebellion and Repression* (New York: Monthly Review Press, 1972).
3. Juan Bosch, *De Cristobal Colon à Fidel Castro* (Madrid: Alfaquara, 1970).
4. Germán Arciniegas, *Latin America, A Cultural History* (New York: Alfred Knopf, 1969).